UNDERNEATH
ENGLISH TOWNS

MARTIN CARVER

UNDERNEATH ENGLISH TOWNS
Interpreting urban archaeology

FITZHOUSE BOOKS
LONDON

For Em and J

© Martin Carver 1987
First published 1987
This edition published 1989 by
Fitzhouse Books, an imprint of
B.T. Batsford Ltd
4 Fitzhardinge Street
London W1H 0AH

Printed in Great Britain by
Courier International Ltd
Tiptree, Essex

British Library Cataloguing in Publication Data

Carver, Martin
    Underneath English towns.
    1. Archaeology—England   2. Cities and
    towns—England   3. England—Antiquities
    I. Title
    936.2'009'732   DA90

    ISBN 0-7134-3637-9
    ISBN 0-7134-3638-7 Pbk

Preface

'And is an archive, then, an instrument not for distributing the truth but for delaying its appearance?' I asked, dumbfounded.

After U. Eco, *The Name of the Rose*

The predecessors of modern towns were themselves once proud and busy places; that much we can read or guess without recourse to archaeology. What archaeology can do is bring those places to life, describe and, to a certain extent, explain their fortunes, and offer these conclusions for historical scrutiny. One thing is clear from this investigation, undeveloped though it still might be, which will pre-empt the chapters that follow – there is no inexorable progress in English town life. Civic authorities who might be hoping to read of a steady improvement in civilisation from the time of Claudius to the twentieth-century Town Planning Acts are going to be disappointed. It is a story of frustrated greed, cyclical decline and occasional disaster; the English town emerges from its ruins underground as a passive artefact, propped, cajoled or pump-primed into temporary functions through the artificial aid of a wealth and power which decidedly preferred the green belt.

Our evidence for this particular view is also very particular – abandoned middens, pilfered buildings and disused drains – evidence whose interpretation is by no means simple or unequivocal. But it is new, and it is different; different from the account books of government officials, from the chauvinist proclamations of civic champions, from the eclectic jottings of clerical diarists, and from the watercolour sketches of early tourists. The evidence of archaeology speaks with its own materialist voice, giving its own generalised view on matters often far removed from the preoccupations of the surviving historical record.

The enquiring spirit of the archaeologist is generally directed to what is strange or unknown, so that the Roman trade network and its specialist industries, the missing link of the Dark Ages, the English new towns of the tenth century, and the rise of medieval craftsmen have tended to get the priority in town digging; while the more recent centuries, in any case better known to history, have been rather taken for granted. That is, on many occasions their layers have been taken away in skips.

I intend no criticism here, having done the same thing myself many times, I believe rightly, given the constraints of time and money and given the pure curiosity which provides research with the necessary adrenalin. It does mean, however, that with a few famous exceptions like Chichester, the post-medieval and modern periods have been little embellished by new urban archaeology, and their material culture has not yet been linked to that of the immediately preceding period. We shall certainly regret this – not just because of the collectors' passion for completeness, but because archaeology is capable of shining an independent beam of light on one of the most interesting episodes of human behaviour – the transition from feudalism to capitalism.

This survey therefore stops at the end of the Middle Ages, and even for the 1500 years it does cover, *c.* 40 to 1540 AD, it is not an attempt at history. It is an introduction to the world of urban archaeology, and therefore has something to say about its achievements, and even more about its potential. It is intended for everyone who has worked as a volunteer on a dig; for visitors who look over the fence; for developers who are waiting for their site back; for contractors commissioned to build on it; for engineers, civil or otherwise; for local government and central government officers who have to justify the whole business, and for the press who want a good story.

The material used in this book derives mainly from urban excavations carried out in the last 25 years, over 75 per cent of which were unpublished at the time of writing. I have therefore used the interim and ephemeral reports that have been issued from time to time and offer a blanket apology to all those whose discoveries I have ignored, misconstrued or misrepresented as a result. References to the information used will be found under the name of the town in the *Gazetteer* (p. 144) and in the *Sources* (*p. 151*) which follow. A tribute is owed to Andrew and Wendy Selkirk whose periodical *Current Archaeology* has done much to ensure that research topics are kept on the boil during the long business of writing up. Liz Hooper of Birmingham University has done far more to help this book to press than provide many excellent illustrations, and I am very grateful to her.

I would like to offer my special thanks to the Inspectors of the Department of Environment's Ancient Monuments Inspectorate (now *English Heritage*), and to Peter Addyman, Martin Biddle, Rosemary Cramp, Philip Rahtz and Graham Webster, who gave me my chance to work in towns; and to Simon Esmonde Cleary who kindly weeded the text and made several of its generalisations less unreasonable. Generalisation, sometimes of a speculative and unsubstantiated kind, remains, in order to offer the kiss of life to some of the drabber data. I have tried, wherever possible, to signal the approach of these dangerous passages.

Moreton Morrell, 1986

Contents

List of illustrations

I
Underneath English towns

Pity the poor visitor to an archaeological site in one of England's historic towns. His curiosity is aroused in the street, where hand-painted advertisements, perhaps a quaint array of photographs, and an impressive list of sponsorship credits announce that this is a Roman or a medieval 'dig'. Once through the hoarding, however, he encounters a scene of irredeemable dereliction. A large brown rectangular gap lies in the land, cut about with pits, interlaced with wandering plank-paths and bolstered by pieces of scaffolding. Here and there a short run of barely recognisable walling, a cluster of wooden stakes, or a patch of bright pebbles or burnt clay relieve the dark brown carved cubes and scoured sockets. Everything is decked with little white labels, investing the peaks and hollows and shafts with some unstated significance. This straight-sided quarry contains a tableau of people of both sexes, mainly in their twenties, who dress as though recently rounded up from a refugee camp, and move as though under sedation. They strike a variety of curious attitudes, many kneeling with bowed heads scratching the ground like chickens, others apparently trapped beneath heavy drawing-boards, others shovelling earth from deep holes, others dejectedly setting forth with wheel-barrows on the long climb to the summit of an adjacent hillock of homogenous debris. It is a scene which manifests system rather than purpose, and of a controlling discipline there can be no doubt. It must be either the outstation of a corrective institution or an avant garde street-theatre rehearsing in the absence of its director. Meanwhile the enthusiastic and gesticulating site guide, periodically overwhelmed by the roar of traffic or lapsing into technical obscurity, speaks of roads, temples, houses and palaces, of Roman plaster, Saxon stake-holes, medieval culverts and Victorian cellars, hoping, it would seem, to restore morale with a recitation of antique images, inspiring, audacious but by no means obviously relevant.

The impression is understandable, but false. These are some of the most skilled professionals currently working out of doors. Excavators and their visitors must take their archaeology as they find it, and this is how it generally is: smashed, perforated and decayed beyond repair, and to all but the trained eye, beyond recognition. Many of the things discovered do, of course, presently remain difficult to interpret and can be spoken about only in the provisional language of the explorer. It is the feeling of entering into the unknown that gives archaeological investigation its special excitement. But if this is to be a journey of more than innocent rapture, we shall need a guide-book, however basic, and a great deal can now be said about what a Roman, Saxon or medieval town might have looked like. Before considering the opaque deposit itself, it will be helpful to have a few of these 'antique images' in mind.

The Romans, at least in the first 200 years of their exploitation of the province of Britannia (first–fourth centuries AD), built to last, and it is no accident that they were responsible for many of Europe's most durable ruins. For the first, and virtually the last time in British history, the planning authority had overall control of the choice of site and its design, and could make an investment in the urban future unrestrained by the local economy. It can be argued that no towns so robust in their fabric or so grand or so systematic and utilitarian in their design were to be seen in England again. We may compare them, to their advantage, with the new towns of the Middle Ages, eighteenth-century redevelopments such as Leamington Spa, or indeed the new towns of the 1960s, such as Milton Keynes.

Many Roman streets, public buildings and private houses were made of selectively quarried stone, high-quality brick and superlative mortar: the York sewer and the foundations of the South gate at Winchester are examples of Roman masonry which almost defeated modern demolition. This durability was recognised and famous in the ages in between. Admired by the Anglo-Saxons, whose poet praised (or conceivably satirised) the remains of Roman

1 *A lorry jammed in the Roman Arch at Newport, Lincoln. About two-thirds of the arch is now underground, due to the accumulated debris of the Anglo-Saxon, medieval and later town (Picture: Tom Baker)*

Bath as 'the work of giants', it continued to influence the topography of very many places at least until the eighteenth century. Some Roman defensive town walls are thought to have remained generally visible, if not functional, to the end of the Middle Ages; Roman houses were still around in ninth-century Lincoln; the walls of the fort on the future site of Manchester were still standing 3m (10ft) high at 'Castelfield' in 1765, while Roman masonry still survives to a height of 5.8m (19ft) in the multangular tower at York. The outline of crenellation, thought to be Roman, has been traced in the north wall of the church of St Mary Northgate, Canterbury, which had used the Roman defensive wall in its construction. In 1971 a lorry contrived to become jammed in the Newport arch at Lincoln (*Fig. 1*). Had the lorry been driving beneath this Roman arch at Roman street level, it would have experienced less difficulty. With the addition of traffic lights, a Roman town with its urban throughways, pedestrian areas and shopping precincts, its municipal rubbish tips, main sewers and public water supply (via aqueducts and piping) could have supported a modern urban society – indeed, in some instances abroad it still does.

Great contrast is offered by the rustic city dwellers, such as they were, of the eight centuries that followed the collapse of the Roman administration. The people of the *Early Middle Ages* (fourth–eleventh centuries AD) undoubtedly made continuing or occasional use of Roman buildings, but often seem to the archaeologist to have left as little mark on them as sparrows on a parapet. At a certain date, probably during the fifth century, early medieval people appeared to have temporarily lost the art or will to make mortar, bricks, tile, and masoned stone, and the unrepaired buildings no doubt eventually became a hazard rather than a shelter. Early medieval buildings were predominantly of timber, founded on posts which were secured in holes in the ground, or jointed to horizontal beams which were laid either in the earth or on dwarf walls of unmortared stones. The artist's reconstruction of the seventh-century palace at Yeavering or the large, if ephemeral, timber hall built on the demolished basilica at Wroxeter, seem to offer early medieval secular architecture at its best. Stone building returned only with the churches of the Christian Anglo-Saxons where, in addition to timber, they might employ stone foundations, including reused Roman ashlar, mortared rubble walls, plaster, window glass and perhaps even roof tiles – in short, the techniques of Roman construction relearned from abroad.

Such were the architectural options when, in the tenth century, towns became necessary again; and for all the ephemeral character of their buildings, they might have been grand and busy places. Expert carpentry, whitewash and paint, pebble yards and streets, well-tended gardens, and the dignity of a colourful cavalcade – all create a glamorous and imposing vision. We should not be too ready to condemn the early Middle Ages as chaotic or squalid. No period of ostensibly civilised life has been made to seem more remote by silence or more distant by decay.

With the *full Middle Ages* (eleventh–sixteenth centuries) we return to an epoch whose urban fabric we can more clearly see. Chester has kept its town walls, York its gate, and a hundred towns still have their cathedrals, churches or castles. All these are competently constructed in mortared stone, and it is their durabilty that has mainly encouraged their continuous use by the townspeople: for in English urban life, economy has generally overruled taste or sentiment. The majority of medieval urban constructions, including even that of prestigious buildings, was, however, still carried on in timber and earthwork. Stafford retained its defensive timber palisade until the seventeenth century. Worcester's first castle was a mound of earth 18m (59ft) high constructed by the Normans, and it remained beside the cathedral till the nineteenth century; such Norman *mottes* can still be seen at Tamworth and Baile Hill, York. Only a few medieval stone town-houses have survived to our own day – the 'Jew's house' in Lincoln and Bennet's Hall at Shrewsbury are examples. There may have been a great many more, but what we expect and what we generally find is a continuous rebuilding in timber-framing along the street frontages: the houses of the working citizens. Such townsmen were generally resident in long parcels of land (tenements), regular in their dimensions and still traceable on early town maps. With a house comprising both dwelling and workshop, sideways-on or gable-end-on to the street, and a garden, yard or smallholding to the rear, such tenements might measure 5m (16ft) broad x 50m (164ft) long. The study of these tenements is one of the chief recurring benefits of medieval archaeology in towns. In them were practised not only the necessary daily functions of human life but every conceivable trade or craft, each activity leaving its little parcel of diagnostic debris. These tenement sequences provide a fossilised census of artisans in different parts of the country through five centuries or more.

To the archaeologist it is the end of tenement life and the movement of manufacture outside the city walls which signals the real end of the Middle Ages, although it did not happen until the seventeenth century in many cases, in others never. Whether occasioned by conflagration, as in London in 1666, or by battle, as in Worcester in 1651, or merely by an excess of purchasing power, parts of many towns were replanned in the *post-medieval* period (seventeenth–nineteenth centuries AD) and towns as a whole became very different places. Brick was reintroduced into England from Holland in the fifteenth century, and by the seventeenth century was widely available. The towering jettied timber town-houses of the Elizabethan *nouveau riche* were gradually translated into brick and stone. Cellars became more commonplace and large rubbish pits and latrines were dug into those remaining open spaces in the tenements not yet covered by the rambling outbuildings of the enormous inns and prestigious residences of merchants.

For the archaeologist, it was the Victorians who made the greatest physical impact on urban space after the Romans; and, like the Romans, they built to last. The archaeology of the period is characterised by deep, extremely solid foundations of brick and mortar, by large drains and sewers, stepped cellars and deep wells. The substructures of our own century are, of course, on a larger scale – an underground railway or car park – but those of the Victorians were seemingly ubiquitous. Strip away the concrete and tarmac of a modern English town, and there, punctuated by paved streets and the occasional stone mansion, is an extensive city of brick, its ambitious scale comparable only with the *civitas capital* of an earlier empire.

Such a generalised sequence of urban images, even if valid, scarcely explains to our visitor, now growing restless beside the hoarding, what it is that he actually sees. For all the eloquence of his guide (who is, after all, short of funds), the scene is not one of romantic ruins redolent of lost civilisations, but resembles rather a giant Black Forest gateau on which someone has been practising with a pogo-stick. It is necessary to try to understand the transformation which produces urban strata since only thus can we follow the thread back from these opaque layers to the living city. I should not pretend that we do actually understand all the processes involved in this transformation; we can only say at present that some can be observed and others guessed, that we are still learning and that the study of decay itself is of some considerable interest.

Many things get buried during the life of an urban community, including, of course, human corpses (generally isolated in cemeteries), and domestic rubbish placed in pits to eliminate it from the living space. Once under the ground, decay starts immediately and proceeds at a greater or lesser rate depending on a variety of factors such as the acidity and permeability of the enclosing soil, and, of course, what the discarded objects are made of. In general, organic materials go first and most easily, so that a timber post quickly becomes a socket filled with dark earth; and a timber water-pipe leaves its rusted iron collar joints, a dark stain running between them, and the trench in which it was originally laid. Precious metals and their alloys, although rarely discarded, survive better than iron, and pottery and stone survive best of all. Variations on this theme are extensive. Anaerobic (i.e. airtight) conditions result in the total preservation of not only timber but also textiles, leather, plant matter and even flesh. Iron can also carry the ghost of wood or textile 'ferrified' in its original shape. Human bone has a wide variety of survival, from crisp white skeletons showing clear pathological detail, to graves containing nothing visible but the crown of a tooth. Animal bone survival can depend on the species of the animal and the particular member, as well as the ambient conditions of the deposit. Philip Armitage has calculated that horn sheaths, indicators of an important industry, may survive only fifteen years in some London soils. The very act of digging a hole, disturbing the relics of a civilisation already buried and thereby mixing ancient and contemporary detritus, alters the character of the deposit, accelerating or, less frequently, inhibiting further decay.

Decay is only one of the agencies at work in obscuring for the archaeologist the people he is trying to study. An urban community does not bury or discard everything it uses, and there are indeed a number of objects in our museums, some more than 1000 years old, like the Fuller Brooch in the British Museum, which have never been buried. When the opportunity allows, displaced householders will take their valuables with them. It does not always allow – and nothing is more satisfying to the archaeologist than an ancient catastrophe – a destructive fire or flood or the special circumstances generated by an earthquake or an erupting volcano. All these are comparatively rare in England. The English city generally constructs its deposits in other ways, the most significant of which is also the most deliberate: the systematic demolition of the old and

its replacement by the new, that goes under the general terms of urban 'redevelopment' or 'renewal'. At least three processes have been well documented; the first consists of dismantling existing buildings, known particularly where it occurs below ground as 'robbing'. The deserted Roman port at *Clausentum* (Bitterne) was sytematically quarried for stone, brick and tile by the inhabitants of the new medieval town of Southampton nearby; the brick for St Albans Abbey was collected from the abandoned town of Verulamium; while at Bishop Hill in York, stone, brick, tile and even the *pilae* of the hypocausts and the linings of the drains were dug out of the old Roman buildings by Anglo-Saxons engaged in the construction of their neighbouring churches at St Mary Senior and St Mary Junior. Sometimes Roman foundations (indestructible or not) were simply incorporated into the new buildings: at Colchester, the Norman castle was built round the podium of the temple of Claudius. Beside the Walbrook in London, nineteenth-century foundations rested on the stub of the demolished third-century *Mithraeum*.

Redevelopment was frequently accompanied by a levelling up or levelling down of the ground surface. At Chichester, a new Flavian city with its ordered grid of streets was erected on a platform of rammed gravel 1m (39in) thick which sealed the remains of the first Roman city and a legionary fortress. In Winchester, on a smaller scale, the topsoil of the fourteenth-century Warden's garden at Winchester College was taken up and relaid over a deposit of stones – presumably to improve drainage. The streets themselves often rose as layers of greenish mud, churned by feet and hooves, being periodically sealed by new surfaces of pebble metalling, as has been seen in late-Roman Worcester and medieval Winchester, providing at the same time a valuable sequence of unintentionally dropped artefacts. Of less advantage to the archaeologist are frequent levellings down, sometimes referred to as 'denudation', which might be occasioned by builders seeking firm platforms for timber-framed houses, as happened in thirteenth-century Shrewsbury. More devastating was the wholesale removal of strata from large areas of the town which took place at the hands of the great developers. Among the first and most energetic of these was the Norman aristocracy, whose large earthen mottes were often quarried from the adjacent tenements, and whose extensive baileys removed scores of others. The motte at Worcester consisted of 6000cu. m (7848cu. yd) of earth and debris quarried from the adjacent Roman and Saxon town. At Durham, the peninsula was first levelled for the construction of the motte, and then again by Ranulf Flambard in the twelfth century, who 'made as clear and level as a field' the space between the motte and the cathedral which had been 'invaded by numerous dwellings – less the church be soiled by their filth or imperilled by their fires'.

Such denudation was common, unfortunately so, because such 'filth and fires' represent the stuff of good archaeological sequences. Far less common was the gradual rise of living debris such as characterises the great 'Tell' settlements of the Middle East, and is often erroneously expected in English towns too. The English city-dweller generally created a chicken-run rather than an anthill; only in rather special and isolated circumstances do deep deposits form. A churchyard is the best known example of ground rising from repeated digging, modern churchgoers having to step down three or four steps to arrive at the medieval floor level. The digging of rubbish pits can cause a similar rise in ground surface through the same process as the digging of graves, and such a rise has been noticed for example along the streets of

Cheapside and Cornhill in London, and in central Chester.

Also confined to particular parts of towns are the infilling of natural depressions, hollows, stream valleys or re-entrants. In this case the impermeability of the natural subsoil and the great depth of the deposit itself sometimes being the additional asset of anaerobic preservation. Such deposits have become justly famous for the richness of the organic artefacts and vegetation captured there. The Walbrook, a little stream running southward through the City of London, was already half buried when the *Mithraeum* was constructed there in the third century AD, and the valley subsequently received tons of dumped Roman leatherwork and other debris. Similarly, at the London waterfront along the Thames, an early quay, now some 10m (33ft) below the pavement, incorporated a preserved timber cill-beam 8m (26ft) long. Anglian and Viking encroachment into the valley of the river Foss at York allowed the preservation of deep sequences of workshops, midden heaps and the relics of a dozen crafts, all of which gave the Coppergate excavations their especially rewarding quality.

2 *A hypothetical slice of urban deposit, showing different types of buried feature, differently preserved (Drawn by Liz Hooper)*

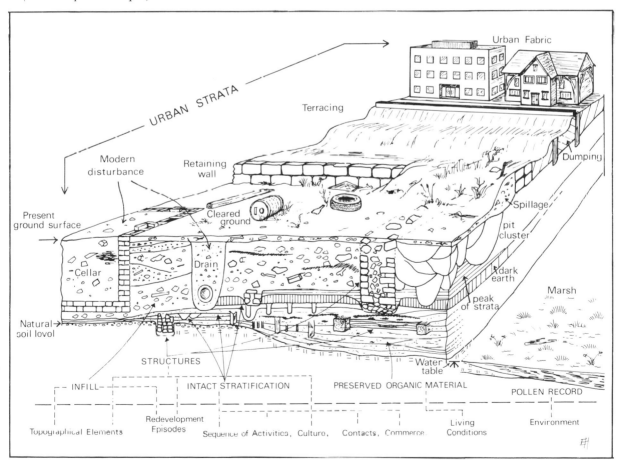

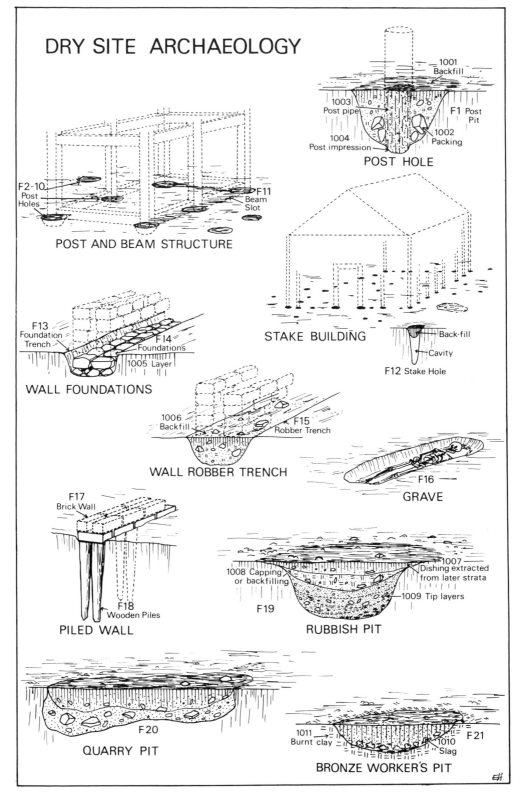

3-6 *Types of buried construction found in towns*
     (Drawn by Liz Hooper)

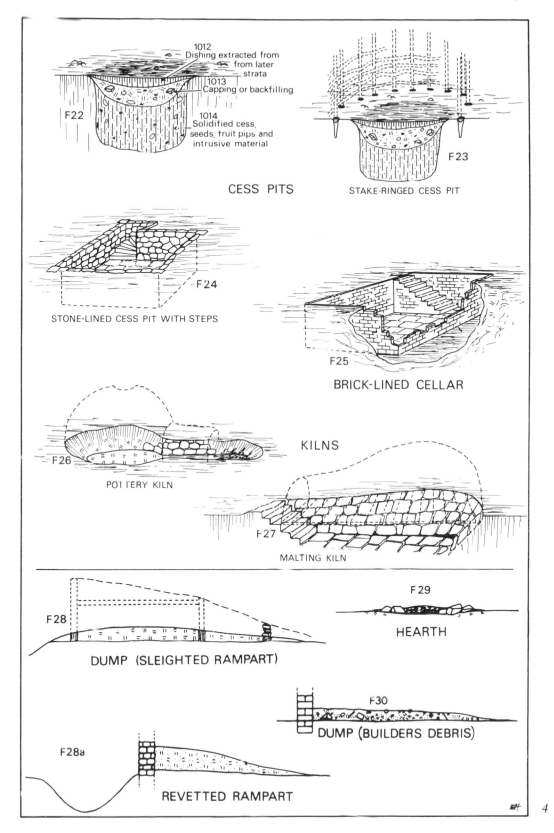

1012
Dishing extracted from
from later
strata
1013
Capping or backfilling

F22

1014
Solidified cess,
seeds, fruit pips and
intrusive material

CESS PITS

F23

STAKE-RINGED CESS PIT

F24

STONE-LINED CESS PIT WITH STEPS

F25

BRICK-LINED CELLAR

KILNS

F26

POTTERY KILN

F27

MALTING KILN

F28

F29

HEARTH

DUMP (SLEIGHTED RAMPART)

F30

DUMP (BUILDERS DEBRIS)

F28a

REVETTED RAMPART

4

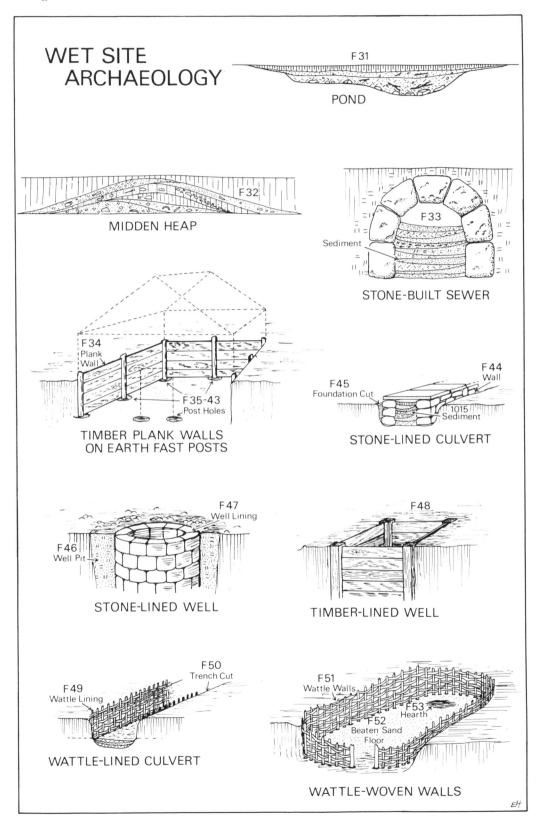

WET SITE
ARCHAEOLOGY

F 31
POND

F 32
MIDDEN HEAP

F 33
Sediment
STONE-BUILT SEWER

F 34
Plank
Wall
F 35-43
Post Holes
TIMBER PLANK WALLS
ON EARTH FAST POSTS

F 44
Wall
F 45
Foundation Cut
1015
Sediment
STONE-LINED CULVERT

F 47
Well Lining
F 46
Well Pit
STONE-LINED WELL

F 48
TIMBER-LINED WELL

F 50
Trench Cut
F 49
Wattle Lining
WATTLE-LINED CULVERT

F 51
Wattle Walls
F 53
Hearth
F 52
Beaten Sand
Floor
WATTLE-WOVEN WALLS

5

EH

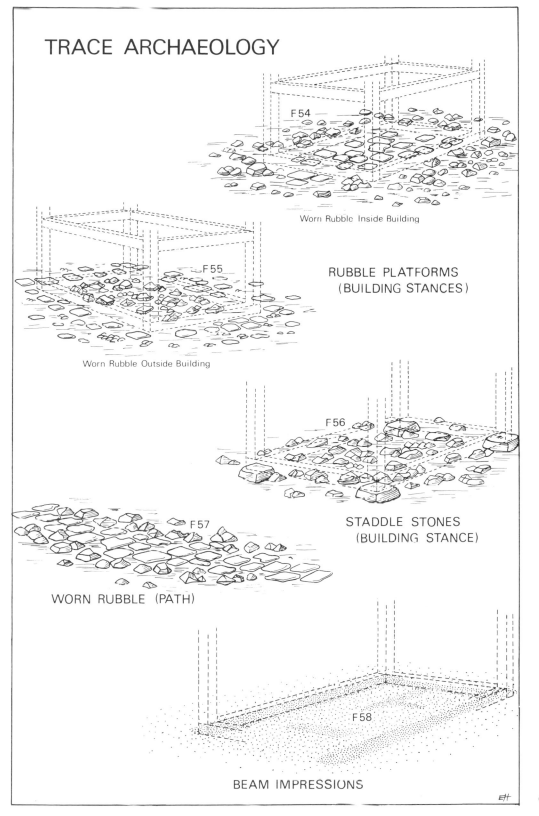

TRACE ARCHAEOLOGY

F 54

Worn Rubble Inside Building

RUBBLE PLATFORMS
(BUILDING STANCES)

F 55

Worn Rubble Outside Building

F 56

STADDLE STONES
(BUILDING STANCE)

F 57

WORN RUBBLE (PATH)

F 58

BEAM IMPRESSIONS

6

At Durham a row of Anglo-Saxon tenements, with full organic preservation, was discovered beneath the cellars of a theatre in Saddler Street on the slopes beneath the castle, sandwiched in damp sand without the complications caused by water-logging. With their all-pervading warm sweet smell, posts and stakes and wattlework bright with birch-bark and touched with blue vivianite, their discarded plants, pressed as between the pages of a book, their wood chippings, pieces of cloth and leather offcuts, these sites are the jewels in the crown of urban archaeology.

The transformation which confronts a site visitor is not, therefore, one of dark brown bathos, but one of prodigious variety; variety of survival, variety in the situations allowing survival, and variety in the resulting structures and activities, all of which are capable of resolution by the accustomed eye. Some of the structures which archaeologists actually find are illustrated here (*Figs. 3-6*), labelled by the terms generally used to describe them. If the reader finds these terms heavy-handed, let me assure him that an agreed terminology does not yet exist, so that a visual glossary of at least those names used or abused in this book will be useful.

Much of the difficulty lies in the fact that a structure discovered in the ground cannot always be immediately identified by its function – 'rubbish pit', 'latrine pit', 'beam slot' – until later on when the analysis of its contents is complete. This is the reason for the use, on site, of neutral words such as 'context' (layer or homogenous mass of material), 'feature' (manmade shape of some kind), 'stratigraphic unit' (strata of all kinds and the boundaries between them), and so on. The excavator descends, layer by layer, going gradually backwards in time, thus the meticulous drawings, written descriptions and photographs of everything she sees. No trace, no stain, no patch, no dump, no footprint is without potential significance in this sequence of manmade episodes. Each is given a name, number and a little white label. Fig. 2 provides a worm's eye view of a slice of urban deposit such as the site visitor rarely gets, and Figs. 3-6 are of different types of features, the basic building blocks of urban sequences. Some attempt has been made to evoke their original shapes by carrying up in feint lines the parts which have vanished.

These vanished portions are a salutary reminder of how fragmentary is the evidence in which we trade, and how the urban archaeologist cannot hope to make sense of it without intimate co-operation with the disciplines of biology, architecture and documentary research. So much is missing, and much of what there is cannot easily be understood. The so-called 'dark earth', for example, an apparently homogenous layer of soil covering parts of many abandoned Roman towns and separating them from their medieval successors, has been variously interpreted as the build-up of humus in an overgrown ruin, as soil imported for horticulture, as flood deposit and as the tippings from generations of hearths. It may, in the event, be all or none of these things, and it takes micro-analytical skill to determine which. Much of Roman and medieval life, and not the least interesting or significant for the inhabitants, took place upstairs where the archaeologist is rarely permitted to go. Architectural analysis, no less dependent on systematic methods of sequencing than excavation, can recover this part of the record in those buildings that remain, and provide analogies and functions for the substructures collected by excavators. Comprehensive architectural studies such as J. T. Smith's in Shrewsbury and Alan Carter's in Norwich provide the source from which archaeologists can appreciate the probable form of demolished medieval houses, their varied function and their distribution throughout the changing social milieu of the urban fabric. Ultimately, none of these disciplines can afford to work in ignorance of the framework provided by the documentary record. At once explanatory and questioning of the hypotheses generated by archaeologists, biologists and architectural historians, the documentary record remains, for the medieval period at least, the manifesto of contemporary opinion with which all other evidence must eventually be reconciled.

These disciplines, therefore, form, or should form, an interlocking system of scholarship at the level of synthesis; but this is not to say that each cannot be pursued alone, and in many historical periods they have to be.

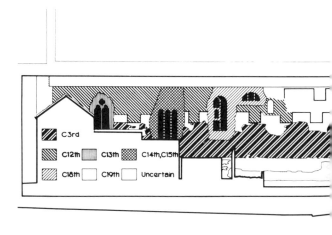

C3rd

C12th   C13th   C14th, C15th

C18th   C19th   Uncertain

The chapters which follow are concerned with the contribution of archaeology, which, as will be seen, is a contribution mainly derived from traces left on the ground or beneath it. But this does constitute an astonishing repertoire, often enough – the reader must judge – for archaeology to tell its own faltering story.

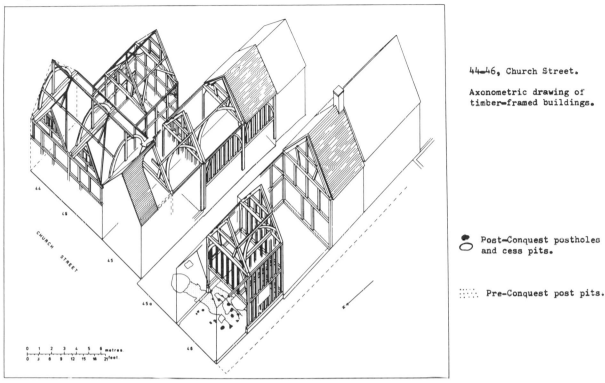

44–46, Church Street.

Axonometric drawing of timber-framed buildings.

Post-Conquest postholes and cess pits.

Pre-Conquest post pits.

7 *A medieval house and features buried below it recorded in Tamworth by Bob Meeson*

8 *Sixteen centuries of walling conserved in the nave of the church of St Mary Northgate, Canterbury. The earliest wall of the third century AD carries a hint of crenellation – it was part of the Roman town wall (Canterbury Archaeological Trust)*

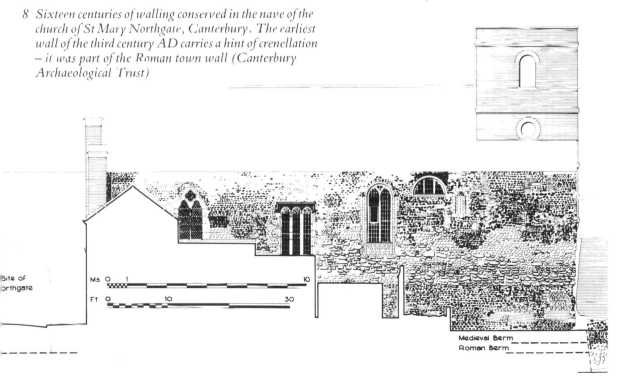

II
Vericomodium:
Roman ideal and reality

Whenever archaeologists go out looking for trends, they find variety. We need these trends and typologies and historical models so as to bring some order into the disjointed babble that is a relict material culture, studied remotely, a babble made still less accessible by filtration through the jargon experts have created. While other disciplines seek to refine their facts with the pure white heat of simple prose, archaeologists seem to rebury theirs in mounds of secondhand verbal slag. The Romanist, in particular, like some latter-day Holofernes, likes to protect his (generally unenvied) expertise by disguising it. When asked to introduce you to Roman Britain, he takes you on a perambulation through *Verulamium* observing that the *mortaria* found in *insula* xxii are more *Flavian* than *Antonine* in type and the *cloaca* was lined with *tegulae*, halting eventually in the *frigidarium* not, as you might hope, to extract a cold bottle of *vinum*, but to pour the final bucket of cold water on visitor and bather alike.

At least, so runs the prejudice that the working archaeologist often encounters. But there are, of course, excellent reasons for the use of Latin words: Latin was the official language of the province of Britain, and the school-leavers of the present century are probably the first of its inhabitants since then who have had little knowledge of it. Many of the places where people lived in Roman Britain and many of the types of objects they used in daily life no longer exist, so it is logical to use the names that were used then. Although this language adds to the strangeness of the study, it should not be allowed to create distance. In the end it is the people who matter, and the archaeologist's contention is that an intimate knowledge of their material remains will bring the people of Roman Britain nearer. By their rubbish shall we know them. In fact, what often impresses is the similarity of so many of their problems and achievements to our own.

Pompeii, the Roman city buried by the eruption of Vesuvius in AD 79, excavated from 1863 onwards, and more recently the subject of a number of notable

9 *A street in Pompeii, south Italy, once buried by the eruption of Vesuvius in AD 79 (Pictorial colour Slides Ltd)*

films, has to a certain extent fossilised the modern image of the Roman town, much as its own last days were more literally fossilised by volcanic ash. We might expect (if only because we have seen the films) a stage-set of smart squares and boulevards in which much of the population ceaselessly wander up and down dressed in sheets and sandals, shouting at each other. It is true that, even when dead and dug up, Roman towns do give out an extraordinary sense of community, one that in England at least is not easily matched by anything that came later. Aristotle argued that 'in order to decide questions of justice, and in order to distribute the offices according to merit, it is necessary for citizens to know each other's personal character'. The modern Englishman would no doubt prefer to associate this idea with a village or club, but a village is far too small to hold the kind of cultivated community that the Greeks and Romans invented, and that many European peoples, including the British, found very much to their liking. There all attempts at generalisation must end. If the sense of 'urban community' is common to all parts of the Roman Empire, the towns themselves were extremely varied: technically varied, varied in their degree of investment, their style, and above all

10 *Buildings of the vicus along the road leading out of the Roman fort of Old Carlisle (Picture by Nick Higham and Barry Jones)*

in the function which each was called upon to exercise. If town-houses in Roman Pompeii, Gloucester and London could be tall and grand, built in brick and stone with marble fascias, and provided with a courtyard with a garden and fountain, those at Braintree and Chelmsford had thatched roofs, white-washed walls and were timbered throughout.

'Roman town' would not indeed be a concept that a citizen of Britannia would have immediately acknowledged. The range of settlement-types and the circumstances which brought them into being were wide. Many, from Exeter to Carlisle, began life as forts on the axes of advance of those major military campaigns which reduced native British opposition to varied states of compliance during the first century AD. The military establishments at York, Lincoln and Exeter were large robust fortresses serving as legionary bases and supply depots: others might be more temporary bases. Outside the gates of the camp, on the main approach road, a group of followers would settle, earning a living initially by providing those rather particular services of which soldiers abroad are most in need. The process by which such places evolved from garrison to town is charmingly evoked in the case of Cirencester, whose affluent cavalry unit was probably instrumental in the transfer from the native hillfort at Bagendon of not only the nodal point of commercial oportunity, but the equally nodal point of social ambition. Within two generations of the Roman takeover, the native centre of the *Dobunni* was deserted and the town of *Corinium Dobunnorum*

with its baths and amphitheatre was flourishing. It might seem incredible, even pitiable, that the tough and romantic rural Britons should desert the noble independence of their hillfort to sit about in steamy rooms attempting to make polite conversation in broken Latin. In theory there are no limits to the horrific social mutants which can be created by money and snobbery, particularly on this island; but it may be that both images are overdrawn. When it came to elite sports, large defended settlements or glamorous and powerful women (such as Cartimandua or Boudica), it is doubtful if the British had everything to learn from the Romans. It would be wrong to think of the coming of Rome as an enforced cultural transformation for the individual Briton, who would no doubt regard the experience of a bath at Cirencester with the same equanimity as a bathe at Bagendon. Remembering the rapid rate of technical change in the twentieth century, we must be careful not to underestimate the great adaptablity of human beings, who can use a horse, a bicycle, a tram, a train and a car to commute to work in a single lifetime. Equally interesting is that, of itself, the much later decline of technology seems in its turn to have inflicted little damage on the self-esteem of leaders. The society of Roman Britain consisted, after all, of Britons rather than Romans, and we must imagine the same people that had opposed the Roman invaders taking on the technical and social opportunities brought by defeat, among them the not entirely novel adventure of town life.

Digging in Roman towns nearly always encounters pre-Roman settlement of some kind, only London, unlikely as this may seem, being claimed hitherto as having no prehistoric antecendent. In many cases the early settlement may appear coincidental, as with neolithic cultivation under Carlisle, or the middle Iron Age settlement under Ilchester. 'Iron Age' cultivation under Chester or Chelmsford shows that a new settlement there is more likely than not. But in the case of a natural (or supernatural) asset of some kind it seems reasonable to believe that a settlement of the later British Iron Age has continued, and not necessarily under new management. Examples are the salt-works at Droitwich, or the sacred spring at Buxton. There are, moreover, an increasing number of contacts with earlier settlements beneath Roman towns, particularly in the south and east, which suggest that a late Iron Age system had been partly exploited and redeveloped: the fortification at Orams Arbour, Winchester, which preceded *Venta Belgarum*; houses and streets, the latter marked with wheel-ruts and hoof-prints beneath *Durovernum Cantiacorum* (Canterbury); two phases of occupation under the forum and basilica at Silchester, which even in its first phase as *Calleva Atrebatum* contrived a certain 'native' character. At *Verulamium* (St Albans), the pre-Roman establishment has been suggested as a palace or sacred site, a pre-echo of one of the ways in which towns were reborn, 1000 years later, in the new nation of England. Chichester, already the scene of native activity, was chosen by that most romanised native of the south coast, Cogidubnus, as the site of his Italianate palace and garden.

However, the new urban network was based mainly on the garrisons' supply depots and the communication system of the army. Few of the successful towns of Roman Britain are likely to prove innocent of a fort, and most have already provided evidence of one. In many towns the garrison continued to be a prominent aspect of urban society long after the conquest itself had faded from living memory. Choosing a site for a fort demands its own criteria, and strategic sitings at river crossings often required expensive redevelopment to adapt or improve the area for town life. This the Roman administration (and its military technicians) was able to achieve; marshy ground was drained at Alchester and Southwark, while work at Cirencester included the diversion of the River Churn into the town ditch.

Digging for the origins of Roman towns encounters subtle variations of these overall themes of military establishment, public investment and native development, and the initial period of growth, lasting nearly a century, must have been a time of varied skylines. The documentary record, such as it is, gives some guide to the hierarchy which formed the declared or subconscious planning targets for the province. Chartered towns, designated *colonia* or *municipium*, were founded at

Verulamium (St Albans), York, Lincoln, Gloucester, and Colchester; while regional centres (analogous to county towns) were designated as capitals of their *civitas* – this latter word referring to the hinterland of the native tribal group (as in *Corinium Dobunnorum* – Corinium of the Dobunni) rather than to, as in school text books, a city. Such capitals once flourished where Exeter, Dorchester, Winchester, Chichester, Canterbury, Cirencester and Leicester have succeeded them. Others at Wroxeter, Silchester and Castor-by-Norwich now lie in open country far from their modern successors. Such constitutional status might express itself in terms of town planning, monuments, buildings or activities – but since image and reality were probably now and again separated by the cloak of civic pride, it will not always be easy to give names to what we find. Neither do the named towns represent the whole urban network. There were forty or more other settlements in addition to those just named, some always undefended, which played a vital role in that economy which made towns both possible and necessary.

The components of the principal Roman towns are presented here (*Fig. 11*) in the form of a 'Michelin guide', checked against the list of named places in Britannia. Each of these components, or something very like them, can be found at places other than towns – a Roman fort, for example, might have a temple, and a fort and a villa would have their species of bath-house. But where many occur together, in styles designed to serve a civil population, we can usually detect with them a busy, cultivated, wealth-creating ambience, the unmistakable emotional atmosphere of town life. All the regional capitals in the province probably had most of the components, and although we might still have doubts about Aldborough, the recent work at Chelmsford, likewise an uncertain capital, shows how quickly diligent research can establish the real personality of a place.

The most significant attribute of the Roman town was the *forum*, analogous to a town square or market place, and indeed both of these things. But most important was its social function, comparable with a students' union or a village pub: where to hear the latest joke or see the latest pretty face, where to stir up a spot of antipathy or tout for business – in short a forum of opinion. It is not easy to imagine the point of a forum other than by taking part in the evening *passagiata* in a southern French or Italian town, where it is clear from the smiles, the greetings, the asides and the busy wayward eyes. In a small modern town such as Arles or Mantova it is probable that Aristotle's adage still holds: by the age of forty, one would expect to know who everybody living there is. It would probably be very much harder for this

Name (People)	Status	Present Place	Known Amenities to date
Caesaromagus (?Trinovantum)	Capital	Chelmsford, Ex.	(?) …
Calleva (Atrebatum)	Capital	Silchester, Ha.	(43) …
Camulodunum	Colonia	Colchester, Ex.	(44) …
Corinium (Dobunnorum)	Capital	Cirencester	(97) …
Durnovaria (?Durotrigum)	Capital	Dorchester, Dor.	(?) …
Durovernum (Cantiacorum)	Capital	Canterbury, Kt.	(40) …
Eboracum	Colonia	York	(?) …
Glevum	Colonia	Gloucester	(17) …
Isca (Dumnoniorum)	Capital	Exeter, Dn.	(40) …
Isurium (Brigantum)	Capital	Aldborough	(22) …
Lindum	Colonia	Lincoln	(18) …
Londinium		London	(137) …
Luguvalium (?Carvetiorum)	Capital	Carlisle	(28) …
Moridunum (?Demetarum)	Capital	Carmarthen	(?) …
Noviomagus (Regnensium)	Capital	Chichester	(40) …
Petuaria (?Parisorum)	Capital	Brough-on-Humber	(5) …
Ratae (Coritanorum)	Capital	Leicester	(40) …
Venta (Belgarum)	Capital	Winchester	(58) …
Venta (Icenorum)	Capital	Caistor-by-Norwich	(14) …
Venta (Silurum)	Capital	Caerwent	(18) …
Verulamium	Colonia	St. Albans	(80) …
Viroconium (Cornoviorum)	Capital	Wroxeter	(80) …

Legend of symbols used in the "Known Amenities to date" column:

Maximum Defended Area (in hectares) · Forum (size in hectares) · Amphitheatre · Theatre · Aqueduct · Baths
Mansio · Sewers · Temple · Grid of Streets · Houses · Shops · Crafts · Triumphal Arch · Waterfront
Mithraeum M · Palace P · Statues · Naval Base

11 A 'Michelin guide' to the towns of Roman Britain showing the principal evidence discovered at the time of going to press (Carver/Hooper)

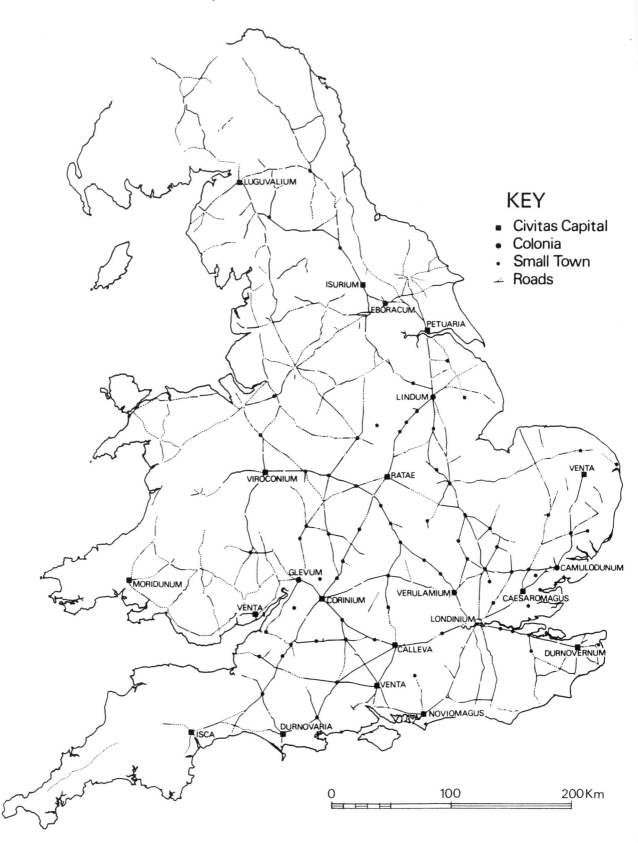

KEY
- ■ Civitas Capital
- ● Colonia
- • Small Town
- ⸝⸍ Roads

LUGUVALIUM

ISURIUM

EBORACUM

PETUARIA

LINDUM

VENTA

VIROCONIUM

RATAE

MORIDUNUM

GLEVUM

VERULAMIUM

CAMULODUNUM

VENTA

CORINIUM

CAESAROMAGUS

LONDINIUM

CALLEVA

DURNOVERNUM

VENTA

ISCA

DURNOVARIA

NOVIOMAGUS

0   100   200 Km

type of citizen to imagine what forces could possibly hold together a certain type of modern northern European town, which has no forum, where strangers are always in the majority, and all that they share is payment of rates to the same local authority, and protection by the same police force and fire brigade. Paternal provisions of the nineteenth century, such as the 'people's park' at Halifax, where the common man could take an improving stroll at the end of his working day, were little more than dim parody of Roman social dynamics.

When encountered underground, a forum comprises a few acres of cold stone – little more than a large courtyard which may have been surfaced from time to time with flagstones or cobbles or brick. But because of its role as the heart of the community, the site, shape and destiny of the forum is particularly informative. Its size gives some idea of the status of the town (as compared with other towns) and our 'Michelin guide' gives the pecking order of the sixteen fora so far located in Britain. The strata of which the forum is composed should offer,

like the street, an index of urban preferences throughout the town's life. Curiously, perhaps because of its disconcerting size and the fact that it was regularly cleaned, there have been very few long narratives from British fora, although we could guess something of what to expect. The originals were clearly laid out in the expectation of a certain population, so that the relatively small fora at Caistor or Caerwent have been read as an indication of how far the Romans had reduced the populous, if fractious, members of the *Iceni* and *Silures*. The construction of the open square, and colonnade surrounding it, was in stone – as in mid-second-century Gloucester, which acquired a large equestrian statue at the same time. In certain later periods, the forum might have been exploited with less formality – encroached on by huts, latrines and market stalls which would leave their traces in the form of wear-patterns, slots, pits and sockets. This type of evidence (which requires meticulous excavation) could be seen as a downgrading of urban life (it certainly would be in the opinion of a die-hard imperialist seeing the town square invaded by the *suk*) or conversely an economic asset – the post-holes being caused by the seasonal arrival of a fair, which was prized and welcomed.

12 *Roman London, showing the site of the fort, forum, baths, palace and the temple of Mithras (Museum of London)*

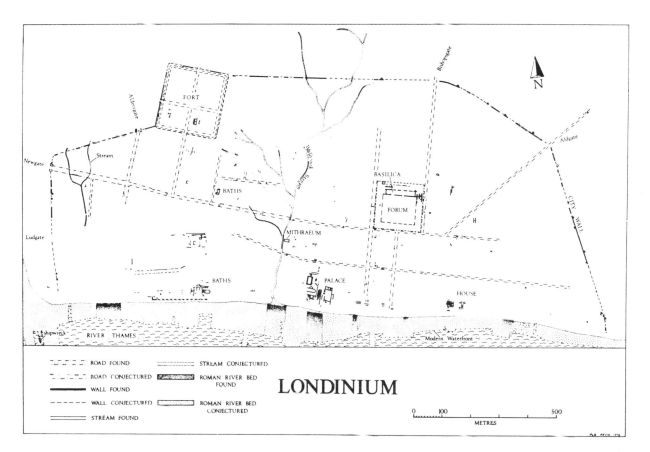

LONDINIUM

ROAD FOUND
ROAD CONJECTURED
WALL FOUND
WALL CONJECTURED
STREAM FOUND
STREAM CONJECTURED
ROMAN RIVER BED FOUND
ROMAN RIVER BED CONJECTURED

0   100   500
METRES

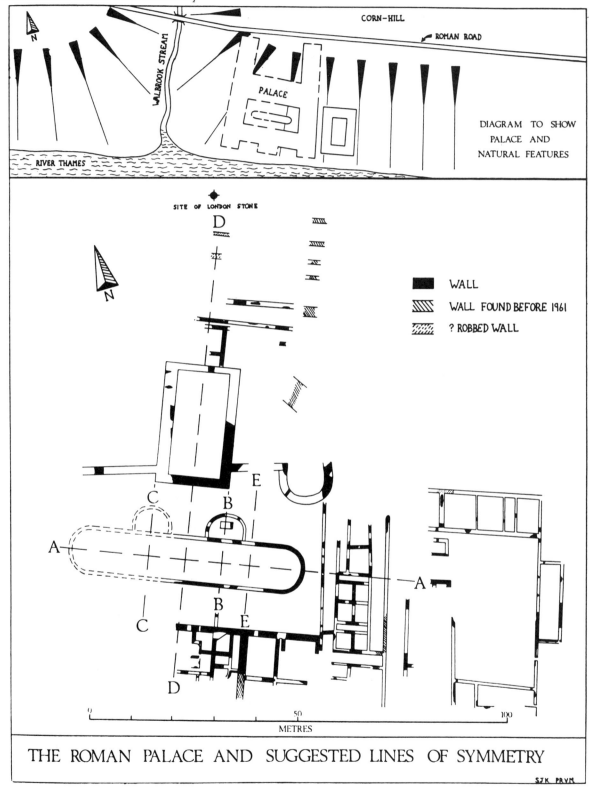

13 *The Roman palace and the London Stone; plan of the
buildings revealed by excavations by Peter Marsden
(Museum of London)*

Along one side of the forum, a large building – usually *the* largest building in the town – is found, the *basilica*. The London basilica, thought to be the largest Roman building north of the Alps, lies partly beneath Leadenhall market, where its foundations were seen in the nineteenth century. In 1977 it was mapped, and in 1986 a major excavation has begun at Leadenhall Street. The story of any basilica is even more potentially evocative than the courtyard in front of it. This enormous hall, used for local government, the administration of justice, and religious worship, had an abstract influence on later centuries, particularly the Middle Ages, which perhaps deserves further study. It was a sort of combined palace, parliament, town hall, law-court and cathedral. Beside the basilica at *Verulamium* at least three temples were built into the *forum*; the basilica at Caerwent had a large shrine added. Thus merchants and travellers could conveniently seek secular and divine sanction for their projects at the same time.

It would not be expected, however, that a society so complex as the Roman would leave all the trappings of authority concentrated in one building for us to find. The governor of the province had at least one town palace – the one discovered beneath Cannon Street Station in London – although it seems inherently probable in a countryside studded with large country houses (the 'villas'), that the equivalent of Sandringham or Chequers awaits discovery in the Chilterns or Kent. The London palace covered more than 1.2ha (3 acres) and was constructed on three different levels overlooking the Thames. It had an ornamental garden with a pool (built on a concrete raft 1.8m [6ft] thick), which was 50m x 10m (164ft x 33ft) in extent. There was a quay, perhaps with a colonnade along the Thames. The well-appointed reception halls and residential chambers were equipped with central-heating and sewers. Other monumental symbols of Roman rule are also encountered from time to time, such as the Temple of the deified Claudius at Colchester, destroyed by Boudicca, and the London arch, recently realised by Tom Blagg from stones found reused in the riverside revetment wall.

But, had one enquired of a citizen of the day where the real political business was conducted, the answer might well have been – in the baths. The Romans and the British provincials were intensely clubable, and the public baths, such as adorned all the major towns, performed a function analogous to the Selangor Club in British Singapore. Not everyone finds it easier to discuss politics sitting naked in hot water, but it seems to have created an appealing tradition. In our own day, the Kennedy cabinet used to meet in a swimming pool, and many people

14 *Triumphal Arch at London, reconstructed from stone found in the riverside wall, by Tom Blagg (Museum of London)*

apparently find it possible to do business on a golf course.

The baths themselves do not suggest exclusivity, rather the opposite, from their size, but excavated examples show that many activities could be contained in this great warm busy building at the same time. There were gymnasia and open spaces, presumably dedicated to games, but the principal experience available was 'a bath' and it is this part of the building that leaves the most durable remains. Many of the Roman town monuments we still have, such as the Old Work at Wroxeter, or the Jewry Wall at Leicester, belonged originally to public baths. A series of heated rooms gradually increases the temperature of the bather, who consequently begins to sweat. Oiling and scraping the skin with a 'strigil' can then take place, followed by a cold plunge to close the pores and generate the final feeling of exhilaration and well-being. It is the most sophisticated version of the sauna bath, a European custom that is found from Birmingham to Finland , and endured from the Bronze Age to the present day. A cross between a sports centre and a massage parlour, the baths were important enough to civic morale to attract public money for their elaborate construction, and considerable running costs. John Wacher estimates a use by 500 people a day at

Leicester, and assumes that the furnaces would be run continuously.

It is hardly surprising that where large numbers of naked people meet every day in warm rooms there should be reports of scandalous behaviour – as in the time of the Emperor Hadrian, who reacted by decreeing separate bathing times for men and women. There were, however, plenty of other recreations available to the Romano-British citizen – indeed, recreation and amenity have left a mark on the archaeological record as permanent as that of the organising hand responsible for *fora* or town walls. Amphitheatres and theatres both provided subsidised entertainment, but of different kinds. Amphitheatres arrived early and at least six regional capitals (out of twenty-one) are known to have had them. At Dorchester it was the prehistoric earthwork at Maumbury Rings that was adapted; at Caerwent and elsewhere they were built in timber, earth, and stone from new. The amphitheatre at Silchester had an initial capacity of about 9000 persons. In the central space was the *arena* (= sand). Analogous to a football stadium, but with a wider repertoire, competitions, gladiatorial combat, games, and bloodsports which are now less fashionable, such as bear-baiting and executions, took place in them. The design, for the entertainment and containment of large numbers of roaring emotional people, has never been bettered, although then, as now, the spectators were sometimes sufficiently moved to fight and kill one another.

The theatre provided more spiritual entertainment and was usually attached to a temple, and only Canterbury, Colchester and Verulamium are known to have had one. Here the performance was mannered and masked, and presumably required a knowlege of Latin, although it is known that native

15 *Roman town wall at Caerwent (Pictorial Colour Slides Ltd)*

religious festivals, probably providing, as they were to do for many centuries, the basis of British theatre, also took place there. The Romano-British religious scene is certainly one of great complexity and must have undergone a continuous if highly influential evolution from the first confrontation of the deified Emperor Claudius with the gods of Iron Age Britain, to the adoption of Christianity. The un-Romanised Britons are not thought to have built many temples, but natural features are known to have been important to them. The springs under Bath and Buxton collected so many belongings – coins, bracelets and so on – that they must have retained their role as places to make offerings right through the Roman period, and perhaps beyond. The more classical type of temple appropriate to Roman gods, with podium and pediment, appears to be rare. Architecturally the compromise between Roman and native religion produced a very characteristic building, with a plan in the form of two concentric squares – the Romano-Celtic temple. The notable religious complexes at Gosbecks, near Colchester, and Chelmsford, were contained with a precinct where the fusion of tradition and new ideas gave rise to other special types of architecture, by no means easy to interpret. Temple life was probably important to the citizens, and the buildings themselves gave an imposing presence, either outside the town walls, or inside, as in the example of Lower Brook Street, Winchester, with its associated wooden effigy of Epona.

A successfully imported Eastern religion was *Mithraism*, a forerunner and rival to Christianity, originating in Persia and featuring a human/divine hero (Mithras), often depicted performing his symbolic act of killing a bull. *Mithraea*, which resembled Christian churches in that they had a participating congregation who faced a sanctuary at one end, and featured initiation and penance, have possibly been contacted at Leicester and Carlisle, but the most famous, if perhaps atypical example, is that excavated by W.F. Grimes in the City of London. It was 17.2m (56½ft) long with an apse at the west end, buttressed against the infilled slopes of the Walbrook. The visitor entered from the street at the east end and found himself (the religion was for men only) in a nave with a raised aisle on either side. At the south-west corner near the entrance, was a font. Other gods, such as Serapis, Mercury and Bacchus were apparently admitted to the pantheon, since fragments of their statues were found. Amongst the liturgical plate were candlesticks, daggers, stone stoops and a silver gilt canister with a strainer – all presumably equipment required in the ritual sacrifice of some animal, perhaps chickens, the bones of which were found.

16 *Roman shops excavated at Newgate Street, London*
(Museum of London)

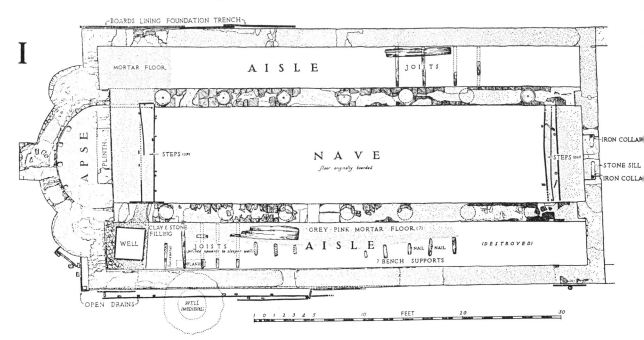

I

BOARDS LINING FOUNDATION TRENCH

MORTAR FLOOR

A I S L E

JOISTS

APSE

PLINTH

STEPS (UP)

N A V E
floor originally boarded

STEPS (DN)

IRON COLLAR

STONE SILL

IRON COLLAR

WELL

CLAY & STONE FILLING

J O I S T S
pitched upwards to sleeper walls

PLANK

GREY PINK MORTAR FLOOR (?)

A I S L E

(DESTROYED)

NAIL NAIL

? BENCH SUPPORTS

OPEN DRAINS

WELL (MEDIEVAL)

1 0 1 2 3 4 5   10   FEET   20   30

17 *The London Mithraeum excavated by W.F. Grimes
during the first great archaeological campaign in the
city in the 1950s (Courtesy of W.F. Grimes & RKP)*

The silver canister was found concealed within the north wall, and the building showed other signs of preparation against an impending desecration. Their most likely antagonists were the Christians, also belonging to an Eastern religious sect, and a militant one, who were to gain official status empire-wide under Constantine. They appear, nevertheless, to have left remarkably few architectural traces on Roman Britain in general, or in the towns in particular. One small building in Silchester and another in Caerwent have been claimed as churches, and material signs of Roman Christianity have also been discerned in Dorchester, Lincoln and at Colchester where a suspected *cella memoriae*, or reliquary building, has been found in a cemetery outside the walls. None of these examples, however, seems to manifest the architecture of influence. In the fourth century at least, after Christianity became the official religion, commonsense would expect a central and demonstrative Christian presence. Major Roman churches may of course await discovery, but there is little evidence for the most expected hypothesis: that the Christian church installed itself in the central basilica, whence it was to re-emerge in spirit and in architectural aspiration as the medieval cathedral.

The most striking difference among many for the modern traveller approaching a Roman town would be the enclosures of tombs outside it. In this it must have resembled the modern towns of Italy or Provence, the stone structures and effigies of dead citizens contained by precinct walls which almost obscured the walker's view of the town. The Roman law that the dead should be buried outside the town appears to have been strictly followed, even during the Constantinian period, and it was this that sometimes gave rise to a curious shift of the town centre. Where a church or *martyrium* was built in the Christianised extramural cemetery, its fame and success as a place of worship might attract a new nucleus around it: the town came over to join its cemetery. This happened at places on the Continent (Tours and Xanten are examples) and it ought to have happened in England, too, if any kind of Christian continuity can be sustained. St Albans, where Martin and Birthe Biddle are now at work, is the likeliest candidate, but as Grimes pointed out and recent research has further illuminated, St Bride's and St Martin-in-the-Fields outside the walls of London City may also have provided just such a nucleus, and the subsequent location of a Middle-Saxon centre there may be more than coincidence.

The burial of the dead was one aspect of that organising hand which gave to Roman towns a specially coherent structure. Other aspects have been envied or occasionally disparaged by town planners

– streets and street plans, the provision of a water supply, sewers and drainage, the disposal of rubbish and the building of the town walls. Of course, here as elsewhere there is a gap between theory and practice, and a contrast too between the beginning, middle and end of the Roman period.

In the years culminating in the heady days of Hadrian in the early second century, urban development was forthright and uncompromising. The land itself would be moulded to take a blueprint: rivers diverted and hillsides terraced into habitable platforms, as at Lincoln and York. Waterfronts were constructed to handle the cargo of ocean-going vessels – London has given the most striking example. Streets and *fora* might be paved. The water supply and sewers, essentially a linked system, were triumphs of engineering. Good-quality drinking water was, like the baths they supplied, an essential prerequisite of public health. The aqueduct supplying Dorchester was 19km (11¾ miles) long and could deliver 58,900cu. m (77,000 cu. yd) of water a day. Waste water flushed the sewers through a series of feeder channels; a major duct at York found in 1972 was large enough for a man to walk down, and constructed in masoned blocks of

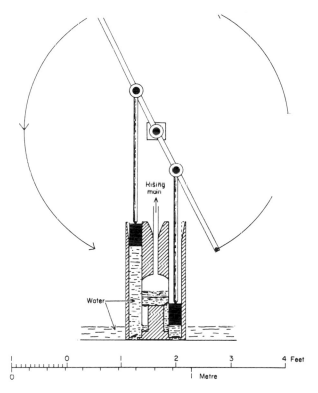

18 *A suggested reconstruction of the forcepump from Silchester used to raise water for the town supply (J. Wacher)*

millstone grit. It was a planned city, a very commodius ideal, which was, needless to say, not achieved immediately or perhaps even wanted everywhere. Not all Roman roads were paved or indeed straight; renewable cobbling with pebbles or gravel, or, as at Worcester, with iron slag, was more common, and their archaeology consequently more helpful. Successive surfacing of the road leading to the fort at Deansgate (Manchester) through the *vicus*, left stratified surfaces 1.5m (5ft) thick. They bore the marks of wheeled traffic as well as the wear of innumerable boots. Similarly, drains and culverts could be of timber or brushwood as at Southwark, as well as mortared stone and tile as at York. An octagonal stone fountain has been identified at Lincoln, but such a fine feature of continental street life remains rare. Wells and some private water supplies were allowed or contrived as the pipe-lines show: wooden with iron collar joints at Wroxeter and Worcester, or lead or pottery set in concrete.

Within this controlled framework, the archetypal machine for living in, the messy life of real people – soldiers, shopkeepers, merchants, estate managers – took its varied course. But in this detailed evidence, Roman towns are surprisingly reticent compared with their later counterparts. The personal debris on which we rely to distinguish rich from poor and noble from artisan, was rarely dropped or buried where it was used. The sewers themselves, if in general use, concentrate and scramble the personal biota diagnostic of diet; rubbish pits are rare too, probably because the refuse-disposal system was generally efficient, causing much of the domestic rubbish to end up on municipal tips outside the walls – as in the example found in an abandoned quarry at Cirencester. One suspects that the domestic and industrial waste recovered by archaeologists, though rich and varied, scarcely does justice to the enormous economic machine that powered the Roman towns.

But there remain the houses, in Roman as in medieval Britain the prime urban attributes, and an inadequate term for the rich variety of domestic and artisan establishments which infilled the skeleton provided by the streets and the great landmarks such as the basilica, temple, amphitheatre and baths. At Gloucester and Dorchester, Italianate courtyard houses have been encountered, and at York on either side of the Ouse there were large mansions with apsidal rooms, heating systems and mosaics. The mansio at Chelmsford was a large courtyard house with its own baths, taking up nearly a quarter of the enclosed area. The 'painted' house at the Dover *vicus* preserved a fine set of frescos, while a house in St

19   The Roman sewer found beneath Church Street, York (York Archaeological Trust)

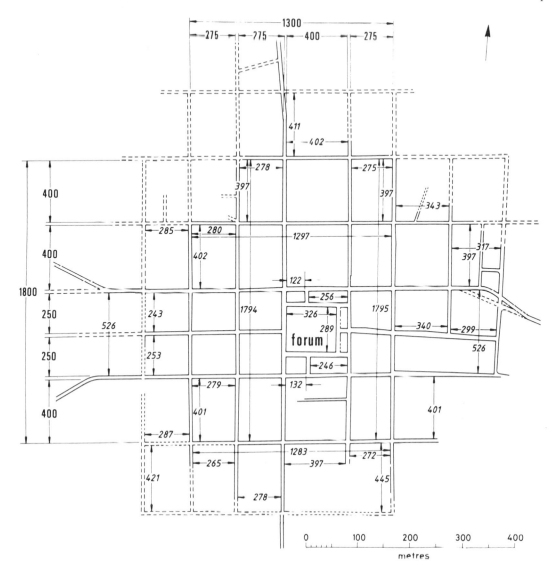

20 *Laying out a town: the street system at Silchester in Standard Roman feet (After Crummy in Grew and Hobley, 1985)*

21 Part of a painted ceiling from Verulamium (St Albans) (Verulamium Museum)

Albans had a painted ceiling as well as painted walls.

But the more characteristic town-houses, and those which arguably housed the economic motor for the urban machine, consisted of strip developments of tenements, containing residence, shop, workshop and backyard, and separated from each other by a network of pedestrian alleyways. The structures might be timber-framed, founded on 'dwarf' walls, with clay floors and daub panels, and roofs of thatch, but for all that could still achieve impressive facades, using well-finished carpentry, rendering and whitewash, to rival or even to match those similarly finished but rendered in stone. Examples from Braintree, Chelmsford, Great Dunmow and across the River Thames from *Londinium*, at Southwark, demonstrate the formula to which the Middle Ages would return.

The most demonstrative of all the Roman urban developments, and the one which came to symbolise the town for the next one and a half millennia, was the wall which contained it. Roman towns did not begin with a wall, as one assumes with the hillforts that preceded them or the Anglo-Saxon *burhs* that

22 *Interval tower on the Roman wall at York,*
  excavated by the York Archaeological Trust
  (York Archaeological Trust)

followed. The wall was added to enclose most, or part, or sometimes only a small part of pre-existing and presumably flourishing Roman settlement. The psychological effect of such a barrier can be imagined. It created, out of a familiar amenity, a defensible enclave where space was at a premium, and ensured that from now on there would be two conditions of men – those on the inside and those without. Although one of the motives for building a wall may have been protective in the military sense, there were other protective aspects, for example commerce and class, that prompted this particular expression of civic pride. As with other elements of the Roman town, the components of the defensive system were general (ditch, rampart, wall and gate), but the way they were realised differed from place to place and century to century, potentially giving an index to the arrival of the defensive habit and its provocation throughout the province. A great deal of research of varied quality has therefore gone on chasing walls, but many problems remain, and for good archaeological reasons. The defensive fabric is of great size, durable in time and notoriously difficult to date.

The first defences visited on Exeter were constructed in earth and timber in the late second century; in the legionary fortress at York the turf

23 *The multiangular tower at York. The small neat stone-work in the lower half of the tower is Roman, while the tower was repaired, restored and carried up again to its present height in the Middle Ages (Picture: P.A. Rahtz)*

rampart was later faced with blocks in millstone grit, while in the south-west the wall was constructed in limestone ashlar over oak piles. The interval tower, excavated by the York Archaeological Trust, was 20.2 x 9.4m (66¼ x 30¾ft) in plan, while the nearby multangular corner tower, raised and repaired in the Middle Ages, still dominates the Abbey Gardens. Gates were the control points, as well as ornamental arches, and were sometimes built first. They were realised in timber, as at Carlisle, or stone, as at Lincoln, whose Newport arch still (just) stands. An exciting discovery at Canterbury was the crenellation fossilised in St Mary's Church, Northgate, which perhaps belonged to the Roman city wall itself. The work of constructing a town wall was formidable – particularly where the construction was in stone – a colossal investment which must, where it had occurred, have inhibited further development of the town centre for economic reasons alone. Unlike elsewhere in the Empire, the earth and timber rampart remained common in Britannia, although this may have also reflected British taste and competence rather than lack of investment. When more of Roman Britain is revealed, it may appear as somewhat unfinished architecturally in comparison with other provinces, and the British continuum from the Iron Age to the fifth century may begin to show through more clearly.

With every Romano-British town having such an individual and complex reaction to urban ideas, every Romano-British town is a precious asset. If basilica and forum, gatehouse and bath have begun

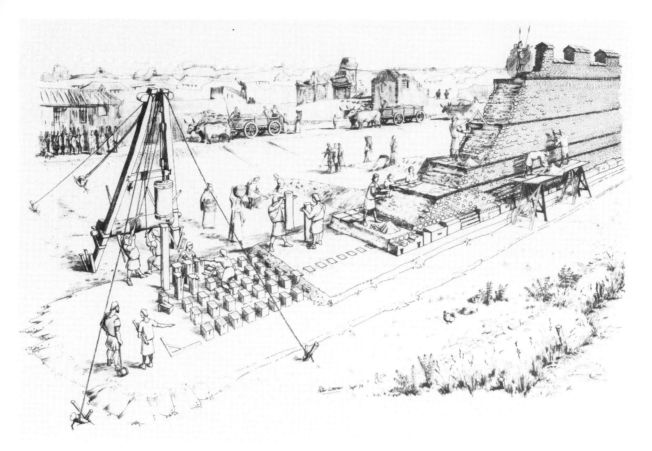

24 The Roman riverside wall at London under construction: an evocation by Peter Warner (Museum of London)

to seem predictable and tedious from a distance, they are not so, close up. The individual destinies now being collected, particularly from the shops and artisan's tenements, will one day connect to give a setting and a system significant for everything that followed. No period has more crucial evidence for understanding such a system than the later centuries of Roman towns. In may ways, the first, second and third centuries AD are analogous to the seventeenth, eighteenth and nineteenth centuries in British town life, and it is always difficult to remember that centuries then were just as long in duration as centuries now. A citizen of first-century Cirencester may have started his career as a clerk to a retired cavalry sergeant, and ended it as a wealthy merchant, proud to be of Dobunnic stock but as proud as any Roman of the clean white classical buildings, straight streets and open spaces of his capital. His son and grandson lived in a world of accelerating affluence and urban pretension, the walls severing their view of the countryside that supported them. Still running a family business and no doubt master of several others, a third-century descendant might have constructed a country villa and moved into it with a small group of dependants, leaving his tenants to fight for the family's profit in a crowded market place.

It may be that the fourth-century Roman town, into which the tenth generation of this hypothetical family steps, has not left a very fair account of itself, because in many ways its messages are read in the layers of the dereliction that was to follow. There is, nevertheless, a clear indication that something fundamental had happened to the Roman ideal. Official buildings had been were demolished and quarried for stone; the defences had been refurbished or installed in every major settlement; the streets were covered in trampled mud and resurfaced with pebbles; heavy industry, especially ironworking, had come inside the walls, and sometimes, as at Silchester, inside the basilica itself, and cattle were slaughtered in street markets. It was a more crowded, more busy and more dirty place. In many respects the fourth-century town could have evolved without effort as an asset of medieval feudalism, housing another thirty generations for whom its crenellated walls and towers were home. But in this corner of the Empire, it did not. Somewhere between the third and sixth centuries the Roman urban machine ground to a halt. Britain became England, and the urban process would have to begin all over again.

III
Dark earth and Dark Ages

The withdrawal of the Roman administration from the province of Britannia in AD 410 is noted in recorded history by a celebrated rescript of the Emperor Honorius. It meant that all and any expectations of economic or military rescue that the province may have had of Rome were put in doubt. What happened to the towns? A great deal of archaeological energy has been put into this problem, in a way the most central and the most particular to the history of settlement on this island. Five hundred puzzling years separate the ordered formality of the Roman *civitas* capital from the Anglo-Saxon city of the next chapter, and archaeological investigation can throw much light on them.

Of course, the official statement from Honorius probably did not come as a surprise to everyone, and there is no reason why it should have produced an immediate change in lifestyle. Britain had been a Roman province for four centuries and commonsense (if nothing else) tells us that the news was not greeted as a signal to put away one's toga, smash all the pottery in the kitchen, empty the small change on the floor and take to the hills. In four centuries, towns, and provincial reaction to Imperial edicts, had changed a good deal. However, the impression gained from such evidence that we have, is that there had already been a widespread economic decline, and that, within a generation of the famous rescript, towns were largely deserted.

Many theories have been put forward to explain this episode, probably the most devastating social upheaval that the inhabitants of Britain have experienced in the last 2000 years, and archaeologists have used those theories partly to direct, partly to test, and partly to explain their own findings. Some prefer practical explanations, like flooding. Heavy silt layers have indeed been recorded at a number of places: Chester, Droitwich, Gloucester, Staines, Spalding and London. But this may have been an effect of neglect rather than its cause. Others feel that military aggression inside and outside the Empire,

inspired by greed, Imperial ambition and a general sense of adventure, was quite sufficient to put an end to civilised posturing once they were no longer held in check by the central army machine. For England the confrontation is provided by the immigrant Anglo-Saxons, thought to be settling from the fifth century onwards in the east, with the indigenous British, who may themselves have become migrant, predatory and 'heroic'. Others suggest that the Roman army was already such a cosmopolitan affair that factions arose within it, self-interest for a group providing a more powerful motivation than the well-being of an impersonal formation like the Empire. Others have blamed Christianity, which, like other Eastern religions, introduced an other-worldliness into professional ethics. Many of the best brains became non-combatant, and their followers put the abstract dominion of God before that of the Emperor. Another hypothetical agent is bubonic plague, which decimated the population, perhaps particularly its many slaves, forced up the price of labour and encouraged people to leave the cities, never to return. And a modern vision of the onset of the Dark Ages is, perhaps not surprisingly, that of a community brought down by insidious inflation, eventually provoking the cutting and cessation of public funds, with the consequent collapse of officially promoted trade, swiftly followed by famine, unrest and anarchy.

All or any of these factors may have been provoked or inflamed by the most elusive and pervasive influence of all – that of public mood and morale. An economic system may be made unworkable simply because people no longer trust each other. It will take another five generations of archaeologists, exploiting every possible opportunity for research, to determine how far any of these factors, military, economic, religious or political, really provoked the fundamental changes of fifth-century Britain. What is clear is that the effort will be worthwhile. Every archaeological success throws some light on human behaviour – that is largely the point of it – and few things can be more absorbing and instructive than the behaviour of humans during a prolonged disaster. At the time, what people felt they needed were tales of heroes, and this they gave themselves, together with the occasional lambasting of all and sundry by incensed commentators such as Gildas. Later, that is in our own time, we who have no burnt property in Corinium, or relatives killed in raids or by the plague, can compose tales of a more dispassionate kind from the traces left underground.

In practice, these are also tales which have a strong seasoning of fiction, because what we actually find, at least in towns, is precious little. Sandwiched between the ruins of the robust Roman temples, houses and streets, and the foundations of the later first-millennium timber and stone churches and houses which succeeded them, little more can generally be distinguished than layers of dark brown earth, and building rubble, often finely broken and crushed. These layers vary in composition and thickness from town to town, but have been proposed as a general phenomenon with an over-riding characteristic – they are inscrutable and archaeologists can only make sense of them with the greatest difficulty.

It is natural to use imagination as the jumping-off point for this piece of detection; and imagination suggests a number of models for the post-Roman town, each more or less plausible and each providing a particular line of research. Imagine, for example, that the sturdy buildings of the Roman town simply continued to be used by a resident population who also used the inherited artefacts of their parents. By the time they reached the third and fourth generations in the sixth century, the population would have been living largely with antiques; the mass-produced cooking-pot obtainable in a fourth-century market would have become a treasured heirloom, brought out only for large family gatherings.

Speculative or fortuitous conservation of this kind may well have occurred, since Roman objects found their way into the pagan graves of the following centuries. But it seems scarcely consistent with human nature to remain so obstinately nostalgic. Military pressure and the displacement of the old community by a new one would provide another explanation – but where is its crockery? We would have to say that the new material culture, whatever it was, was such that it does not normally survive – the users of leather bottles and wooden bowls. A few large bronze cauldrons have suggested to some people that there was a change in eating habits, reflecting in turn a change in social structure: no more family groups, each with its dinner service, but big rambling extended interbred tribes with large

communal stews, dished out centrally. Looking at crockery alone, the evolution of meals from an array of plates containing titbits, to large cooking pots, the evolution from salad to stew, happened at some time in the first millennium AD, so perhaps had already begun by the fifth century. However, waterlogged deposits with food remains and the expected range of wood and leather vessels that contained them have yet to appear.

The continuous use of stone buildings is plausible, since they were certainly designed to last. How far can we see the traces on them of post-Roman occupation? The trouble is that the upper storeys, where town life could have continued for centuries, are usually thoroughly demolished by the time we get to them. The insertion of a floor, a partition, the making of a window or fireplace would certainly have left their marks, but they are not easy marks to distinguish in a pile of rubble. Only when repairs and improvements went below ground can we pick up their traces. The streets of Lincoln were made up after AD 392. A courtyard in St Albans was still in use, and a water-pipe laid there in the fifth century or later. The York principia building in the fortress is thought to have been used until the seventh century. The Southgate at Winchester was still functioning in the fifth or sixth century. 'Saxon' huts, generally fifth-century in date, have been found in Canterbury, Dorchester and Colchester, as well as smaller Roman towns such as that at Heybridge. On the other hand, the medieval streets of Exeter, Gloucester, York and London ignore their Roman predecessors, which at York had accumulated a deposit of silt 0.5m (20in) deep. The amount of empty space recorded in sixth- to ninth-century cities is now considerable. There is also some reason to believe that the continued occupation of Roman buildings in Britain's towns was not very probable. Robust they may have been, but even the most robust buildings have structural members which need replacement from time to time. No roof tiles, no brick, no cement, yet alone mosaic or wall plaster, seems to have been manufactured after the fifth century, and there must surely have come a time when such buildings became more of a death trap than an amenity.

One view of this lack of any materials to repair buildings is that the relevant techniques were 'lost' as a result of a general amnesia, and this idea receives a little support from some curious discoveries at York and elsewhere. Here, areas of crushed plaster and mortar have been found in post-Roman levels, suggesting pitiful attempts at reconstitution by mixing with water. If true, this evokes in retrospect a highly compartmentalised Roman society, where many elementary techniques were in the hands of a skill-conscious few. But it would be premature to sneer. Not everyone in our present over-educated community knows how to make mortar out of limestone, or how to manufacture pottery or coins, and even those that do might find it difficult if separated from their workshops.

Within the archaeological profession there is always an eloquent lobby (which has one eye on the history of the subject) which is wholly sceptical of negative explanations. The whole material culture of the Dark Ages is there, and is present, moreover, in the Roman towns; we just don't know how to see it. One way it can remain invisible is by resembling exactly what went before, which argument requires you to believe that the Roman lifestyle was carried on into the fifth, sixth or even seventh centuries in the form of potteries making pots, coiners making coins and masons making buildings, that resemble in every particular those that were made 300 years earlier. There are well-known continental parallels for this kind of conservating activity, such as the Pietra-ollare (soapstone) bowls of the alpine area of Italy which were manufactured from the first century to the nineteenth century AD; or the Maria Theresa dollar, still made in the Near East, and still carrying the date (1780) of its last issue; or some buildings, particularly churches like Santa Maria Foris Portas at Castel Seprio, for which any date between the fourth and tenth century is stylistically possible. It is not altogether impossible that antiques were recreated, particularly for buildings, where a deliberate attempt to recreate Roman styles and techniques was made by the tradition-conscious Carolingian court. In England there are some oddities, like the Anglian tower at York, grafted onto the Roman city wall and constructed in a style that is nearer Roman than medieval. But they are uncommon and uncertain, and it is fairly unlikely that in England, at least, there is a large well-disguised corpus of pseudo-Roman things awaiting discovery. The things themselves have been well studied by generations of archaeologists, and it is incredible that the centuries should have failed to introduce some minute changes into the fabric and style of pots, metalwork or buildings. Apart from which, people were certainly living and leaving traces elsewhere. York might not have produced any pottery datable between the fifth and ninth centuries, but areas of Northampton have produced more than 2000 sherds from this time.

Another type of invisibility is more probable with buildings, as with artefacts – that caused by the disappearance of ephemeral materials. Buildings in timber leave little enough trace if the posts were originally set into the ground, since the wood rots away and only the post-hole survives. But what if frame buildings were used, whose only contact with the ground were that of the cill–beam supporting the superstructure? Then we can imagine whole settlements of substantial buildings, braced and studded with timber, panelled with daub, and roofed with straw – all materials which can and do disappear without trace. Just such a settlement has been inferred at Wroxeter, seated on the rubble of the demolished Baths Basilica building. Ingenious and meticulous recording of large areas by Philip Barker was responsible for the observation of linear arrangements of small stones, level blocks set in arrays, and patterns of wear on rubble platforms. The small stones collect against the line of a cill–beam, and remain after the wall has vanished; level blocks serve to support a frame building above the ground, like staddlestones support a granary; and the wear-patterns tell of paths made by habitual journeys – to the front door, to the garden, to the outside lavatory. The rubble beneath the building can show up as a square or a rectangle which is 'fresher', less trodden; and on occasions thin parallel lines of soil can be seen, the dust brushed down over the years between the floorboards. Such 'building stances' have been detected at other places (and belonging to other periods), but Wroxeter is by far the most ambitious evocation of an intangible Dark Age conurbation.

It is no wonder that excavators have searched long and hard for this type of Wroxeter ghost-city in the rubble layers of collapsed Roman buildings, but, it must be said, with very little success. Could it be that the areas available in a living city are too small to catch sight of these subtle regularities in the rubble? Or is it the fact that these other towns later revived, and their new occupants punched the delicate pattern full of holes – the perforation by later pits and pipe-trenches that makes the Dark Age occupation incomprehensible? This is certainly possible, and is one reason why archaeologists strive for large open areas in places where continuity is suspected.

On a large number of these opaque rubble sites, the still more opaque dark earth lies above. A favourite interpretation used to be that this earth was nothing more than the natural mould caused by centuries of overgrown trees, bushes and weeds: the dark earth was itself the diagnosis of an abandoned city. The place-name Silchester, which the Anglo-Saxons gave to *Calleva Atrebatum*, is evocative in this respect: 'fortress of the willows'; fortress, because the Roman wall still stood, and willows, because the ruins were overgrown by willow trees and shrubs, their roots and branches gradually undermining and dismantling the brick and stone walls. However, 'Calleva' itself means woody place, so the Saxon place-name may imply exactly the opposite: contact

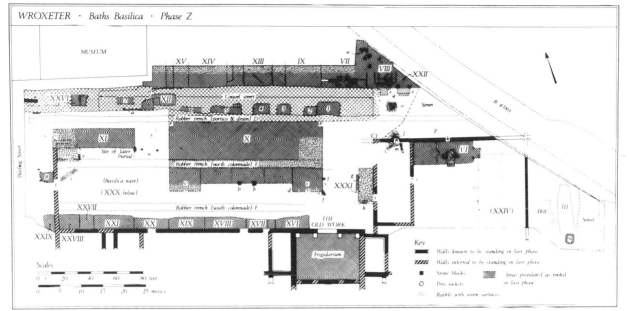

25 *A strictly provisional interpretation by Philip Barker of the plan of timber buildings and a street, the traces of which he has detected on the rubble of the largely demolished Roman town at Wroxeter. These buildings are thought to have been erected in the fifth century AD (Courtesy of P.A. Barker)*

and communication with a live civic community.

In many places, moreover, the dark earth is virtually innocent of building stone, being finely mixed and containing small fragments of tile and pottery. Careful examination by soil scientists has been taking place over the last few years to try to reach a more certain understanding of how such a deposit came to be there. Some first results from the London team are of the greatest interest – the soil is dark because it contains large amounts of finely divided charcoal, the tippings of countless domestic fires. So, whereas the imagined timber buildings remain generally elusive, there is here some reason to suppose that someone was still in the town – enough people for sufficient time to build up a substantial deposit from burnt firewood and ash.

The moment has not yet arrived to say exactly where the truth lies about the use of towns between the fourth century and the eighth. Some of the very best work – the most careful thinking and digging – is currently in progress. Although considerable areas have now been examined with negative results, the Roman town was a big place and it remains possible that a British community continued to exploit only a very small portion of it, putting the rest under cultivation. As Martin Biddle has suggested, these may be 'princely' groups, exercising a relict authority. It may be that discoveries such as the

church built centrally in the forum of Lincoln will eventually lead us to their halls. In the long timber building beneath the Blackfriars in Carlisle we may already have one. If the research momentum can be maintained over the next few decades, archaeologists will be capable of giving answers which will rewrite, or write for the first time, this odd period of English history, featuring the fundamental regression or reconstruction of civilisation and being of the greatest interest to anyone alive today. But it would be wrong to leave the subject merely as a little bag of hypotheses and disclaimers, because that implies that it is more of a headache than an inspiration. In fact, it is an excellent field for speculation.

A nice statement of the Dark Age problem is given by Bu'lock in his account of the hiatus in the story of Manchester:

We start where the archaeologists leave off, with the fourth-century *Castrum* over at the junction of the Irwell and the Medlock and its associated *Vicus* extending some way to the north between the main highway, modern Deansgate. There follow several dim centuries, during which British, English and Scandinavian travellers and settlers come and go, mysteriously, upon a darkened stage, on which we realise that the scenery is somehow being rearranged. When the lights go up we find the medieval manor-house, precursor of modern Chetham's standing at the other end of Deansgate, where the Irk joins the Irwell, with its chapel and the tenements of its dependants surrounded by fields, wastelands and woods. The walls of *Mancunium* are an overgrown ruin while the vicus is now called Aldport and woods and coppices stretch from modern Quay street to Knott Mill.

To this I shall now give an archaeologist's reaction and offer some explanations both for what might have happened and for the curious traces we actually find.

None of the discussions so far has taken adequate account of the predatory and acquisitive inclinations of human beings. The main effect to be seen, surely, in an inadequately policed city would be vandalism and the pillaging of materials. This was the principal way in which 'the scenery was rearranged' – the cities were largely dismantled. This does not always have to be done in a piecemeal or clandestine fashion; some of these robbed-out sites are so large that one wonders whether some authority outside the city had a proprietorial claim upon it as a resource – a kind of official building supply depot. Looking at an extensively robbed site like that in the York *colonia* at

26 Shifting central places in the north Shropshire plain. The Wrekin *was an Iron Age hillfort, associated with the Cornovii; Viroconium Cornoviorum (Wroxeter) was their Roman capital; near* Atcham, *the cropmark of a settlement, probably middle-Saxon, has been seen from the air, while a late Anglo-Saxon* burh *was established at Shrewsbury, which remains the centre for the county (Drawn by Liz Hooper)*

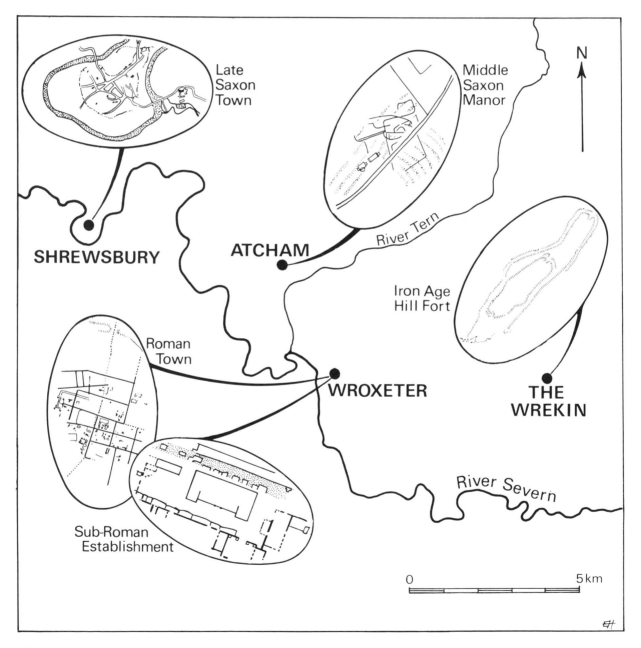

27 *A corn-dryer, re-using a Roman altar, excavated by Philip Rahtz beneath Anglo-Saxon and later defensive banks at Hereford (Hereford Museum)*

Bishop Hill, where even the drain-linings and hypocaust tiles had gone – apparently to the adjacent churches of St Mary – it is easy to believe that quarrying Roman buildings was an accredited activity, and at some periods even controlled to the advantage of the exchequer. It is even possible that the timber ghost-city at Wroxeter with its building platforms, little hearths, sorted rubble and gravel cul-de-sac, made apparently of sifted mortar, owes much to organised robbing. The stone walls of the basilica (all, that is, but the Old Work which still stands, and the masoned blocks reused as a portico), must have gone somewhere, before the principal ranges of timber buildings were erected. Perhaps what we are really seeing are the temporary premises of a late Roman or Dark Age demolition company. Where did all this Roman stone, brick and tile go? Much of it certainly went into other buildings, including early Saxon churches, as can be seen at Wroxeter itself, nearby Atcham and many more examples throughout the country. It must also have been used in many other buildings, Roman or Saxon, which have since vanished. It reappears in other Dark Age structures, such as the corn dryers, perhaps eighth-century, which incorporated Roman altars and lay underneath the Saxon rampart at Hereford. Dispersed all over the hinterland of a Roman city, it would soon lose, in the entropy of its use and reuse, most of the tell-tale signs of its Roman origins.

If the 'trace-occupation' on rubble could sometimes be attributed to casual or systematic robbing, what of the dark earth that occurs elsewhere? Here we can introduce two new factors into the discussion. First, such dark layers are not confined to the post-Roman period: identical episodes have turned up, for example, in medieval Lichfield and seventeenth-century Stafford where they bear distinct traces of cultivation. Secondly, techniques of seriation (see Chapter 9) do suggest that these layers (examples from Worcester and Stafford) contain very high diversity – in other words many different types of pottery from previous periods, abraded and broken small. The interpretation is again that of cultivation. In some of these later examples it seems inevitable that the soil was actually imported into the town – that at Stafford, a sand and gravel site, contained a great deal of clay – and we have a documented Dark Age example from Tours, where the Bishop imported soil to construct a vineyard within the walls. This idea does not conflict with the evidence for tipped ash, which would have been a normal fertilising routine.

If these interpretations are valid we still have a big problem to solve before we can illuminate this piece of urban history. We might guess that much activity observable between the fifth and tenth centuries in towns is due to robbing and horticulture, but we do not know exactly when these things took place. Neither stone-robbers nor cultivators are given to dropping large numbers of datable objects. Where the next tangible activity in the town was the late Saxon development, we have a bracket of 500 years. But in other cases, not until the twelfth, sixteenth or nineteenth centuries does recognisable urban life begin again.

This brief archaeological picture suggests that most parts of most towns were finally abandoned, as towns, soon after the 'official end' of Roman administration. Then, or earlier, or later, they were exploited as quarries for building materials; after this, parts were laid out as gardens or more extensive areas of cultivation. Some places must have been exploited in this way within the fifth to ninth centuries, and there we have to suppose a private estate or manor of a kind for which Winchester, as so often, provides the model. Martin Biddle's presentation of his post-Roman sequence at Lower Brook Street has yet to be fully published, and will be infinitely more valuable and informative than any summary that can be made here. But it would seem (from the interim report that has appeared) that we have here *a* part of *a* town where the settlement fabric of the sixth to eighth centuries coincided with what went before and after: a burial, a workshop, an early church; perhaps nearby a hall and outbuildings. This would provide a reflection within the walls of an establishment which is otherwise overwhelmingly rural; the 'palace sites', manors or 'villae regalis' which were the favoured settlement type of the middle-Saxon aristocracy. Such re-exploitation might be spiritually close to the administrative role of the Roman town, as a centre of regional authority, or it might have been considerably more remote, more in the pragmatic spirit of the late twelfth-century lord of the manor who adapted and fortified the amphitheatre at Silchester, constructing his 12m (39ft) long hall in the arena.

Such ideas might suggest a prolonged interruption of town life, but not always an interruption in the use of the town – as a useful ruin, and as an enclave for an old or a new artistocracy, spaciously arranged like a walled park. It might be an indication of how quickly the rural Anglo-Saxon mentality dominated the culture over most of England in the years following the fifth century. They knew how to make pottery and metalwork, but they preferred to build in timber and did not want or need town life. No doubt the self-confidence and self-interest of these heroic and belligerent Germanic communities provoked a memory in the British soul of their own similar pre-Roman Iron Age past; and soon every-one was doing it. The towns were recognised for what they were and what they had been, as their Anglo-Saxon names show. In the seventh century, St Cuthbert was still able to admire the Roman fountain at Carlisle, as the guest of its citizens. But the new mode of living was based on the drinking hall and the loyal gang, adventurous deeds of acquisition and exploitation, and imaginary genealogies leading from and to immortal greatness. It was who you knew and what you had done, not where you lived that mattered. The new mood of the new politics was far more important to the ambitious, and indeed to everyone, than the ability to make mortar.

IV
The early English town

To those that love the natural world, and find a comfort in its beauty and its violence that is almost religious, the Dark Ages exercise a dangerous fascination. The disused arterial road system, the submerged square miles of factory farms, the derelict cities and abandoned industries, the irrelevance of all this grand design and its replacement by wild oak forest, meadows and mud flats teeming with game, has an enduring appeal. Not since the mesolithic period can England have seemed so green. Even if not strictly accurate, the concept had real roots: hunting and the possession of large tracts of land (however unproductive) were a fundamental motivation of the new society of the post-Roman era, and remained so for many centuries. And if, as a concomitant of belonging to this natural world, the new society was initially held together by a personal allegiance rather than wages, this too was a feeling of 'right behaviour' experienced at all levels that took a very long time to change. Urban life, when it reappeared at the end of the first millennium AD, would be very differently motivated to the civilisation of Rome.

Such a huntsman's paradise, in reality largely ordered and owned, can never have been free from disruption by political ambition. The roads to urbanism that emerged in the seventh century and later were many and various, and we see the new urban centres with considerable difficulty. The documentation is sparse, so sparse that it was possible to doubt, in this century, that the Anglo-Saxons had towns at all. The Anglo-Saxon Chronicle speaks of something called a *burh*, but tells us very little about it, giving rise to an uncertainty compounded by a change in the meaning of the word itself between the seventh and twelfth centuries. When in AD 755 Cyneheard fights Cunewulf in Hampshire, the latter is visiting his mistress in the *byrig* of *Merantune*, a small defended enclosure containing a hall and a few outbuildings. A century later, Alfred's *burhs*, although also defensive, were much larger and part of a strategic network

established in Wessex. A similar system apparently extended over the Midlands during its reconquest, by other members of his family, from the Danes. The later forms – *bury* or *burgh* – are found attached to defended monuments like hillforts which were not necessarily towns, and perhaps to towns which were not necessarily defended. Werfrith's *burh* at Worcester was established 'for the protection of all the people' and some of the King's income from the community was sacrificed to build it. Commerce, on the other hand, took place in a *port*, but a *port* could be situated within a *burh*. It was in the *burhs* that the mints were sited when the country returned fully to a coinage economy in the tenth century. The impression that emerges is that *burhs* were initially defensive or strategic in function, but many simultaneously or later performed as commercial centres.

As so often, archaeology tells a slightly more varied story. Where, for example, the defended enclosures (or *burhs*) have been located, some appear to be almost empty inside, although occupation may be encountered nearby: Cricklade, Christchurch, Buckingham, Maldon and Wareham are examples. It is inevitable that what we actually find – the pits, ditches and post-holes of timber buildings – can be equated only partly with the scant historical images, but the work of the last few decades has provided the fragments of a consistent picture. The different paths to the new urbanism cross, intersect, and run parallel from time to time, but each can be distinguished and appears in isolated prominence from time to time. The needs of authority, of strategic force, of the Church, of craft production and of commerce, whether acting individually or together, pressed into being a range of settlements which are towns by any other name.

Authority is the most difficult to observe archaeologically. Large imposing buildings within central places imply it, and are visible enough in the Roman period. In the post-Roman centuries we have an analogue in the 'palace' sites such as Yeavering,

Map ref	Present Place	Saxon Name	Origin	Known Amenities to Date
1	Abingdon	Abbandun	Middle Saxon	
2	Aylesbury	Aegelesburg		
3	Bedford	Bedanford	Edward's burh	
4	Beverley	Beoforlic	?Middle Saxon	
5	Bath	Bathum		
6	Bristol	Brycgstow		
7	Buckingham	Buccingahamm		
8	Burpham, Sx.	Burham		
9	Canterbury	Cantwaraburg	Middle Saxon	
10	Chester	Legaceaster	Aethelflaed's burh	
11	Chichester	Cisseceaster	Wessex burh	
12	Chirbury, Shr.	Cyricbyrig	Aethelflaed's burh	
13	Colchester	Colneceaster	Edward's burh	
14	Cricklade	Creccagelad	Wessex burh	
15	Doncaster		(Roman)	
16	Durham	Dunholm	(Minster)	
17	Eddisbury, Ches.	Eadesbyrig	Aethelflaed's burh	
18	N. Elmham, Nor.	Elmham	(Minster)	
19	Exeter	Escanceaster	Wessex burh	
20	Gloucester	Gleawancaster	Wessex burh	
21	Great Yarmouth			
22	Hereford	Hereford		
23	Hertford	Heorotford	Edward's burh	
24	Ilchester		(Roman)	
25	Ipswich	Gipeswic	Wic	
26	Lichfield	Liccidfeld	(Middle Saxon)	
27	Lincoln	Lindcylene	(Middle Saxon)	
28	London	Lunden	Wic	
29	Lydford			
30	Newbury		(Middle Saxon)	
31	Northampton	Hamtun	Middle Saxon	
32	Norwich		(Middle Saxon)	
33	Nottingham	Snotingaham	(Middle Saxon)	
34	Oxford	Oxnaford	Wessex burh	
35	Porchester	Porteceaster		
36	Rhuddlan			
37	Romsey			
38	Shrewsbury	Scrobbesbyrig		
39	South Cadbury			
40	Southampton	Hamtun	Wic	
41	Stafford	Staethford	Aethelflaed's burh	
42	Stamford	Stanford	Edward's burh	
43	Steyning			

	Present Place	Saxon Name	Origin	Known Amenities to Date
44	St Albans			(symbols)
45	S. Neots			(symbols)
46	Tamworth	Tamoworthig	(Middle Saxon)	(symbols)
47	Thetford	Theodford		(symbols)
48	Torksey	Turescesieg		(symbols)
49	Wallingford	Wealingaford	Wessex burh	(symbols)
50	Wareham	Werham	Wessex burh	(symbols)
51	Wells	Wyllwm		(symbols)
52	Winchester	Witanceaster	Wessex burh	(symbols)
53	Worcester	Weogornaceaster	(Middle Saxon)	(symbols)
54	York	Eoforwic	Wic	(symbols)

Planning ⊞   Defences ⚒   Streets ◁   Property Boundaries ⫿   Church ⌂

Minster ⌂   Cemetery +   Pottery Kilns ⌒ᴷ   Other Industry ⚒   Environmental ∅

Organic Preservation O   Collegiate Buildings ⚏   Latrines ⊔   Animal Pens ⫫

Commerce ⚘   Fishing ⌒   Mortar Mixers ⊕   Halls ⋔   Iron Smelting ⌐   Ovens ⌒

Bread Ovens ⌒ᴮ   Water Mill ✳   Pottery Workshop ʊ   Houses ⋔   Wells ⊔   Cellars ⊔

Domestic ✱   Waterfront ⊨   Gate ⊡   Drains ▪   Shoemaking ◁   Belltower ▣

Bellmaking ⌐

28 *A 'Michelin guide' to the late Saxon burhs, the earliest English towns (Carver/Hooper)*

the 'villa regalis' which contained a central and often monumental hall from which power could be wielded, as the heroic literature of the age suggests. The problem is that we do not know how many places of this kind there were, or whether they formed a system. The fact that few were mentioned by name by Bede does not mean that there were few. Like their medieval successors, those people with power in the middle-Saxon period may have held that power by virtue of a very large number of such manors, and divided their time between them, albeit unevenly. Together, the holding gained by inheritance, gift, purchase or homicide need not have formed a system in the sense of an urban hinterland with its central place. The wide dispersal of property-holdings is apparent in William the Conqueror's Domesday survey, however much some ambitious persons may have been working to achieve an intergrated power block. Beside this picture, we must set Martin Biddle's arguments for a continuity of authority, in certain places at least, and above all in certain Roman towns. Places like London, York, Colchester, Winchester, St Albans, perhaps even Gloucester, Exeter and Worcester, for example, derelict or not, should not have lost their potency to attract authority, particularly for the new Roman Church, and some actual administration may have been exercised from them.

It would appear likely that some places which became English towns grew directly out of something like a 'villa regalis'. H.M. Chadwick translated this term as 'royal village', and some eighty years ago pointed to a number of examples (cited in charters and other Anglo-Saxon documents), some of which became towns, and others not: Wilton, (South)hampton, Dorchester, Micheldever and Canterbury. He reaches the conclusion that 'in earlier times most of the places mentioned in the Burghal Hidage (i.e. the *burhs* of southern England) must have been merely royal estates or villages'. Grenville Astill, studying the towns of Berkshire, has detected a number of candidates other than named *burhs*, where proto-urban functions were practised – places like Lambourne, Thatcham or Cookham. It would not be surprising in fact, if somewhere underneath every English town lies a royal village (or villa), which, in its own residential style, had already exercised many of those centralising functions which are later thought of as urban. By one of those coincidences in which archaeologists delight there was a 'late Saxon farm' in Whitehall, actually under Downing Street, in what was to become the national centre of 'West Minster'. If we were right about the 'dark earth', then a royal village might be laid out inside the walls of a Roman town at the expense of the Roman fabric,

29 *The middle-Saxon and later halls excavated at the west end of St Peter's church, Northampton. The earliest building, analogous to contemporary rural 'palaces', points to a central authority as one kind of urban origin (Northampton Development Corporation)*

Winchester presenting the best image so far of these successor centres to Roman authority. Those that developed in the countryside away from Roman towns have a far more chequered career, and we are hardly in a position yet to chart their progress. The 'royal villa' itself has a dispersed character that is not easy to hunt (or date) underneath a modern town. It may have looked like Yeavering or Cheddar, or Catholme, which were themselves successions of timber buildings by no means simple to unravel. The size of Yeavering is similar to a small medieval county town, but the density of occupation strikingly sparse in comparison. A discovery like the magnificent hall at Northampton, reminiscent of those at Yeavering or Cheddar, at the west end of the most important church in the town, perhaps gives a clue to the siting of these buildings elsewhere. Other halls, such as those discovered at Nottingham and Waltham, may also prove to be the nodal point of the embryonic English town. Documentary surveys and casual finds hint at their existence at Tamworth, Stamford and elsewhere.

Recent work at Stafford has cast light from a different direction on the same idea of an urban origin from a manor site. There, just north of the central minster church (and the presumed site of the hall that went with it), a sequence of features was encountered which ran from the Roman period to the eighteenth century and which were almost exclusively concerned with processing grain. Roman (or plausibly post-Roman) four-posters for grain storage are succeeded by late Saxon ovens making bread. An enormous dump of burnt grain characterises the Norman phase, and in the Middle Ages corn dryers and malting kilns were in use. The area emerges into the light of documentary day as the site of a tithe barn. The 'royal villa' here appears to have inherited its function as a collecting station for the agricultural wealth of the neighbourhood from a

Roman predecessor, and retained it long afterwards. This type of sequence is possibly echoed at Stamford (Lincs.) where a grain-drying kiln, a bakery and a pottery kiln were among the early features found within a fortified enclosure beneath the medieval castle.

Stafford, like Stamford, became a *burh*, one of those mentioned in the Anglo-Saxon Chronicle as having been fortified by Aethelflaeda, Alfred's daughter. The defences applied to such places, while certainly strategic, may have been equally essential to protect a royal resource – in this case bread. Perhaps the construction of the *burh* at Worcester 'for all the people' should be read in this somewhat cynical light. The function of *burhs* in any case implies physical defences of some kind, and much archaeological effort has been expended looking for them, especially in named places. Some *burhs* were built in former Roman towns, such as Chester, where the work presumably involved the repair of the surviving Roman walls, but curiously little evidence for such refortification has turned up. Part of the sequence of banks following the construction of the Anglian tower on the Roman wall at York belonged to this period. Doncaster is an example of a refortified Roman defensive system. The Anglo-Saxons also occasionally chose earlier types of

30 The sequence of Anglo-Saxon and medieval defences excavated at Hereford, as realised by Ron Shoesmith (Hereford Museum)

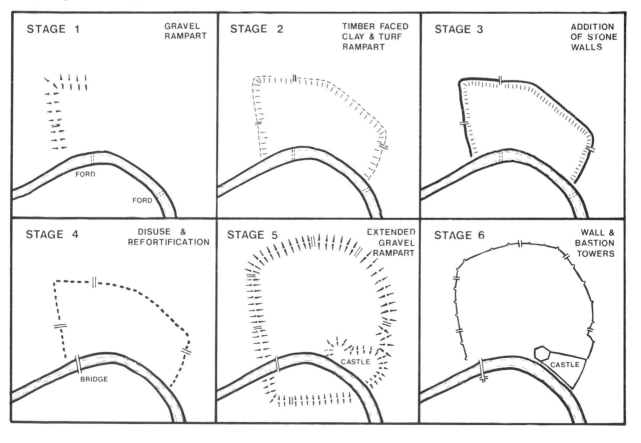

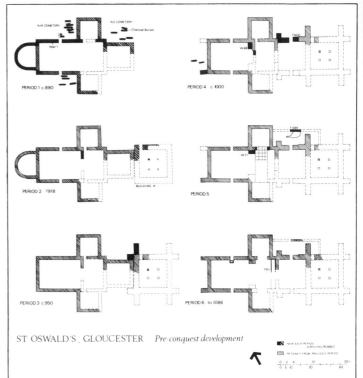

31 Plan and elevation of the late Saxon church of St
Oswald's, Gloucester, drawn by Richard Bryant
(Carolyn Heighway)

fortification to re-exploit, such as the hillfort at South Cadbury, but their own taste and their own style becomes more visible when they develop a 'green-field' site.

The people whose ancestors constructed Offa's Dyke should have understood something of the planning and resources required to build a major earthwork, but the pre-Norman town defences so far encountered do not exactly match up to expectations. Sequences excavated at Hereford, Tamworth, Wareham, Cricklade and Nottingham all have a rather experimental and sometimes ad hoc appearance. The earliest examples, which should lie in the ninth century AD, are, like Offa's Dyke, essentially dump ramparts, revetted with turf and fronted by a ditch but on rather a small scale. Certainly none except Rhuddlan and Nottingham has yet approached the 10m (33ft) ditch and 6m (20ft) high rampart suggested by the recently excavated sector of Wat's Dyke. In the Hereford sequence, the technique of construction advanced rapidly, the simple gravel rampart of the mid-ninth century being replaced, fifty years later, by one of clay with turf and timber revetment, enclosing a larger area. By the mid-tenth century a drystone revetment is in place as a technical improvement. At Cricklade a patch of worn stones suggested that there had been a tower on an inside corner of the defensive circuit. Such materials do not make an enduring monument in the same way as Roman stone walls, but nevertheless the course of late-Saxon defences left a mark on the urban topography; not least because they were followed in whole, or in part, in many cases, by town-wall builders for the next 600 years. At Tamworth, the excavated array of post-holes in a gap in the defended perimeter has been argued to belong to a gate, and a type of timber 'wild-west' superstructure suggested for it. More reconstructions of this type are certainly needed for gates, as for revetted earthworks and timber halls, before the profile of the late-Saxon defended town can be imagined as it would be seen by an approaching traveller.

One feature would certainly command such a skyline – the towers of the Minster and other churches, such as still survive at St Michael at the Northgate in Oxford and elsewhere. They were built in mortared rubble, with stone strip work, and evidence from manuscript illustrations suggest that they were rendered and whitewashed, with oak shingle roofs and a weathercock on the tower. The documented dedications suggest that churches were numerous in some centres, and may represent a way of classifying the towns. There were at least 13 late-Saxon foundations in York, five in Worcester, over 30 in London, but only one in Stafford. It is less

certain, of course, what such a classification might mean. If at first sight an equation is made with population – there were more churches because there were more people who needed to go to church – it is as likely that the number of churches represent the number of independent estates in secular or ecclesiastical possession. The rights and the revenue of each may have been disputed: not all enjoyed official right of burial, for example, although those that did not might have ignored the fact. The church, like a modern multi-national company, could to some extent lay its own development strategy over towns big and small. Archaeologically this implies a special approach and a special reading. Church foundations, when excavated, provide excellent sequences and a powerful index of affluence and respect from the moment a church was first needed. Their cemeteries are the chief source of information we have for the health and stature of the medieval population. But the whole set of churches from a particular town is an even more powerful monitor of the population and its class divisions and their distribution – which is one reason why churches attract archaeological attention to the degree they do, and why the whole set, rather than bits of a few examples, should be our target.

For the early citizen, the church buildings provided a framework for life in this world as well as in the next, a framework already developed in the countryside and carrying with it into the town the spirit and the emblem of the community. The size and style of these buildings, and the conurbation of those that served them, produced their own hierarchy of settlement status in and outside the town, varying from large monasteries in their own setting, to dominant minsters, such as the Old Minster at Winchester, and the smaller parish churches such as St Mary in Tanner Street. The process was still more marked in the later Middle Ages, but we can suppose that for the Anglo-Saxons too, the church towers, with their weathercocks and bells, presented an alternative landscape of power, money and spiritual health, separate from the royal, military and commercial networks which otherwise governed their lives, and almost unimaginable in England today.

How far were the new towns of Anglo-Saxon England organised places, with the planning of streets and areas dedicated to different activities and power groups? Once again Martin Biddle's work is crucial, since it is his study of rectilinear street plans which has made the late-Saxon planned town a real possibility, not only in Winchester but in other former Roman towns such as Chichester, Colchester and Exeter, and on green-field sites such as Wallingford and Wareham. These street grids do not have the rigid geometry of Roman or thirteenth-century planners but there is evidence of something deliberate, a partition or zonation of activity by a system of streets, which was itself a major undertaking. Biddle has calculated that the Winchester town plan involved over 8km (5 miles) of streets, requiring 8000 tonnes of flint cobbles. We are still some way from knowing the full significance, distribution and function of these plans, but they do offer a characteristic which can truly be called urban. Together wtih the defences, the Anglo-Saxon town plan provides the main contrast with large rural settlements such as Catholme or North Elmham, which are not known to have been towns. Once again the independent evolution of this characteristic can be noted. The planned street grid is not to be found everywhere, and in many investigated examples certainly did not exist. They appear to be confined to the towns of Wessex, and Martin Biddle and David Hill have made a good case for their association with the *burhs* promoted, perhaps invented, by King Alfred.

Another organising tendency, whose origins are much harder to place, is the laying out of tenements – those long strips of properties so reminiscent of strips of cultivation laid out in the fields, and which have such a vital part to play in the development of industry. At York, the Anglo-Scandinavian tenements were separated by fences – visible in this case because of the preservation of wood – and at Colchester the case has been made for a standard measurement being employed, already this early. At Hereford, the long tenements, fossilised as elsewhere in the maps of the nineteenth century, seem to overlie an earlier system of larger, more chunky parcels of land – the *masurae* – and it is these which perhaps belong to the earliest system of planning and tenure.

Whatever their geometry, the appearance of these regulated properties fronting onto the streets is of paramount importance in the development of town life. They announce that, in all senses, the founders of a town meant business. The commercial function follows yet another seemingly independent strand of aspiration and achievement, using the town and being used by it. Somewhere between the reappearance of the first crafts in an urban context and the busy medieval city 200 years later, commerce becomes the main rationale of the town – the 'urban motor' of Chapter VI. But the way in which this happened – a primary goal of archaeological research – is still highly equivocal and modern interpretations of it are bound to be influenced, if not intoxicated, by modern political readings of history.

For some, very little happened, or was likely to

happen, without the initiative of patrons; towns were a way of promoting and rationalising the exchange of produce and the manufacture of goods which ultimately benefitted them. For others, a craftsman belonged to a continuum which inept political control could diminish but not eliminate, and towns provided an opportunity for output, co-operation and invention that only awaited the stimulation of a certain population pressure. Both these assessments could be true at the same time and there may be other factors, such as external pressure for trade with Europe and Scandinavia, which bore on the new English aristocracy, and encouraged the arrival of immigrant trading colonies. To judge the relative influence of each factor using archaeological methods would require the big picture, which we are far from having as yet – paint over the whole canvas rather than the inconsequential and differently coloured patches which twenty years of hard work have so far achieved.

The early trading centres are all the more impressive because they are the first urban attributes to make an appearance, and do so on their own before defences, street planning or the clustering of churches. They appear in the seventh century, two centuries before the new towns became a regular part of the English settlement pattern. The two best known examples are Ipswich, and Southampton's predecessor *Hamwih*, where large gatherings of houses and activities are known.

At Hamwih, far more than Ipswich, contacts with the Continent, mainly but not exclusively pottery, are on a scale which can scarcely be anything but commercial. Similar entrepôts or trading centres

32 Late Saxon planned towns and other burhs from excavated topographical and documentary evidence (Biddle and Hill, 1971, and elsewhere)

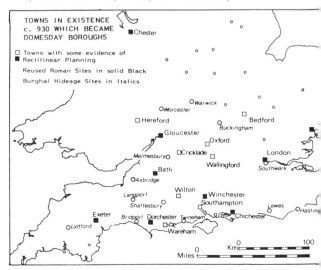

must have existed at London and York, and there are others whose sites are now abandoned, or lost or forgotten, such as Quentovic across the Channel, and possibly Fordwich and Sandwich in Kent. It is more difficult to find evidence of production, as opposed to exchange, in this early period and it remains possible that here, and in York and London, parts of the settlements we are seeing are actually colonies of foreign merchants. The very large

33 Ninth-century sunken-floored building from London (Museum of London)

deposit of oyster shells which has been found underneath Poole, large enough to suggest a centralised industry, and places such as Droitwich exploiting a localised resource (in this case salt), must represent the earliest indigenous production centres.

In the century of the new urbanism, the tenth, centres for overseas trade are still few, but active. Pottery might be the most visible import, as always, but glass, amber, stone querns and silk were brought into places like York, London and Lincoln, where the best evidence has been found. Oysters and sea fish were brought as far inland as places such as

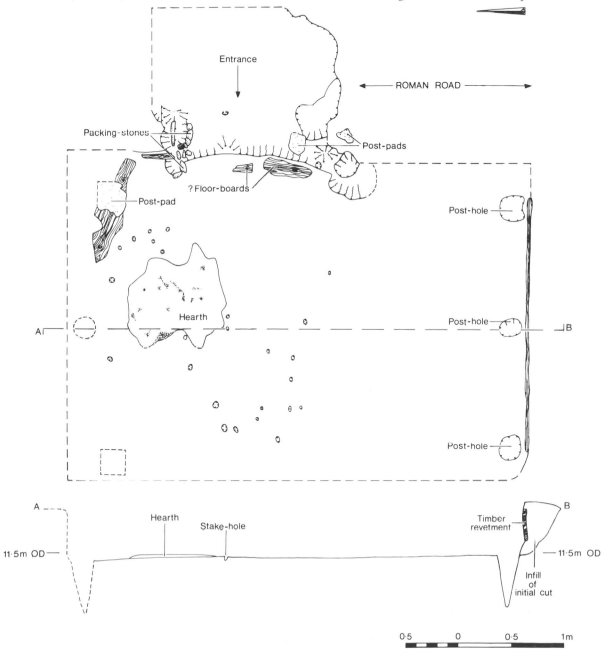

Durham, implying some kind of regular and fairly rapid marketing operation. In some instances at least, the confrontation with imports must have itself been the inspiration for new crafts. The burgeoning late-Saxon pottery industry, whilst not confined exclusively to towns, certainly took root there and pottery was traded or sent to a wide hinterland. The names of the famous types – Stamford ware, Thetford ware, Torksey ware, Winchester ware, Northampton ware – are names deriving from new late-Saxon towns, and this is unlikely to be an accident of research. Nor is the variety of early crafts that urban archaeology has so far brought to light: iron, copper, leadworking in Stamford and Northampton, bone and antler working in York and Lincoln, tanning, spinning, weaving, baking, and making coins, barrels and wooden bowls. The towns which have produced sites with full preservation naturally have the lion's share of the new discoveries – but it is likely that they provide a window on the others.

We might guess three types of working area in the late-Saxon town – the *waterfront* where boats were beached; *industrial zones* for centralised manufacturing, and *workshops* within the houses themselves. The evidence comes mainly from timber structures, and a wide repertoire of pits – round and oval, deep and shallow, with timber posts as revetment or superstructure, clay-lined or clay-domed – a repertoire which is increasing all the time. With exceptions such as the ninth-century goldsmith's house at Lower Brook Street, Winchester, the buildings distinguished are all in timber – post-built or frame-built, with wattle panels or sometimes plank cavity walls, as at York. An example from the 'G.P.O. site' in London was a frame-building 9m (29ft) long, with a partition. Sometimes the walls of the building were simple wattle-work, used to revet the hillside as at Durham. Floors might be of clay or rammed pebbles and many examples have central hearths, the smoke presumably finding its way out of a roof of thatch or timber shingles. Perhaps the only specialised town building, in that it turns up in towns, was the cellar, although this, like the rest of the architecture, had its rural antecedents. These rectangular pits up to 10m (33ft) long may be revetted with timber posts or stakes; a London example had an access via a set of steps. They occur in the most developed centres – Canterbury, London, Gloucester – but are thought to be less an indication of population pressure than an indication of the need to store wine.

It is not yet clear how waterfront, industrial areas and workshops relate to hall, minster and the *burh* defences. A very provisional model could be proposed, in which hall and minster occupy the fortified *burh* area, with the waterfront, industrial area and residential craft zone sited outside at perhaps different points of access. But there are likely to be numerous variations on this theme. Where old Roman defences provide the blueprint, all components may be situated within them; where two or even three defended enclosures are present (for example at Nottingham), we have yet to discover how the functions and classes of people might be distributed between them. There is variety too in the very intensity of urbanisation – some places attracting a genuinely commercial quarter, others little more than 'designated villages', with loosely federated cottage industries and farms.

One has only to contrast two recent urban campaigns to get the flavour of this variety. York in the tenth century had a large and busy industrial zone beside the river Foss where an astonishing range of goods was being manufactured; some, like the silk from home–bred silkworms (mulberry was found), were inspired directly by the imports brought in along the Ouse and on to the hardstanding beside the Foss. To the north of this commercial suburb, the vestiges of the Roman legionary fortress now provided an ordered enclave of another kind: the sector of authority and the Church. Such complementary settlements need not everywhere have been physically joined: Martin Biddle has proposed that Winchester and Hamwih form just such a twin system in an earlier period, and others have followed his idea, proposing Worcester/Droitwich, Canterbury/Fordwich and Bury St Edmunds/Ipswich as similar twins.

By contrast, a settlement such as late-Saxon Stafford appears as a thinly-disguised expansion of the rural manor which no doubt gave it birth. A central enclave contained the only church, and three centralised crafts: butchery, bread-making and pottery manufacture. Although pottery was probably exported from Stafford to other Mercian centres, there is no evidence of commerce of any kind; and, apart from the sparsely built up area reserved to the *burh*, bypassed by a throughway, no planning or tenements. The *burh* here is little more than a fort, whose immediate and strategic needs were served by a cantonment of tradesmen retained at its gates, like the old Roman *vicus*.

The rhythm of urban invention in the Anglo-Saxon period is therefore curiously reminiscent of that of Roman Britain. Towns grew from a combination, as yet not fully documented, of pre-existing central places, waterside entrepôts, and the strategic network of forts left by a military campaign. In the southern regions (where the campaign began), the defended settlements evolved into ordered civic spaces; while in the less developed

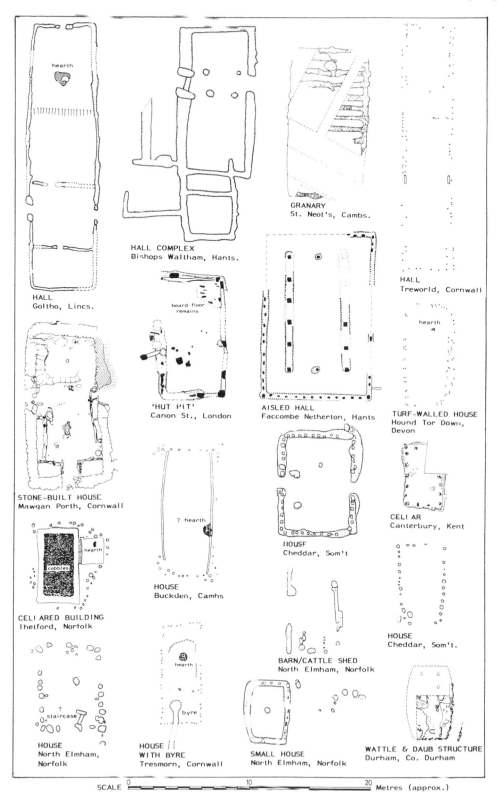

34 *Late Saxon buildings from towns and rural sites*
   (Drawn by Liz Hooper)

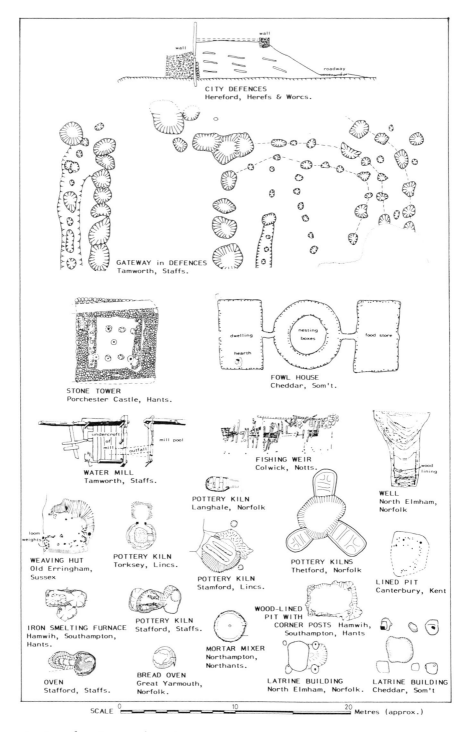

CITY DEFENCES
Hereford, Herefs & Worcs.

GATEWAY in DEFENCES
Tamworth, Staffs.

STONE TOWER
Porchester Castle, Hants.

FOWL HOUSE
Cheddar, Som't.

WATER MILL
Tamworth, Staffs.

FISHING WEIR
Colwick, Notts.

WELL
North Elmham,
Norfolk

POTTERY KILN
Langhale, Norfolk

WEAVING HUT
Old Erringham,
Sussex

POTTERY KILN
Torksey, Lincs.

POTTERY KILN
Stamford, Lincs.

POTTERY KILNS
Thetford, Norfolk

LINED PIT
Canterbury, Kent

IRON SMELTING FURNACE
Hamwih, Southampton,
Hants.

POTTERY KILN
Stafford, Staffs.

MORTAR MIXER
Northampton,
Northants.

WOOD-LINED
PIT WITH
CORNER POSTS Hamwih,
Southampton, Hants

OVEN
Stafford, Staffs.

BREAD OVEN
Great Yarmouth,
Norfolk.

LATRINE BUILDING
North Elmham, Norfolk.

LATRINE BUILDING
Cheddar, Som't

SCALE 0   10   20 Metres (approx.)

35 *Late Saxon structures from town and country*
    (Drawn by Liz Hooper)

north and west, the functional fort with its attendant *vicus* may have endured some considerable time.

If York and Stafford are both 'towns', in default of more precise vocabulary, it is clear that the tenth-century traveller in Anglo-Saxon England would have to keep an open mind when directed to one. It is also likely that the inhabitants would have been surprised to see him: the English town was born, mature, and working, but perhaps not yet ready for tourists.

V
The medieval fabric

We called up our visitor to the Roman towns of Britannia, only after constructing a somewhat laborious and probably quite artificial stage-set; for the post-Roman ruin and Anglo-Saxon new town we could scarcely offer him a vision. England's medieval towns can welcome him from the start. The town wall is the primary image, and rising within it, the towers of motte or castle or churches, a cathedral, monasteries and hospitals – the status symbols of the day. And if not every medieval town always had a wall, a rampart or a palisade, and if some of them had only a few towers and no spire, there is still no doubt that the image of a town demanded a crowded skyline, and it was an image which was admired and pursued in the period itself.

Within the walls, the visitor would look for the privileged, often palatial enclosures of the aristocracy – a castle with precinct wall and gatehouse – and of the church – a cathedral close, or a deanery with its garden. Beside them, between them or beyond them, he would expect to find the market place, and, beside the linking streets and passage-ways, rows of artisans' tenements, where the manufacture and repair of a hundred crafts were practised; and between tenement, meadow, battlement and street, the barter of trade and politics, threading through every urban component like an electric current.

We would now expect that many an idiosyncracy of the medieval town was created, if less visibly, in the pre-Norman centuries, and that this urban arena, in which vested interests could compete and co-exist, was already old by the conquest in 1066. Nevertheless, the transition was not always smooth; archaeology has noticed many sudden changes in the eleventh and twelfth centuries, changes in the urban network, and changes within the towns themselves. The changes are sometimes made plainer by episodes of devastation, followed by an impressive programme of renewal. The devastation is not obvious everywhere and will perhaps prove to be prevalent only in the rebellious areas of the north and

the Midlands. It is noticed, for example, at Durham, Lichfield, Shrewsbury, Worcester, Hereford and Stafford where the late Saxon phases closed suddenly and the town reopened after a tiny interval with something rather different. In many such cases, a large part of the town, up to a fifth of the settled area, might be flattened to receive the motte-and-bailey castle of the conqueror. Elsewhere, quarry pits pound into previously active areas, abandoned long enough (at Stafford) to allow silt to collect in the disused bread ovens. New tenements are laid out with characteristic narrow strips end-on to the street – in places they had never been before. The majority of churches are levelled and rebuilt in the Norman 'Romanesque' style: taller, straighter, more massive, with great square blocks of ashlar and accurately turned and decorated round-headed arches. Mills appear, powered by newly impounded water ways, like the King's Pool at Stafford or the Minster Pool at Lichfield. Within a century, new or redeveloped foundations had been sited countrywide, so as to infill the urban network in parts the Anglo-Saxons did not reach. However much we might like to feel that the Normans had little to teach the cultured English, the evidence for a major programme of urban renewal, at least in the north and Midlands, is overwhelming.

That is not to say that it required the Norman invasion to make it happen. England was already party to the new mood of Europe, which found some of its expression in the embellishment of cities. And this would not be the last such occasion. The Anglo-Saxon aristocracy had relaid the template of an urban system in every English county; others would intermittently use or extend this template to decorate or enrich their personal estates following the fashion of the times. To the archaeologist, town life is hardly the index of progress; it appears as a veritable switch-back from high investment to insidious blight from the tenth century to the twentieth. In Shrewsbury, the periods of high development following that of the Normans were

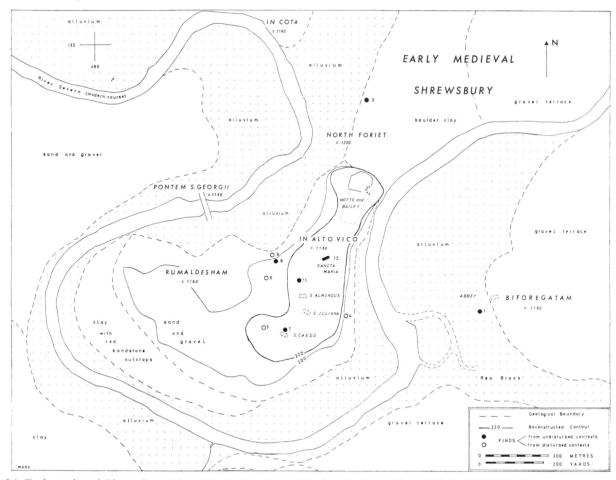

36 Early medieval Shrewsbury: three suggested areas of settlement share this peninsula formed by a loop in the River Severn (Carver, 1978)

the mid-thirteenth century, the late sixteenth century, the eighteenth century, the mid-nineteenth century and the 1960s; in Norwich, they were *c*. 1300, 1470-1503, after a fire in 1507, 1670-1730, the mid-nineteenth century and the 1930s. Future rewards lie in finding and isolating the precise rhythm of growth and decay in particular centres, so as to compare it with that of the countryside.

For the building trade, the mid-thirteenth century must have been something of a boom. More new towns were established in the thirteenth century, if we are to believe the borough handlist – and it is endorsed by archaeological findings – than at any other time in our history. A majority of all known town walls were also laid down in this period. Within existing towns, new suburbs were planned, or old ones replanned. The Norman Romanesque, less than two centuries old, was often demolished or jacketed in the new 'early English' style. In the towns, as in the countryside, building-stone came

the way of the ordinary tenement holder, and, following a number of edicts about fire, tiles were routinely employed on roofs.

If affluence is signalled by new materials and variety of commodities, squalor is more difficult to locate with certainty, since the discarded debris with which archaeologists deal is, of itself, squalid. If a house-floor is found covered in decomposed plants, or insects which depend on rotting flesh, this does not necessarily imply that the inhabitants preferred to live in the atmosphere of an old compost heap. Most of the evidence points rather the other way: clean floors are the rule and rubbish is put into tips or onto midden heaps (see Chapter VII). 'Reduced circumstances' can perhaps be read more easily, not from debatably unhygienic habits, but from the reduced range of materials available, and pottery fabrics which are coarse and local. If this is valid, then the late twelfth and mid-fourteenth centuries can also be periods of poverty, always with the localised exceptions; there are windfall investments which allow the development of a particular property, even a particular town, at a generally unpropitious moment.

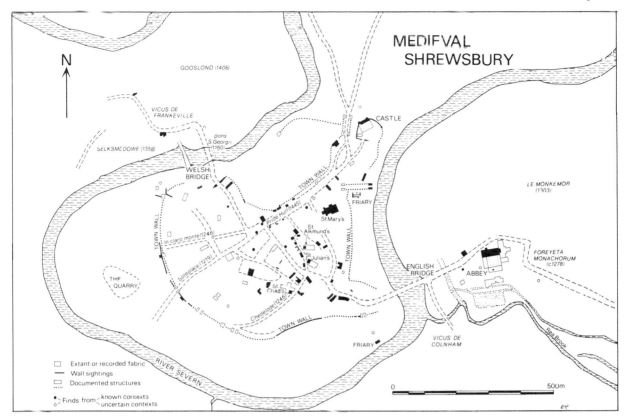

37 *Medieval Shrewsbury. After the Norman Conquest,
the castle and abbey provided two major nucleii for
development. In the thirteenth century, a wall is
thrown around the whole peninsula and a new planned
quarter added to the piecemeal development inside the
walls (Curver, 1978)*

The starting points for medieval towns were
diverse. Some, including the majority of county
towns, grew continuously from the Anglo-Saxon
burh which was already there; others began as
suburbs outside the gates of a castle, analogous to a
Roman *vicus*, as at Bolsover, Castleton or
Newendon; others were villages which acquired or
were awarded urban status – and not necessarily
because they had grown larger; others were planted
as deliberate acts of planning, while Birmingham
began as a moated house. Even where a site is
continuously occupied, the influence of 'planning
periods' can often still be observed. Northampton
and Nottingham, among other examples, show
shifts of the nucleus in a general area of preferred
location, little twitches responding to the periods of
urban renewal. At Shrewsbury, a planned sector

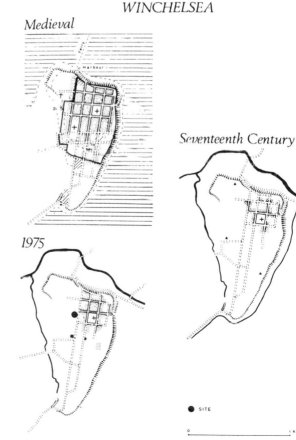

38 *The planned town of Winchelsea, never fully occupied
and gradually abandoned as the sea retreated
(D. Freke)*

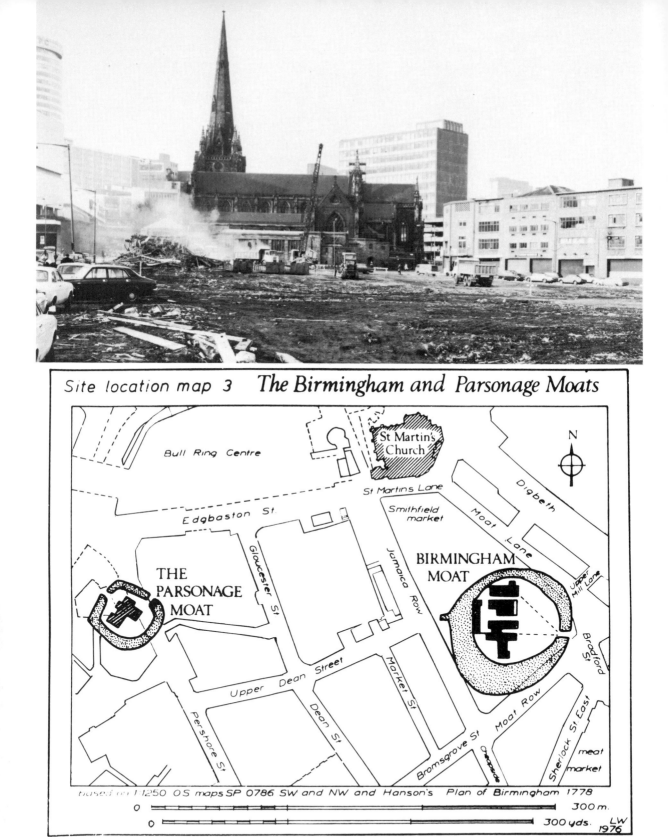

Site location map 3 **The Birmingham and Parsonage Moats**

39 The Birmingham Moat on its discovery near the Bull Ring in 1975 (Lorna Watts)

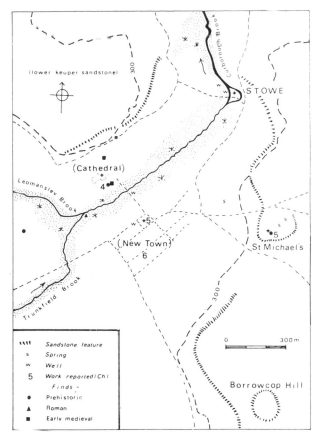

40 The components of early Lichfield. The brook beside the cathedral was dammed to provide a fish-pond and head of water to drive a mill (Carver 1982a)

often fortified enclave, a grand architectural centrepiece surrounded by service buildings, fountains, ornamental walks and gardens. The tenements, in allocated parcels of land off the adjacent streets, were each individual money-making units: house, garden and workshop combined; for in many respects the medieval artisan returned to the urban mode of his Roman antecedents.

Urban castles have received surprisingly little excavation on the grand scale, though there is no reason to suppose they differed greatly in structure from their country cousins. Those with the greatest impact on urban life must have been the Norman mottes – gigantic piles of earth which incorporated the remains of the houses that had been demolished to make way for them. At Shrewsbury fifty tenements – a fifth of the pre-existing settlement – were laid waste and the ground presumably scraped up to make the mound. Mottes remain at Tamworth, Baile Hill in York and elsewhere, and others were demolished in the nineteenth century; but the majority were replaced within a generation by stone keeps, and, by the thirteenth century, by the more sociable arrangement of hall, courtyard and curtain wall. Towards the fourteenth century, a number of towns began to encroach back onto the castle enclave, particularly its ditch. That at Newcastle became the town tip, while buildings have been found actually within the moat, as well as in the bailey, at Wallingford and Banbury. Castle and town wall formed an integrated military system,

41 The town walls of Worcester being recorded in advance of the construction of a ring-road in 1977 (M.O.H. Carver)

within the peninsula was settled for the first time in the thirteenth century. At Lichfield, a new town was laid out in the twelfth century and depopulated in the fourteenth, the citizens at that time exploiting the cathedral close. The new towns – and new suburbs within existing towns, particularly those of the thirteenth century – sometimes did not take. Ambitious Winchelsea, laid out in 1290, was never fully settled before it began to shrink towards its final desertion.

In its heyday, the medieval town was a linked system of the separate worlds which made up society. Those who fought, those who worked and those who prayed, each in their own sector of castle, tenement or abbey, and each with their own hierarchy, were confined in the town, bound together face to face by the town wall. They believed themselves to be interdependent, and the system remained stable as long as the delusion lasted. It produced, as faith often does, a settlement of considerable enterprise, beauty and contrast. Castle, abbey or cathedral church sat in its own spacious and

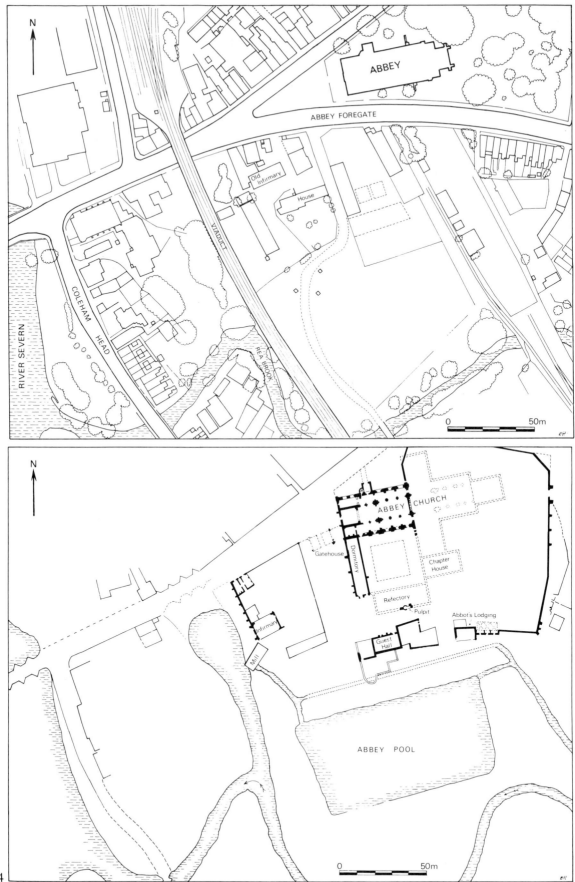

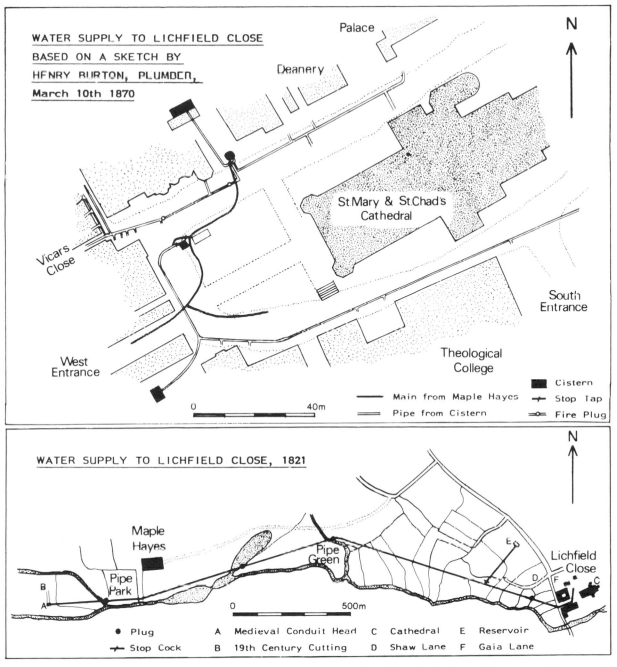

WATER SUPPLY TO LICHFIELD CLOSE
BASED ON A SKETCH BY
HENRY BURTON, PLUMBER,
March 10th 1870

Palace

Deanery

St.Mary & St.Chad's
Cathedral

Vicars
Close

South
Entrance

West
Entrance

Theological
College

0   40m

——— Main from Maple Hayes   ■ Cistern
═══ Pipe from Cistern   ╪ Stop Tap
                                   ⊕ Fire Plug

WATER SUPPLY TO LICHFIELD CLOSE, 1821

N

Maple
Hayes

Pipe
Green

E

Lichfield
Close

Pipe
Park

B

D   F   C

A

0   500m

● Plug   A Medieval Conduit Head   C Cathedral   E Reservoir
╪ Stop Cock   B 19th Century Cutting   D Shaw Lane   F Gaia Lane

*43 The medieval water-supply system to Lichfield
Cathedral close (After J. Gould)*

the defences following a similar evolution of
engineering technique, spread over a similar period
of time, to that of the Romans. The Anglo-Saxon
style of ditch and dump rampart with timber-work
continued, and even as late as the thirteenth century
was still often the first investment. Stone walls

*42 Plan of Shrewsbury Abbey, with later developments
(Birmingham University Field Archaeology Unit)*

followed, often built into the pre-existing earth
rampart and acquiring bastions, square and then
semi-circular, as motivation and money allowed. In
many places the provision of town walls was half-
hearted, and demolition and encroachment
commenced before the defensive circuit was
technically complete. The town ditch did service as a
drain, and a dump, and many became famous for
their flooding, dead dogs and general stink.

Cathedral close and abbey presented aspects no
less proud, spacious and reserved than that of the
castle, and in many cases achieved a greater

65

permanence. Some were themselves defended, or at least marked out by a wall and ditch, or, as at Evesham, by a hedge of thorns. The cathedral church, being the largest building in the city, would be used for secular as well as religious meetings. This could include trading, but it is doubtful whether the medieval church would have allowed the licence apparently prevalent in later St Pauls, in which tradesmen set up stalls and amorous assignations were arranged. The ecclesiastical precincts were famous for their good order, privilege and comfort, which often approached Roman standards. The prior or dean affected a small palace, and the convent or chapter occupied a walled establishment with dormitory, refectory, kitchen, *lavatorium* (for washing), *necessarium* (lavatory), workshops and gardens: a self-contained institution which provided the inspiration for the English university college and public school. A private water supply might be piped in lead pipes, as at Lichfield, which tapped a spring over 1.6km (1 mile) away at Pipe Hayes, or

brought by aquaduct, as in twelfth-century Exeter; and the *necessarium* was served by stone-built sewers, whose rediscovery from time to time provokes tales of secret passages. In the romantic imagination, they could indeed have been used as such by the sequestered clerics of later, more restless, days.

As the lords in their castles were linked with the wealth-creating tenements, whose land or its occupants they directly or indirectly owned, so the Church establishment had an infrastructure of parish churches. Some were of remote origins, by then barely remembered, and others were built to serve newly partitioned and often tiny urban parishes. The Church had an income as a major landlord, and a tourist asset in the cult of relics. Neither was it too proud to collect a direct contribution to its funds at mass, baptism, marriage and burial. Only the last of these is inescapable, which may be the reason why it was the subject of separate control: not every one of the parish churches had the right of burial and sometimes it was only the minster church. Even though settlement and cemetery are combined in the Christian town for the first time in archaeology, we shall have to seek connections between them with some care.

44 The parish church of St Helen on the Walls, York, and its graveyard during excavation (York Archaeological Trust)

45 The college of the Vicars Choral at the Bedern, York,
    during excavation (York Archaeological Trust)

The friaries were generally the last religious houses to arrive on the urban medieval scene, and their allocated land is often outside the town walls. Initially centres of reforming zeal, many went on to steal from abbey and cathedral something of their status, and become well-appointed establishments of their own, smothered by gifts and sought after for burial. The Greyfriars at Oxford where Duns Scotus, Ockham, Grossteste, and Roger Bacon taught, has been excavated to reveal its curious T-shaped church, and fine underground culverts.

All these elements of the medieval town, and more, have been recorded or contacted by archaeologists in recent years: castles at Bedford, Banbury, Wallingford; town walls at Shrewsbury and Worcester; roads at Oxford and Winchester; wharves at King's Lynn and London; the cathedral precinct with its sophisticated hydraulics at Wells; Wolvesey Palace at Winchester; a college of Vicar's Choral at the Bedern in York; an Austin friary (Whitefriars) at Leicester; Dominican friaries (Blackfriars) at Dunstable, Guildford, Newcastle, Norwich, and Great Yarmouth; Franciscan friaries (Greyfriars) at Bristol, Oxford, York, Northampton and Grantham; Carmelite friaries at York, Sandwich and Ludlow, and many parish churches including the complete excavation of St Helen-on-the-Walls, York, and St Benedict's in Norwich.

Some examples are illustrated in these pages, and indeed many others still stand and are currently being recorded and analysed through architectural surveys and documentary research.

The new message being brought by archaeology to these familiar monuments, particularly by excavation, is the evidence of underlying system and social change. Whatever their pretensions, and however blinding these pretensions may seem when enshrined in stylised architecture or diplomas, people still eat, breed, fight, trade and die; and each of these activities leaves a set of archaeological traces to betray them. It is not the plan or even the appearance of a castle or an abbey that tells the story – if that were so then it would be sufficient to keep a few of each and allow the rest to go under office blocks. The story lies in the modifications to the fabric, the buried bodies, the discarded food-bones and pottery, the hearths and furnaces that lie buried in sequence, which form a small part of an evolving system. The Vicar's Choral at the Bedern York, founded in 1252, had initially two long aisled ranges, with a pantry, and a separate square kitchen, brew-house and latrine block set in spacious gardens; by the fourteenth century the aisled ranges had been

46 Medieval barn still standing at the Priory in Taunton (Peter Leach)

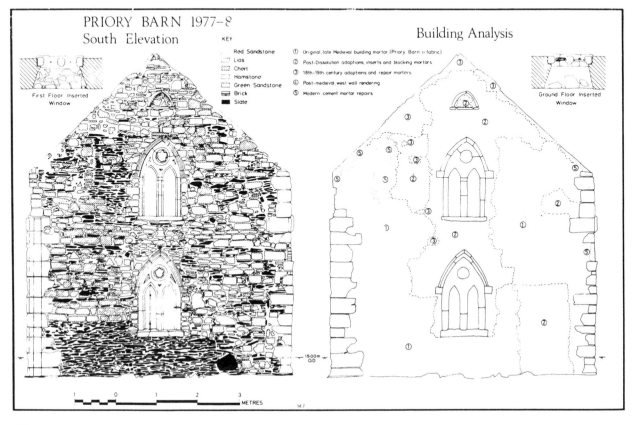

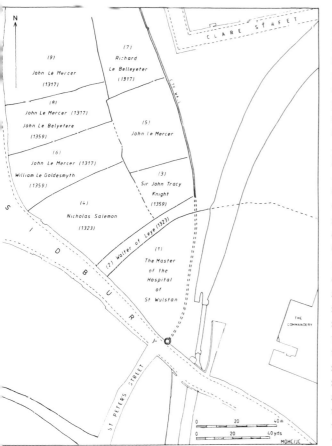

Ordered tenements, laid out in parallel strips with the narrow end against the street, have been identified in embryonic form in Anglo-Saxon towns, and in many places later. A standard or regulated width has been claimed at York, Durham and at Colchester of about four poles (rods or perches). The geographer Terry Slater believes that at least in the Norman and post-Norman periods a standard perch was used, rather than a local version. Adjacent to the street was the house, which might have its gable or its long side along the street itself. At Durham, houses began side-on in the eleventh century and switched to gable-end-on in the twelfth century; at Nottingham houses remained generally side-on; at Winchester twelfth-century gable-end-on gave way to side-on, and then rotated back again. Colin Platt compares the price of side-on to the (cheaper) gable-end-on at Southampton. Practical considerations may also have influenced the alignment: in some cases where the ground rose steeply a house sited gable-end-on to the descending street would have meant more quarrying. But others may have switched, then as now, simply to escape the shadow of their neighbours. Behind the house stretched the open allotment intended, and used, as a smallholding where vegetables were grown, and animals – such as pigs and chickens – were kept. In the early days (tenth to eleventh centuries), vegetable waste was husbanded as middens – a series of food-waste tippings being sealed periodically with sand. The midden heap also acquired dead dogs and cats and the waste products of early crafts such as leather offcuts and cloth. From the twelfth century, rubbish became more plentiful, from the increasingly important crafts, and was buried in pits. The rubbish-pit habit seems to have been discontinued in the fourteenth century, perhaps under the spectre of the Black Death, and the (arguably) no more hygienic town-tip received much of the rubbish until, in the seventeeth century, pit-digging in tenements again returned.

The earliest latrines are also sited in the tenement backs, at first simple pits with two post–holes – presumably to support a seat, as at Stafford – and sometimes surrounded by a wattle-work hut as in Shrewsbury. These earth closets were often cleanable from the time the first models appear, being lined with wattle-work, as at Riggs Hall, Shrewsbury, and the evolution continued in this direction. By the thirteenth century many latrines had moved indoors, and were stone-lined, boarded with wood and had steps for easier cleaning. A timber superstructure supported the user and a supply of cloth offcuts or moss was to hand in the better appointed houses, as at Southampton.

By our standards, the tenement occupier was

47 Medieval tenements and their owners at Sidbury, Worcester, mapped from documents (Carver 1980)

divided into individual houses, each with its own hearth and latrine. The real story of each institution is, potentially, rather more valuable than its stereotyped image.

So far, it is within the third sector of the town, the tenements, that the exploration of *system* has made the most progress, perhaps through an accident of later history. Castle, cathedral and abbey (less so friary) often lie within modern conservation areas, so the majority of rescue operations have been carried out elsewhere, and it is the tenements that have been particularly affected by modern urban renewal. The tenements themselves often have a special archaeological virtue to counter their anonymity. They are tightly constrained by each other, by the public thoroughfare, and by the town wall and, for part of their existence at least, undertook rubbish disposal in their own grounds. Each represents, therefore, a slice of life 500 years long in the same narrow plot, a situation rare in archaeology and of considerable potential for exploring the fortunes of urbanism.

master or mistress of a considerable establishment, and the use of the tenement back must have been a constant source of discussion: whether to grow more vegetables, keep more pigs, build a new latrine or, above all, devote more space to the craft which provided much of the livelihood. The range of crafts practised was very large, although not all have left archaeological traces. In the next chapter some attempt will be made to assess their role in the social system, if mainly in hypothetical terms. Many of the crafts – leather-working, cloth-working, gold-smithing, parchment-making and even bronze-working – would be housed indoors and would not necessarily need the tenement back, except for the disposal of that waste which apprentices were no doubt trained to minimise. The common outdoor crafts, such as iron-smelting, pottery and tile manufacture, do find their way inside the town walls occasionally but presumably were not encouraged to do so, being smokey and a fire hazard. The medieval craftsman appears to have operated largely on a commission basis from his downstairs front room, like tailors and cobblers until recently. Some may have offered goods off the shelf as retail, like a modern shop, as arrangements such as that at Butcher Row in Shrewsbury suggest. But the bulk

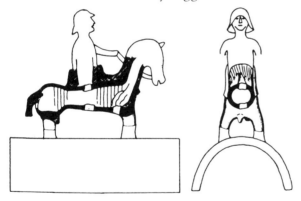

48 *Decorated pottery finial originally from a roof-top in Bedford (D. Baker)*

of the retail trade must have been foodstuffs, and the bulk of these, particularly the imports, were exchanged on market day in market places. Markets and fairs are difficult to identify archaeologically, being mobile and temporary and requiring little digging. Fortunately, they have left plenty of traces in the names of the streets, squares or meadows they once occupied.

From its first appearance, the purpose of the tenement was presumably to make money for its owner who, on some occasions, might be the occupant himself. That tenements themselves were tradeable real estate is shown by the frequent amalgamations and redivisions; the boundaries, marked out by fences and later walls, vary no more than a few inches and, still more remarkable, are reinstated after long periods of redundancy (such as a period of amalgamation) on their original line. It is possible to find, superimposed one on top of the other, a tenth-century oak fence, a medieval stone wall and a Victorian brick wall, property boundaries which endured to the twentieth century.

The houses themselves reflect individual as well as general affluence or depression. Before the thirteenth century, building was predominantly in timber – post-in-hole and post-in-trench construction preceding timber-framing. The timber studs were infilled with wattle-work and plastered with whitewashed daub, while roofs were of thatch or oak shingle, and floors were of beaten earth with a covering of rushes. Upper-storey halls certainly existed by the eleventh century and, more identifiably, timber or stone-revetted cellars. Some stone houses appear in the eleventh century, as at Colchester, and the richer roofs were of green or yellow glazed tiles with finials. By the thirteenth century, building-stone had become more generally available and was employed in foundations to support a timber-frame, if not carried up to form the complete wall. Stone was employed to line latrines and culverts in relatively ordinary dwellings, and tile, its availablity perhaps provoked by new fire regulations, was generally used on roofs. 'Wall-tile' (i.e. brick) first appears as an import at Hull in the thirteenth century, and by the fourteenth century there is a considerable range of building materials available for those who could afford it. At Shrewsbury, a town-house (probably an inn) was constructed on the stub of the levelled town walls with a cellar and ground floor in sandstone ashlar topped by one, and then two, more storeys in timber-framing. Elsewhere in Shrewsbury the rich wool merchants of the fourteenth and fifteenth centuries were building massive houses of timber with two, three or four storeys jettied out into the street to give ever more space for living and trading.

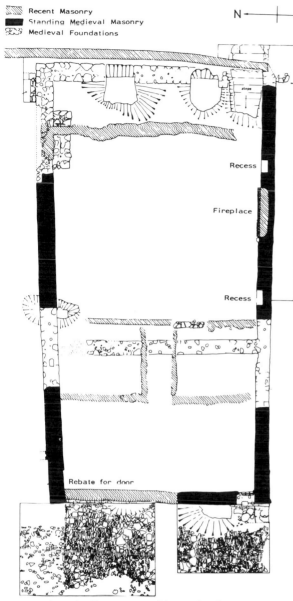

Recent Masonry
Standing Medieval Masonry
Medieval Foundations

N

Recess

Fireplace

Recess

Rebate for door

49 Medieval cellar excavated beneath a house at Winchelsea (D. Freke)

The first brick house in Shrewsbury, Rowley's Mansion, arrived in 1519. These later medieval houses could be beautifully appointed inside, for all their occasionally quaint appearance when restored. Even at the ground floor level, floors of oak boards were supported by earthbound joists, as at Riggs Hall, and ceilings and walls were panelled and carved. Everywhere one can imagine the warm smell of polished wood, candle-wax and porridge.

If the particular contribution of archaeology in bringing the Middle Ages to life had to be isolated, it might be expressed in these terms. Certainly the written records which the town has left for itself are fundamental and provide a framework, although not a directive, for archaeological research. The archaeological attributes are structures, finds, environment and sequence: structure for an indication of function and affluence; finds for an identification of craft and diet; environment, obtained from adjacent pollen traps such as peat bogs, showing the changing woods and fields around; and sequence for the story. We shall see later how the quality of each type of evidence remaining in a particular town can be assessed, as the equivalent of a catalogue of its archives. Of the four, sequence is perhaps the most evocative and offers the most novel information to the historian. Compounded, as it must be, of numbers of tiny sequences drawn from different quarters of the town, there is plenty of room for error in any interpretation reached in this, the early period of systematic urban archaeology. There are common themes and shared trends in the evolution of the medieval town, from the industrious twelfth century to the affluent thirteenth and the disenchantment of the fourteenth; but what has hardly been presented is the very different destinies of towns, from Canterbury to Chester-le-Street; the lag in adopting defences; the sudden accelerated development; the piecemeal desertion and unexpected agriculture that is encountered. There were many more medieval towns than there had been Roman or Anglo-Saxon, and each place had an individual character, developing slowly away from its original function – in short, its own personality. This personality is best approached through patient interdisciplinary studies, for which there is a good tradition in England. This personality is also important for modern citizens, because it still occasionally gleams through in fragments of conserved street plans and timber-frame buildings, and more powerfully in the reconstructions that archaeologists can sometimes now make. The next step is to try and fill these recreated monuments with action and with people.

VI
The urban motor

Picking one's way through the broken buildings, dark layers and dumps which provide the sequence for the four main periods of urban life considered here, one is constantly aware of change, changes in the grandeur of buildings, the style of pottery, the available foodstuffs, the exotic commodities. There is a flavour even in debris which is so strong that an experienced urban excavator can know instinctively where she is in time. 'These foundations have a thirteenth-century feel' she says to the visitor, who laughs charitably – but there is something in what she says. Every feature has the 'feel' of its age, for what we are sensing is a style of life peculiar to a decade or a century, and never quite to be repeated whatever the propensity of later ages for imitation. This is what makes it such an enchanting journey, travelling back through time to a town's origins. But we would all probably make higher claims for it now than mere enchantment. The way towns concentrated the life of their communities, one century on top of another, offers an impartial monitor, an almanac for a whole region. If we could read clearly the meaning behind these constant changes, we might understand how citizens were forced to behave and why; we might know more about their lives than they did.

Much of what follows is hypothetical, occasionally bordering on plain invention. I am writing it to try to illustrate the potential of archaeological method and what it can discover for us; it uses ideas which will be familiar and obvious to many researchers, but less obvious perhaps to many other professionals – policemen, property developers, teachers and town planners – who often wonder where archaeologists think they are going.

Towns, being only settlements of a particular kind, are not essential to human life; they represent a preference which has come and gone and reappeared again in different guises serving different functions and expressing different kinds of communal self-opinion. The number of towns founded at various periods can be deduced from the documentation we

have, numbers modified (in rare cases) by archaeology. The contrasts in these numbers between the Roman and medieval periods may be a contrast in available information or in the size of the population, but it is far more likely to be the contrast between a centralised and a less centralised authority. The thirteenth century is the outright winner for sheer numbers of new places calling themselves

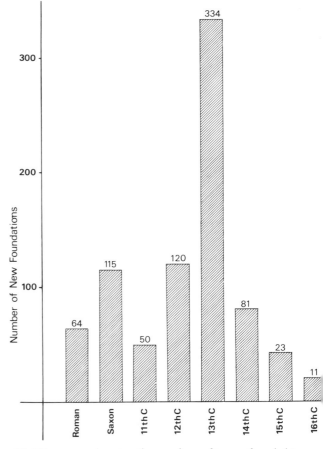

51 *Histogram showing the numbers of towns founded in each century, following documentary records (Carver/Hooper)*

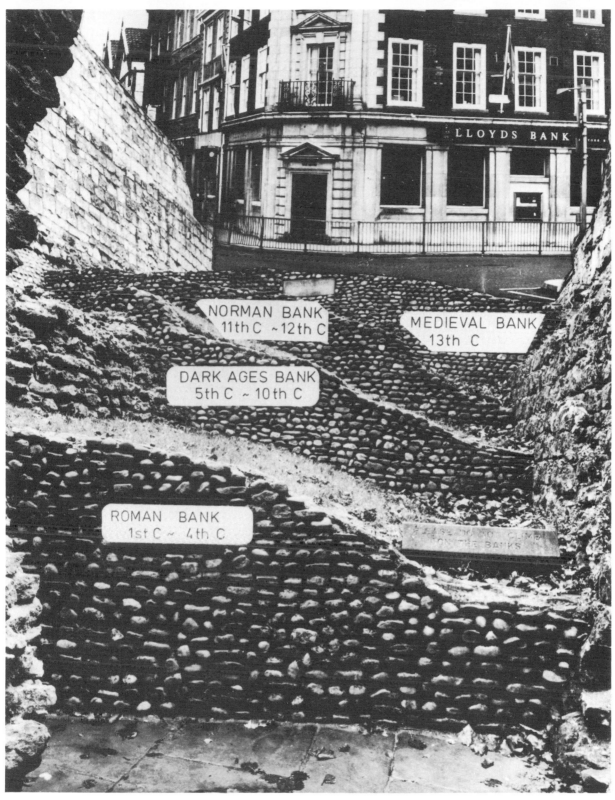

Text on montage labels:

NORMAN BANK
11th C ~ 12th C

MEDIEVAL BANK
13th C

DARK AGES BANK
5th C ~ 10th C

ROMAN BANK
1st C ~ 4th C

LLOYDS BANK

*50 Banking through the ages, a montage by Philip Rahtz.
Such defences were there to protect not just the citizens,
but also their livelihood and the investment of
authorities in the creation of wealth.*

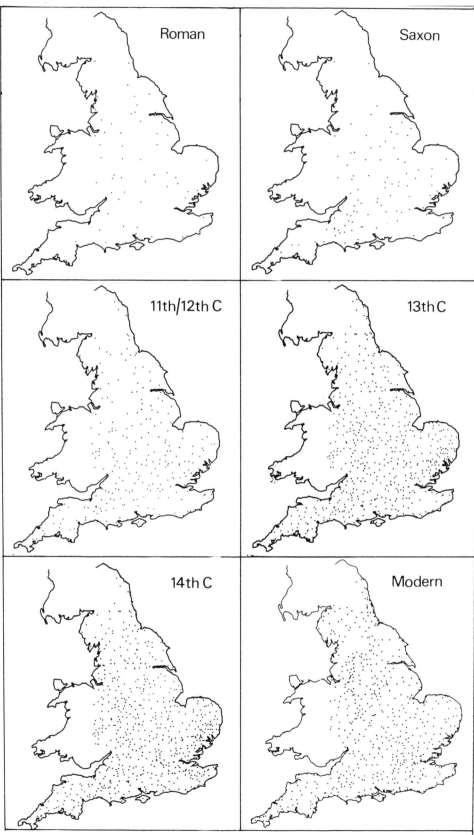

52 *Distribution of urban places thought to be active in six principal periods. (Source: Heighway, 1972; computer plot by Birmingham University Field Archaeology Unit)*

towns, and the country at the time reached saturation point for the urban network it could sustain.

The preferences of town planners in each period were quite differently constrained and expressed. The Romans in most cases were building on top of an existing military network, so the siting and even the layout was to a large extent dictated by that of the forts. These themselves had their own hierarchy and their own rationale – that of an invader providing development opportunities to an initially subject population. This population had already thought of itself as divided into a number of regional peoples: the Coritani, Cornovii, etc., so to a certain extent the patronage of a 'capital' for each region (or *civitas*) provided them with a central place. But the geographically eccentric settlement pattern we still have, with the urban population concentrated into the south-east and thinning out towards Wales and Scotland, is partly a legacy of civilisers who came from across the Channel. The island's capital developed not at some central place in the Midlands, but at a peripheral embarkation point leading to Continental Europe and to the sources of luxury imports. The British in their turn were to create similar patterns out of the natural geography of the land they colonised – great entrepôts on the seaboard like Bombay, Aden, Sydney, Singapore, Hong Kong, designed to canalise resources drawn from the hinterland through a radial system of arterial roads and rivers.

Overlaid on the mainly defunct pattern of Roman urbanism and its road system were those of the English royal entrepreneurs, and these too give a distribution of new foundations that is at least partly inspired by military considerations. The campaigns of Alfred, Edward and Aethelflaed linked the earliest *burhs*; those of Edward I, the boroughs of Wales and Scotland. The earliest English group, and to some extent the later, shows a marked dependence on the rivers – the motorways of their age. In this respect perhaps the most interesting geographical siting is Tamworth, a central place in Anglo-Saxon Mercia, which is sited within striking distance of both the Trent and the Severn basins. With the use of a few canals, no more of a challenge to construct than Offa's Dyke, it would have been possible to reach many parts of the Midlands and the south-west by boat – or rather, possible for every part of the enormous hinterland to deliver tribute to the Mercian heartland. Defensible sites on waterways have a generally different character to those using hills, and many of the new Anglo-Saxon foundations appear to use riverine peninsulas or the confluence between rivers. Such sites are not infrequently partly surrounded by marsh – an effective barrier against energetic aggressors like the Vikings, who came in boats, as King Alfred no doubt discovered for himself in the marshlands of Somerset.

Those foundations which succeeded as towns did so in ways which depended very largely on the institutions within them, and this is one cause of the great variety in their later fortunes. Examined closely, the town is not an integrated community, but an uneasy union of several different enterprises – military, ecclesiastical or mercantile – which were not always contemporary. At Roman Droitwich there were, at various times, a fort at Dodderhill, a villa at Bays Meadow, a saltworks by the Salwarpe, and a civil residential area. Medieval Norwich grew up out of a group of villages, Stamford from three separate forts, pre-Viking, Viking and the *burh* of Edward the Elder. The borough of Nottingham filled the space between the early medieval fortified area, and the Norman castle on its crag to the west; a similar infilling took place at Reigate. In old Roman towns, the establishments of medieval Church and State are found in a corner of the fortified area, perhaps that which had been best preserved, while the townspeople spilled out in an untidy suburb nearer the water. Other Anglo-Saxon towns in their marshbound riverside sites would require reclamation to provide more space for a growing population. Other foundations would fail. Anglo-Saxon Chirbury and medieval Winchlesea were deserted; Colyton shrunk, and Bletchingly became a village. Even in some of the most durable central places, periods of rapid decline have been observed – in Bedford and Stafford in the fourteenth to fifteenth centuries and at Northampton even before the end of the thirteenth century. Are these failings institutional or economic, or are the two things inseparable? Porchester is one of the most interesting cases, because although it performed many functions, elsewhere considered urban, it never seems to have acquired a population. A Roman shore-fort, protected by a wall, it shows evidence of continuity into the seventh century, in the form of a well and buildings with sunken floors. In the tenth century it was declared to be a *burh* with its own mint, and after the Norman Conquest it acquired a castle and a priory which partly survive. But its role as a manufacturing centre or market place is elusive.

The foundation pattern and the successful town pattern are therefore different things. The initial choice of site often seems to have been strategic, but war does not go on everywhere and forever, not even in the first and second millennia, so other factors must have produced the criteria for success. At least one of these factors may already have been subsumed in military planning, namely the need to

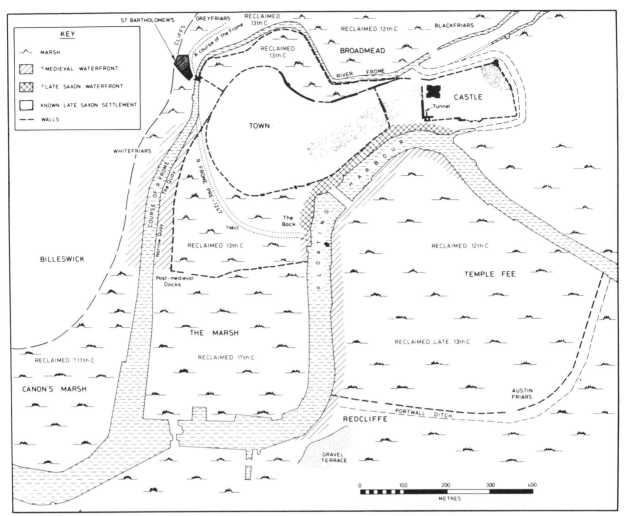

53 *The reclamation of Bristol (Mike Ponsford)*

54 *An Anglo-Saxon silver penny of c.975, showing (left) a bust of Edward, King of the Angles, and (right) the moneyer's mint mark STAEFF (for Stafford)*

protect a pre-existing collecting point for grain or cattle owed in toll, tribute or taxation. It is a somewhat banal picture, our noble county towns having their rationale in providing a secure base for the regional tax collector, and we have only circumstantial evidence that it was so (see Chapter 4). But any attempt to bring to life what drove a town must start with England's principal resource, agricultural produce, most of which was ultimately destined for payment to a lord, a King, a Bishop or an Emperor. These titles are only the changing names for protagonists of a system that was probably already old by the time the Romans came.

If the real point of a town was to collect surplus, then the physical remains we encounter must be, to a great extent, an index of what was done with it. Some suggestions have already been made. Not least of the fascinations of the Anglo-Saxon town is that it is the place where, after a few earlier flourishes, the money economy took off again. All the Anglo-Saxon mints were confined to towns and coins were often stamped with their place of origin as well as the moneyer's name. How would you acquire an Anglo-Saxon penny, and where would you spend it? The coins of the Anglo-Saxons are found, from time to time, in the houses and gardens of the citizens, but not very often compared with the Romans, who appear to have scattered their less easily recycled bronze coinage everywhere. This rarity is still more marked when the numbers of the coins actually in production is considered: James Graham Campbell has estimated the geld paid by England to Viking raiders between 991 and 1014 to amount to 36 million coins. It seems possible that making coins was one convenient way of passing the surplus upwards to the Treasury of the King, or whoever claimed it; and stamping the coin with a mint mark an equally convenient way of assessing the yield of a particular town. The Anglo-Saxons wrote down the equivalence of this yield: four or five pence for a sheep and thirty pence for an ox. The policy of appeasement therefore cost the English people the equivalent of 360,000 sheep a year, which without the towns could scarcely have been collected. When the Scandinavians finally won the war, in the form of the Norman invasion, the urban structure, brand new as it was, was still intact and could be taken over and run by them. In an economic sense, therefore, the towns were the robust framework which allowed the new nation of England to continue.

An alternative to turning surplus wheat and sheep into coins and collecting it, was to reinvest in the town itself. The Romans concentrated on the architecture of power and community, at least in the early years when eager to encourage in the natives the virtues of civilisation. This kind of beneficent demonstration was in later eras confined to the Church, which built cathedrals, hospitals and schools. The English citizen, on his own account, had to wait until the sixteenth century for the provision of the first public latrine. By virtue of its splendour, its position on routeways, and its inherited traditional role, perhaps as a meeting place, the town could certainly function as what modern experts on tourism would call a 'destination area'. But this was hardly sufficient to keep it going, whatever the abstract sense of community, which in England was never in any case highly developed. The real urban motor was industry, and, for the English at least the principal attraction of town life has always been the chance to make money.

Pre-capitalist industry has a low profile, perhaps because it had, perhaps because the documentation is poor, or perhaps because not many historians began life in a factory. Nevertheless, industry is what most people did, and archaeology has a delight in encountering these ordinary doings and their debris. Industry manifests itself broadly as production, manufacture and retail – mines, factories and shops, and it is interesting to see how each has dominated the town in different periods. All aspects are present in the Roman system, although heavy and anti-social production and manufacturing processes such as iron-smelting and making pottery were theoretically excluded. For the Anglo-Saxons the town was the place of production, or at least a place where resources were collected; manufacturing featured slightly, and retail possibly not at all. The medieval town was given over mainly to manufacture, and established retail premises soon also reappear. The emigration of the crafts out of the town and their replacement by shops is perhaps what marks the real end of the medieval city.

'Production' is used here in a very general sense – the exploitation of resources. As well as the general idea of the town as a collecting point for agricultural surplus, we have to consider two other types of resource collection. In some rare cases the resource was actually available in static form on the site. Whereas towns did not generally form, as they did in later times, around coal mines or iron mines, they did develop around brine-springs such as Droitwich, famous from the Iron Age to the nineteenth century for the quality of its salt. The recent work there has shown something of the changing process; in the Iron Age and Roman period the brine was evaporated into tanks and distributed in coarse pottery containers whose distinctive fabric allows an estimate of the area served. Even in the early days a subsidiary industry may have been present: the pickling of carcasses *in situ* in wattle-lined pits. By the later Middle Ages, the principal source for the brine was a large central pit which supplied a number of different operators. In the nineteenth century, the brine was used to serve the public baths of a spa town. Other places which probably flourished by virtue of an on-site resource were the fishing towns, such as early Ipswich or Great Yarmouth, where fishermen's houses have been found. The seventh-century predecessor of Poole with its great deposit of oyster shells (discovered during the examination of a later medieval wool mansion) might also fall into this category. If the deposit was really laid down in a short time (rather than over the centuries like a prehistoric shell midden) then some kind of preservation and distribution of the extracted oysters is implied – although it is hard to see what method could be used to avoid poisoning the early Kings of Wessex.

A second mode of production is the canalising of a new resource into the system by means of commerce. I think it is reasonable to assume here that commerce did not simply spring up through the islanders' love of free enterprise, but was introduced through the acquisitive efforts of more developed communities. Characteristically, the process begins with a visit of merchants with something to sell or exchange, who might sail up river or trade off the beach. A favourite landfall establishes expectations in trader and native alike. It is likely that the pre-Roman coastal trading centre at Hengistbury began in this way, and it is not impossible that those of the Dark Ages did likewise. Hamwih, or, less certainly, Ipswich, may have begun as places primarily intended to receive imports, paid for in whatever treasure or surplus was available, rather than deliberate outlets for exports. The possibility arises

that initially (and only initially) they were not Anglo-Saxon settlements at all, not even the forerunners of Towns, but colonies of Frisian or Frankish merchants, tolerated for what they could offer. The English involvement in York and London is similarly ambivalent, and our archaeology is hardly sensitive enough to tell, in the seventh-century, the difference between an English and a Frisian warehouse. It is often argued that England specialised in invisible exports, or rather exports invisible to archaeology, such as wool, fur, breeding stock and slaves, and something indeed must have been exchanged. It is this puzzle, the role of a commercial impetus to set beside that of the crown, the Church and the craftsmen which makes the archaeology of places like Hamwih, Ipswich, York, Lincoln, London and other potential early ports like Sandwich, Fordwich, and perhaps Bamburgh and Monkwearmouth, so important.

If we cannot see clearly what was going out, we have seen, at least, something of what was coming in. A ship wrecked on Panpudding sands was bound for Roman London and contained Samian pottery from Gaul. A Roman ship could carry 10,000 amphora, for which oil, wine and fish sauce have all been claimed as contents. On the floor of the first-century *forum* excavated at Fenchurch Street was a deposit of burnt grain 1m (39in) thick, thought to be seed imported from the Mediterranean. Other plants or seeds imported into Roman London included nuts and whole cones from the stone pine (perhaps for incense), quince, olives, dried figs, mulberry, walnuts and vines. Dates have been found on the floor of a shop in Colchester, burnt down in about AD 60, the time of the rebellion of Boudica. The range of artefacts reaching London and other major Roman towns was prodigious; from the rubbish pits of London dating between AD 50 and 130, objects have been identified from Italy, Gaul, Greece,

55 A composite section through the excavated riverside revetments of the Thames in London (Museum of London)

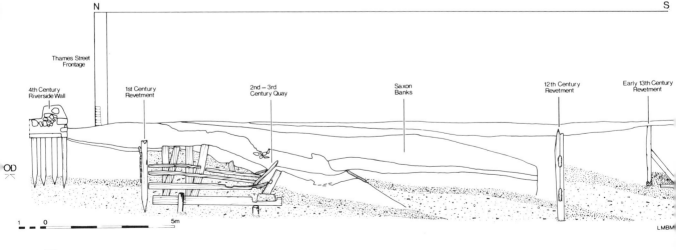

Palestine, Turkey, Syria, Spain and Germany.

The contrast with the post-Roman centuries could hardly be greater. The early English ports show their contacts mainly in the form of pottery and glass from northern France and the Rhineland, although querns of volcanic lava, probably also from Germany (the Niedermendig area), were reaching Tamworth. Higher diversity would appear to arrive with the Vikings in the ninth century and must have benefited from the trade routes they had already established. Silk has been found in Lincoln and York together with whetstones, amber and a cowrie shell from the Red Sea. An Arabic coin, or rather a counterfeit copy of a Samarkand *dirham*, stone cooking bowls from Shetland and hones and walrus ivory from Norway are among other finds from the rich Anglo-Scandinavian sites at York.

The commercial habit grew from then on, the need to import no doubt stimulating the urge to export. Exotic objects have been found in most coastal centres and in a number of inland regional towns from the twelfth century onwards. The exploitation of this particular resource, that brought in by water, had its own topographical influence on the towns that took part. As the boats and landing places changed, so the town adapted itself to receive them and to allow them to unload. Roman overseas cargo ships made use of a robust timber waterfront of which the finest example has been excavated in London. On the river Foss at York was found the base of a Roman crane for unloading up onto the quay. The timber quays built along the Thames' frontage of the city continued to function until their replacement by the stone riverside wall built further

inland in the fourth century. Milne and Hobley have estimated that the Thames at high water was 200m (656ft) wider and 5m (16ft) lower in Roman times, so that the Roman frontage is now buried well below street level on the line of Upper Thames Street. The vessels of the fifth to ninth centuries would use a different method of unloading, being floated up with the tide onto beaches, and pushed off back into the water when unladen. This is probably the context of a shift of activity in post-Roman London, from the derelict docks of the Roman city, to the adjacent site of the aptly named 'Strand', now seen as a middle-Saxon nucleus for London. In the twelfth century, the old city waterfront began to advance again to serve deep-water vessels, and a series of timber and stone revetments was constructed, infilled by rubbish packed behind them in the thirteenth, fourteenth and fifteenth centuries. Gustav Milne has described this progressive encroachment, seen in many European ports, as partly provoked by the need for more space on land to serve the growing maritime trade; partly to counter the increasingly high tides as the river was canalised; partly to overcome silting; but mainly to maintain a sound frontage for an efficient turnaround; for the quay was a source of wealth. It was that at Plymouth, constructed *c.* 1300 (and the first to be excavated in Britain), which allowed the town to emerge from relative obscurity into fame as a significant port, naval base, and embarkation point for the burgeoning pilgrim trade.

Somewhat analogous effects, although perhaps more difficult to observe, were provoked by the needs of inland traffic. A river provided access but also had to be crossed; a ford was compatible with shallow keelless vessels that could be beached and unloaded on the mud, but to unload larger vessels would imply canalisation and a bridge, and vice

56 *Artist's impression of an Anglo-Saxon beaching place excavated in London. Vessels could here be floated on and off with the tide (Museum of London)*

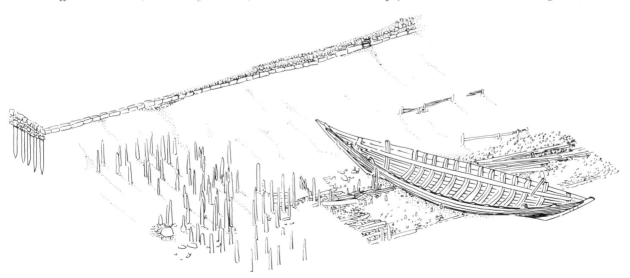

versa. The need for a suitable bridging point (narrow and deep, rather than wide and shallow) would have been one reason to prompt a settlement shift, as from Quatford to Bridgnorth in the eleventh century. At York and Lincoln, as in London, the water-seeking early-medieval boatmen may have been in pursuit of landing space untrammelled by Roman engineering; and similar factors may have influenced many of those places where the centre seems to shift restlessly around the pivot of a generally preferred location, such as at Northampton and Southampton, or at Colchester, where the post-Roman landing place may have been outside the Roman city at Old Heath. It was also perhaps an inability to take part in riverine exchange that led to the desertion of such 'dry sites' as Silchester altogether.

The availability of resources, whether growing in the fields or coming in on the hoof or brought by boat, and the power and political will to exploit them, peopled the towns with Imperial or royal agents, seamen, boatmen and farmers owing rent. We now reach the most significant social group of all – the artisans, the people who, as far back as the archaeological record stretches, have left evidence that they have tried to turn the natural world into something more useful, and to make a living from doing so. It is not only the crafts themselves that are interesting, in a technical sense, but their diversity and success, these being indexes to those peculiar rhythms of liberty and affluence which always appear to be slightly out of phase.

The evidence for urban craft is most abundant in the Middle Ages, perhaps because of the manufacturers' habit of disposing of their waste in their own backyards. The first 1500 years AD saw relatively little technical progress among craftsmen: certainly some techniques were 'lost', such as making concrete in the post-Roman period; and the Romans made machines, such as the Silchester force-pump, which were not to reappear until the fifteenth century. Benedict Biscop, in the seventh century, was obliged to send to Gaul for people who could make glass and build in the 'Roman manner'. But the absence of certain crafts was at least partly an absence of interest and of demand, rather than barbarism or ineptitude. We know, from the Sutton Hoo jewellery, the Lindisfarne gospels or the Wolverhampton cross what the Anglo-Saxons could do with a wide range of materials when they wanted to. The medieval crafts are therefore a reasonable guide to

what was possible in the previous millennium. All were probably invented and practised in the Roman period, and many in the Dark Ages, albeit not necessarily in towns.

Even for the Middle Ages, not all trades leave visible traces. Taking the named occupations collected by Unwin and Salusbury from medieval documentation, a list of eighty-one crafts can be made, of which twenty-three, (such as hatter and haberdasher) would be unlikely to leave much diagnostic archaeology. But the majority relied on raw materials which we can find as offcuts or broken objects, and, very occasionally, the tools of the trade themselves are found. The whole system of crafts can be conveniently inspected in Fig. 58, tabulated by the raw materials that fuelled them: animal, vegetable and mineral. In theory at least there must have been considerable interdependence between them. No less than twenty-five other occupations depended on the butcher for their raw materials, from the soap-makers who needed the tallow, to the leather-workers (lorimer, glover, cordwainer, saddler, etc.), to those making use of the guts for cord, and horns for glue or windows for lanterns (*lanthorns*). Not a lot seems to have been wasted. The discarded horn cores were used for levelling courses when building walls. Cow-hair was also used by the building trade for binding plaster, and by boat-builders for caulking boats. Other forms of interdependence are less obvious: the tanner acquired oak bark from the barker, but the tan burves, when exhausted after a year or two in the tan pit, would find a buyer in the metalsmith, who used them to refine silver (by absorbing the litharge). Even the mason's chippings could be recycled to provide crushed stone temper for pottery, as has been suggested at Worcester.

The commonest crafts captured underground are those which required a hole or which leave durable rubbish. Amongst manufacturing trades, metal-work predominates, since it tends to leave scorched areas and slag. Metallurgical analysis has unravelled the uses to which these areas were put. Of thirty-three second- to third-century furnaces excavated in the suburbs of the Roman fort at Deansgate, Manchester, three were for smelting (heating and hammering iron extract to make it workable), two for lead working and the remainder for smithing: bending and shaping and repairing iron objects from ploughshares to weapons and horseshoes. This activity and its waste product was common in the Roman town, and it is still present within settlements in the middle Saxon period, as at Ramsbury, and in the late Saxon towns. Bronze workers also leave durable debris, particularly the medieval bellmakers (*belyeters*), since the process

57 Artist's impression of fifteenth-century dock at Baynard's Castle, London, with a cargo ship using the quay. Below The quay as excavated (Museum of London)

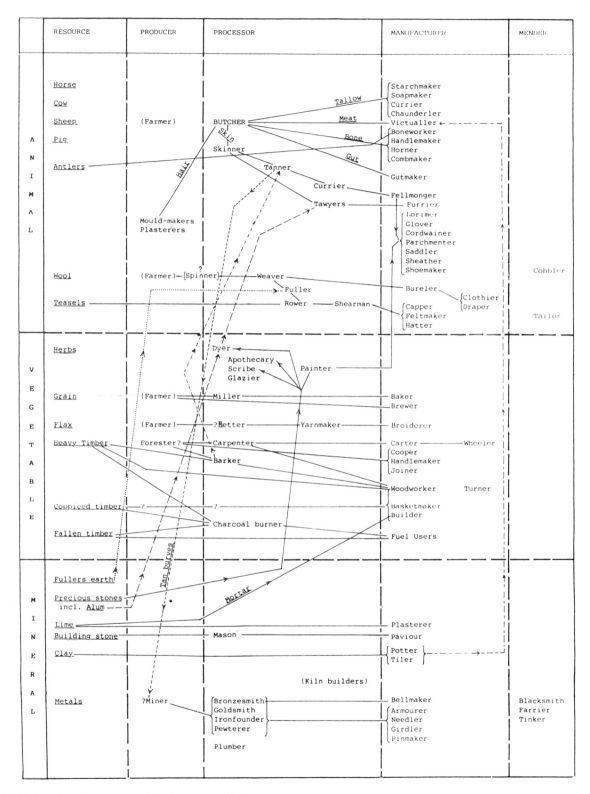

58 *Medieval craftsmen named in documents, their*
    resources and their hypothetical interdependence
    (M.O.H. Carver)

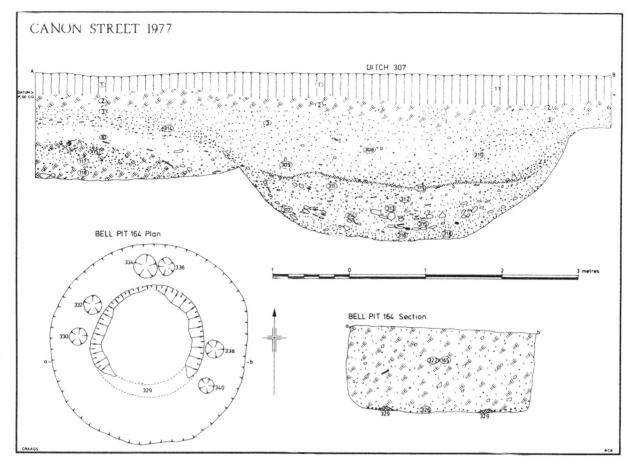

DITCH 307

BELL PIT 164 Plan

BELL PIT 164 Section

59 Medieval bell-pit excavated at Taunton. Pieces of bell-mould, originally supported upside down by posts and frame, were found in the pit (Peter Leach)

required a clay mould supported by a wooden frame in a pit, as at Taunton, Gloucester, and many other places. Some silver-working has been detected in Roman Silchester, and gold-working in Roman London and early medieval Winchester. Bronze workers making bronzes for shoes and belts, pilgrim badges and other ornaments were active in many towns, and pins, wound, crimped or hammered are found everywhere from the fourteenth century.

For the trades which leave more vulnerable archaeological evidence, Anglo-Scandinavian York is the exception which proves what might have been the rule elsewhere. Present there are not only evidence for working iron, bronze, lead, silver and gold, but the cores from turning wooden cups, the offcuts from working amber and jet into ornaments, and horn into handles, and numerous other activities now under close study by its excavators. Bone, antler and horn in particular could be made into objects of almost limitless variety from boxes and buttons to ice-skates.

The building trade was not, of course, confined to towns, although they are good places to observe its fortunes, most powerfully in the buildings themselves. The traces left by builders and builders' supplies are also common. For the Roman period we have a municipal tile works at Gloucester, while second-century Colchester is thought to have been the centre for a school of mosaicists. For the earlier Middle Ages there are mortar mixers at Northampton and others are suspected at Hereford. The thirteenth-century limekiln discovered at Bedford is now an Ancient Monument. Tiles became common, probably following legislation, in the fourteenth century, and tile kilns are known from Worcester. The fifteenth-century stone-lined saw-pit at Hereford is a sign of the medieval builders' general move from split to sawn timber for floor-boards and panels. Among the information nestling in the debris of demolished buildings are the types of stone reaching towns: from the famous quarries at Caen, Beer, Portland, Barnack, Kent and the Isle of Wight for building stone; and from Bridport, Stonesfield, Colyweston and Cornwall for roofing slate.

Citizens must be clothed and fed as well as housed, and although these are common necessities, there is reason to think that here too the towns had a

60 Early medieval objects and waste from manufacture
and lathe-turning in wood and bone at York (Liz
Hooper, after York Archaeological Trust)

61 Early medieval mortar mixer from Northampton (Northampton Development Corporation)

particular role in developing the associated crafts. Cloth was pre-eminent, as is clear from both Roman and medieval documentation. It has been suggested that weaving on a horizontal loom, which superseded weaving on a vertical loom, is particularly connected with increased production from medieval towns. Certainly loom weights, which betray the vertical loom, are rare later, although the traces of this great industry are always fairly modest: a tablet for tablet-weaving from Roman Alcester; textile itself from Anglo-Scandinavian York, including the famous 'Viking sock'; a teasel (for finishing cloth) from the same site; a fragment of fleece from early-medieval Durham; cloth racks from medieval Bristol, and medieval weaving-tools from Newbury are examples. Among monuments still standing is the Fulling Mill at Durham which dates in origin from the fifteenth century. Deposits of fuller's earth (for degreasing wool) are known at Nuffield and Reigate, and fulling pits from Staines. At Lower Brook Street in Winchester, a fourteenth-century dyehouse was excavated. Some evidence has also been found for the linen industry: flax and hemp at York, and the possible 'flax retting' site in early medieval Oxford.

The old leather trades surface as tanning pits, often rectangular and revetted with wattle or stakes, where the skins were cured. They were famous for their smell, using lime, dog turds and elder as well as oak bark to give a vigorous solution. Those situated inside the sandstone caves at Nottingham must have

been particularly noisome to work with, although they had the great technical advantage of a constant temperature, around 54°F (12°C), winter and summer. Leather offcuts are known in quantity from the great waterlogged deposits at York and London, suggesting shoes and sheaths as the principal manufacture. Those found in early medieval Durham show that cobbling, i.e. mending and recycling shoes, was present from the earliest stages. The demand for fur was not necessarily met wholly by imports from the north. Cats and dogs found on midden heaps and town tips as well as in rubbish pits, together with other animals, such as foxes, otters and rabbits, were probably flayed, as is documented in medieval Odense.

The largest and most complex industry and the one which spawned the most dependent trades must have been that concerned with processing food, and connected with it, the one that survives best – pottery. Wheat, rye and barley entered the system as grain and left it as bread or beer, and in between passed through one of the most lucrative occupations of them all – milling. It is perhaps hardly a craft in the same sense as the others, being, it would seem, a jealously guarded monopoly from the earliest days. It was always possible to grind grain by hand, and this must have happened in the post-Roman rural interlude. But it is time-consuming: however muscular the bread-maker, it would seem that town life was impossible without power-driven mills. A Roman mill driven by a donkey is known from Canterbury, and water-mills from Lincoln. Early medieval water-mills with horizontal wheels have been excavated at Tamworth and Old

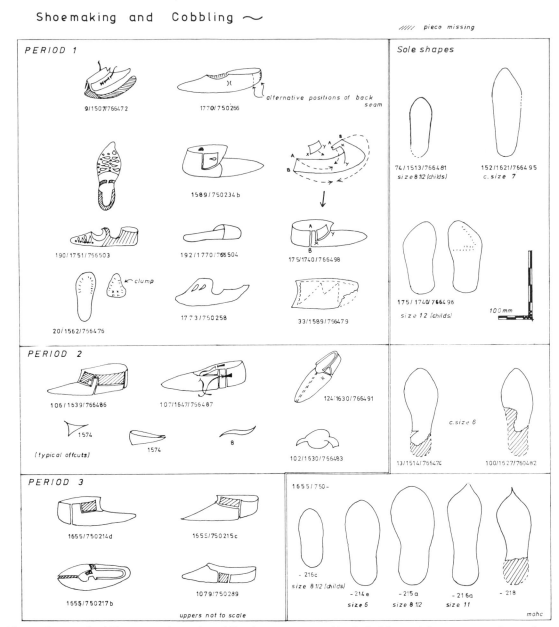

Shoemaking and Cobbling ~

///// piece missing

PERIOD 1

9/1507/766472

1770/750266

alternative positions of back seam

1589/750234 b

A B X Y

B

190/1751/766503

192/1770/765504

175/1740/766498

↓ clump

20/1562/756476

1773/750258

33/1589/756479

Sole shapes

74/1513/766481
size 8 1/2 (childs)

152/1621/766495
c. size 7

175/1740/766498
size 12 (childs)

100 mm

PERIOD 2

106/1539/766486

107/1647/766487

124/1630/766491

1574

(typical offcuts)

1574

8

102/1630/766483

c. size 6

13/1514/766474

100/1527/760482

PERIOD 3

1655/750214d

1655/750215c

1655/750217b

1079/750289

uppers not to scale

1655/750–

– 216c
size 8 1/2 (childs)

– 214e
size 5

– 215a
size 8 1/2

– 216a
size 11

– 218

mohc

62 Shoemaking and cobbling in early medieval Durham (M.O.H. Carver)

Windsor. The wheel is upright again by the twelfth century, using an undershot or overshot drive. When the first windmills appear in the thirteenth century it is likely that the town monopolists began to loose their hold. It is generally assumed that flour was baked into bread in ovens or open hearths of which there are innumerable examples. Baking itself was a centralised craft in the Roman period, as we know from London and Canterbury. A small group of tenth-century low-temperature ovens found in Stafford are also interpreted as evidence for centralised baking. Many examples of medieval hearths and ovens, as from Bedford and Staines, are variously interpreted as for baking and brewing. Characteristically they are small, clay-lined, sometimes shaped like a figure eight, and reused several times, implying a semi-permanent dome. The clay is scorched but not fired and there is no trace of pottery or slag. An interesting group of structures belonging to the fourteenth century, or thereabouts, from Stafford, Stamford and Northampton are also associated with bread or beer production. These are stone-lined, dug into the ground, and stoked below ground, with access by a flight of steps. It is suggested that they are used for drying or roasting grain,

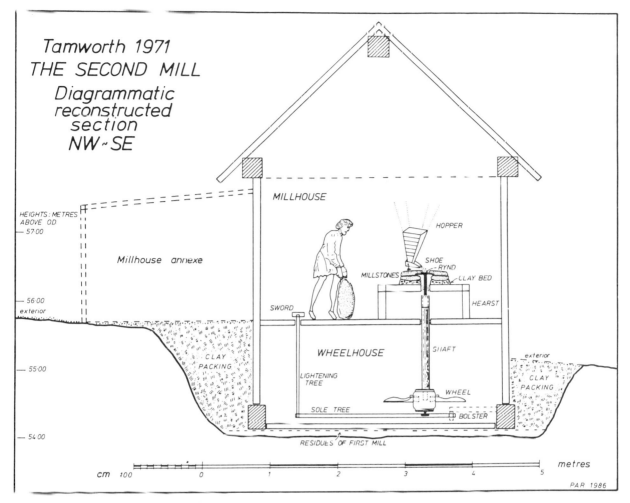

Tamworth 1971
THE SECOND MILL
Diagrammatic
reconstructed
section
NW~SE

HEIGHTS : METRES
ABOVE OD
— 57.00

Millhouse annexe

MILLHOUSE

HOPPER

SHOE
RYND
CLAY BED

MILLSTONES

HEARST

— 56.00
exterior

SWORD

WHEELHOUSE

SHAFT

LIGHTENING
TREE

exterior
CLAY
PACKING

CLAY
PACKING

— 55.00

WHEEL

SOLE TREE

BOLSTER

— 54.00

RESIDUES OF FIRST MILL

cm 100   0   1   2   3   4   5   metres

PAR 1986

63 *An early medieval horizontally-driven mill excavated*
   in Tamworth. Reconstruction by Philip Rahtz

which was spread on a suspended platform of woven
horsehair. They must belong to a tradition begun by
the numerous T-shaped Roman corn dryers known
from rural sites, recalled by the post-Roman example found beneath the early ramparts at Hereford.

Meat arrived on the hoof, and slaughtering on the
spot seems to have been practised from the late
Roman period at Worcester and in early medieval
York. In both cases, this was (perhaps
coincidentally) at or near the spot which later became
known as 'The Shambles' (abattoir). The towns
were probably fed from the adjacent shires, but
Philip Armitage's work on seventeenth-century
London shows how cattle could be brought along
the droveways from all over England. Some years

64 *Bread-oven or corn-dryer from thirteenth-century*
   Hereford (Hereford Museum)

ago the panellists of the television programme *Animal, Vegetable and Mineral* were invited to identify a pair of diminutive leather bootees – those used by the turkeys of more recent times, which were obliged to walk to the London markets from Norfolk. Curing meat for the winter or for transport as a carcass seems to have taken place in Roman Droitwich and Whitchurch, but was presumably otherwise a family responsibility.

The implications for the butchery trade of the many deposits of animal bone recovered from English towns has yet to be fully worked out. The mixed bones from pre-cut joints of beef, mutton and pork dominate, and butchery marks are found, suggesting that they could be purchased in joints from the earliest years of town life. For London, Armitage has suggested a difference between Roman and medieval methods of butchering; in the former the ribs were removed and the carcass quartered on a flat surface; in the latter, the carcass was hung up on a hook and halved along the medial line of the vertebrae. The butcher could then sell off the pieces of the animal required by other trades, but his waste products, particularly the cartloads of entrails, posed a disposal problem, as later medieval lawsuits indicate. More specific deposits of animal limbs, such as ox metatarsals, usually belong to the bone-workers' trades. Sheep metatarsals found in York in association with tanning pits might have been used in the preparation of parchment.

Fish were brought far inland throughout the period. A layer of bones from small herrings (up to 2000 fish) excavated in Anglian York seems to indicate a processing factory of some kind. Fish deposits in early medieval Ipswich, and fish and fish hooks in medieval Great Yarmouth are on a scale which suggests commercial fishmongers and deep sea fishing. Fishing in fresh water may also have reached commercial proportions, but evidence is hard to come by. The medieval fishponds constructed at Stafford and Lichfield seem, from documentary evidence, to be reserved to the King and Bishop respectively, and royal fishermen were licensed.

Closely connected with food production and processing should be the most commonly encountered industry of all – the making of pottery. Of the range of vessels available, some forms would seem to be associated with the transport or storage of food rather than eating it: amphorae in the Roman period, pitchers and cisterns, and possibly jars in the Middle Ages. The bulk of the production was, however, devoted to making utensils for domestic use: plates, pitchers, bowls, cups, lamps and mortaria in the Roman period, cooking pots, bowls and lamps in the early Middle Ages, and a variety of forms, particularly jugs, from the twelfth century onwards. Roman pottery was generally made near, rather than in, the town. Kilns are known from near Canterbury, Colchester and Kelvedon; and at Littlemore, Oxford, a pottery drier was found in what was then a major pottery works on a rural Roman site. Early medieval potteries are often found inside the town itself, and are particularly associated with the *burh* of the ninth and tenth centuries: Thetford ware, Ipswich ware and Torksey ware are the eastern group, with Stafford ware and Northampton ware in the west, and Stamford ware in a class by itself, with its widely distributed pale fabric and yellow or apple-green glaze. The kilns are simple: pits lined with clay, sometimes with a central support, and with a windward flue for the fire. The industry at Stafford was certainly centralised, confined to a 'potting quarter' and provided with wells. The wasters and broken oven fabric were dumped in pits, or on the town tip to the south-east. It is a curious fact that no less than three dumps of wasters at Stafford contained the severed heads of young persons; this smacks of either a particularly well-developed Anglo-Saxon work-ethic, or military discipline. Perhaps also significant is that the distribution of Stafford-type wares, although by no means certainly all made in Stafford, seems to be confined to military *burhs* and the vessels themselves to jars. Stafford was also a collecting point for grain, and had centralised butchering, but how far the pottery was actually intended to contain a distributed food product is not yet known. The other attributes expected of the potter's workshop are more elusive – although medieval examples from Bourne and Lyvedon provide rural analogies. In the eleventh century and later, potteries are more local and more numerous and it is rarer to find them operating from within the town limits. They appear to be among the first craftsmen to serve and the first to abandon the community within the walls.

The artisans, whether enslaved, complacent or enterprising, were the life blood of the urban system; the butcher disembowelling carcasses in the shambles, the bronzesmith making bells, the potter selling pottery from a cart, the weaver, the goldsmith in his stone house and the small boys collecting offal and herbs, were part of a system which they sometimes made, and which sometimes made them. The urban fabric was something they might ignore, or depend upon, or cause to change according to the circumstance of the age. Craft is therefore the staple of urban archaeology and although often viewed merely as a gratifying adjunct to the real business of town history, its potential is far greater. If enough contact can be made with enough crafts in enough towns, we can begin to construct a sequence and a pattern for production and consumption which tells a story of its own, and is not irrelevant to our own economy. It has to be admitted that to try to do this now is somewhat premature – the subject is not well published as yet, and certainly deserves a deeper study – but archaeology is bland without the spice of a little speculation.

The crafts as a whole seem to show a tension between external and internal initiative, the initiative of the investor, be it Emperor or King, and the initiative of the artisan, be it the pursuit of wealth or simply the pursuit of enough to eat. The system shows no evolution, in the biological sense, but is almost completely artificial, its character being largely dependent on doctrinaire politics. This will hardly be greeted as a revelation by the historian, but could be taken as a salutary reminder to prehistorians, many of whom believe that the character of a society is dependent upon the availability of its resources and technical prowess, rather than the other way round.

Within three generations, the Romanised inhabitants of Iron Age Britain reached levels of production and consumption and comfort in cities

which were not to be reached again until the Industrial Revolution, or not even then, perhaps not even yet. The towns were places for manufacture, commerce, recreation and shopping. The shops, with workshops to the rear, spread along the streets, as in St Albans, where examples have been excavated by Professor Frere. One, begun as a business venture after the conquest, was burnt down in Boudica's rebellion, rebuilt and later divided into smaller units by alleys. Like medieval tenements, the shops were long buildings with the narrow end facing the street. Shops were augmented by the market hall or shopping precinct (macellum), as at Wroxeter; in the nearby forum, a fire preserved the unsold contents of a pottery stall: 210 vessels, including mortaria from Mancetter in Warwickshire and samian from central Gaul, together with 100 whetstones. It is possible that particular Roman places were also centres for specialised industries, as were their nineteenth-century counterparts – and some examples have been mentioned: ironworking at Manchester and Worcester; mutton curing at Whitchurch; but the evidence is currently thin. The government in the first and second centuries was powerful enough to promote both extra-mural production and an advanced urban manufacturing system, and the town was its principal motor.

This is why it is, at least in theory, such a significant monitor for the changes of the late Roman period, in which loyalties were shaken and rearranged. By the arrival of the post-Roman centuries, individual leaders had apparently little use for towns, except perhaps as ruins reusable to protect their garden estates. When more centralised power was re-established, and the whole process began again, the first crafts to appear are designed to serve the strict needs of fort and depot. Only in the Anglo-Scandinavian areas in the ninth century do we see at present the diversity likely to mean some release of artisan initiative. Nevertheless, Alan Vince's observations on early English pottery must give us pause (Fig. 66). What do the areas of distribution of the eastern, western, and Thames-valley groups of Saxon wares actually mean? If this were a prehistoric period rather than the tenth century AD, we would suggest tribal areas, and it is, I suppose, possible that they represent the areas under the control of the former Mercian, London and Wessex authorities. Vince's more interesting idea is that the trade and exchange mechanism were there all the time, through the blank centuries of 'invisible' production; only through pottery, the great archaeological survivor, can the arterial routes be seen for the first time, like a barium meal passing through an otherwise invisible digestive system.

In the tenth century appear the first signs of the

65 *Ground plans of Roman urban buildings*
(After Rivet 1964)

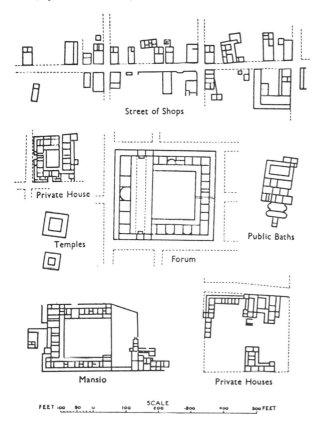

Street of Shops

Private House

Temples

Forum

Public Baths

Mansio

Private Houses

FEET 100 50 0   100   SCALE 200   300   400   500 FEET

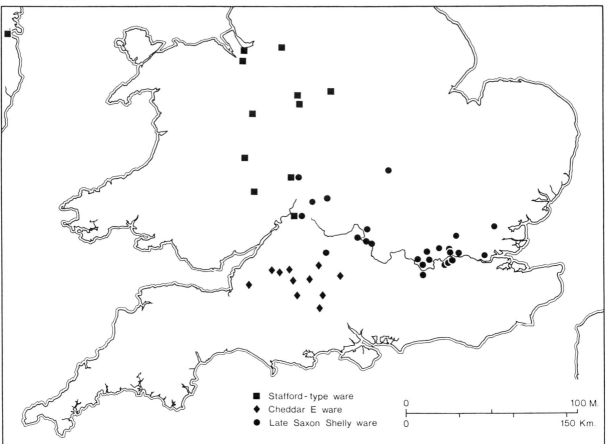

66 *Distribution of three types of late Saxon pottery in the west and south of England. The more numerous eastern English industries (such as Stamford ware and Thetford ware) are not shown on this map (After Alan Vince)*

more deliberate promotion of artisan activity, operating from ordered tenements in the towns of Alfred's Wessex and Anglo-Scandinavian York. Other parts of the country have to wait until the eleventh or twelfth century, when this new development arrives with the greater contrast. Not only the ordered tenements, but other major developments, are put in train to provide a successful base for the urban industries: streams, for example, dammed to provide a 'vivarium' for fish and a head to drive the mill. At Winchester such developments were already happening in the late Saxon period. The new crafts appear to congregate together from an early period – the eleventh or twelfth century, according to information from the Winton Domesday – which presumably helped to attract and meet commissions; but it is not impossible that these zones, too, were allocated by the sponsoring authority.

Medieval towns did not necessarily become more

more specialised or dedicated to a wider hinterland as time went on. In the major ports the diversity increased, while elsewhere the number of towns multiplied, their hinterlands presumably decreased in size and the basic range of recurring staples were found in each. Only in the fourteenth and fifteenth centuries does special success mark out some, such as the great wool and cloth towns of Winchester, Lincoln, Huntingdon, Worcester and Darlington, while others declined into obscurity.

This is the period which we would dearly love to observe in finer focus, the period after the Black Death when craft distribution seems so uneven compared with a century before. In some places, steadily increasing diversity; in others, apparent dereliction, even desertion. The suspicion must be that some craftsmen no longer depended on the official sanction of an urban base and were peddling their valued labour in other sites. It was the Roman cycle of investment, growth and decline repeated again 1000 years later, but with a different outcome. Where the tenements continued to flourish, amalgamations are noted, as with the bronze–workers in Sidbury, Worcester, where, one, then two, and finally three adjacent tenements go over to the production of bells and buckles. Somewhere

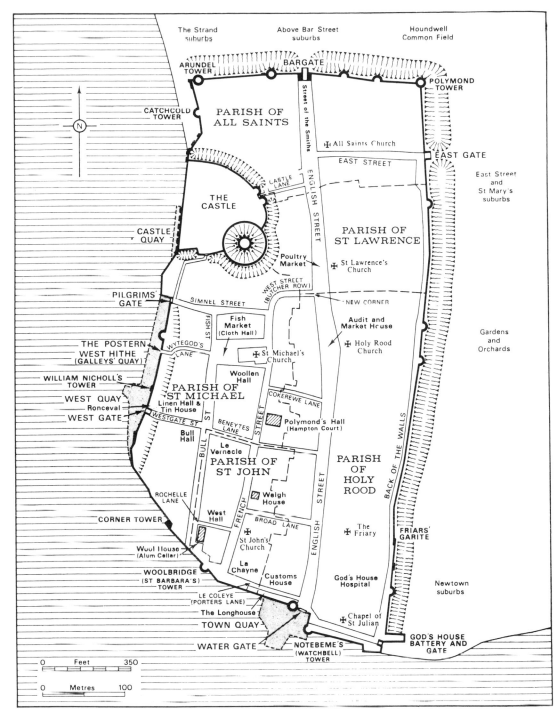

*67 Streets, parishes and quarters in late medieval
Southampton (Platt and Coleman-Smith, 1975)*

behind this amalgamation is a new type of person,
the embryonic entrepreneur.

Those places which were unlucky in their regions
or their investors, continued to struggle. By the
Elizabethan period we hear of petitions to the crown
to support failing industries such as that at Stafford
(which made woolly caps). The Elizabethan
authorities also attempted to alleviate the
unemployment problem with state-sponsored
projects, such as cloth-making. These early MSC
schemes lasted eight or nine years, and seem to set a
rhythm of stimulation and indifference which has
been tediously repeated ever since.

VII
Private lives

From time to time, in our search for generalities amongst the strata, we come face to face with signs of the individual. These encounters are somewhat one-sided, the urban archaeologist, even the most resolutely scientific, being pleasantly moved but the individual remaining obstinately nameless and faceless. Some feel that this anonymity is no less than the dead deserve; many of these people could afford little enough dignity in life, without being disinterred and slandered in the name of science. But to others, individuality is what makes human beings human, and every fugitive nuance is precious; the colour of a girl's hair, a habit of collecting shells, a game played with scratched stones on a cracked mosaic, all these things are preserved and we are sometimes lucky enough to detect them or to stumble across them. Besides which, there are personal questions of a particular kind which *can* actually be asked. Even if we cannot say 'Were you good looking?', we can ask 'Were you tall?' or 'Were you rich?' or 'Did you have syphilis?'.

The evidence for the character of people comes in many different forms. Occasionally we find pieces of the live person, like the locks of hair, one blonde and one brunette, from Saxo-Norman Durham. Sometimes they leave their names, like L. Viducius Placidus of Rouen, a Roman *negotiator* whose inscription was found built into a post-medieval lime-kiln in York; or the twelfth-century 'Snarr the toll collector' whose seal was found in the same city; or the thirteenth-century Richard of Southwick who abandoned such a remarkable menagerie in his latrine pit at Southampton (see below). Moneyers in the Anglo-Saxon period put their names on the coins, from which we can follow the career of a few: Lul of East Anglia, Eaba of Canterbury, Godwine of Winchester. There is some evidence that the moneyer's trade stayed in the family, with the descendants striking for both English and Danish Kings. Sometimes we find Roman graffiti, like 'ac quis te cinae (de)' (and who's a little sod – you!) or 'equa ella culo' (f*ck that horse) at Leicester, which

68 Man buried with his dog in Roman Ilchester (Peter Leach)

92

can be construed as fairly personal. But the main evidence for people is less specific, although more plentiful: evidence for diet, personal hygiene, the inside of houses, and, above all, the special evidence which comes from cemeteries.

In death, as in life, not everyone is expressive of their own personality, or fortune, although there are a few rare examples. A man in Roman Ilchester was buried with his dog; a young girl from medieval London had died in pregnancy; and a young man in early medieval Ipswich fell through the ice while skating on the Orwell and was found as a skeleton with the bone skates still attached to his foot-bones. More generally it is the burial rite adopted and the state of the body which say something of people's

general beliefs and circumstances. The greater the number of burials examined, the more clearly human conditions can be observed, and the more evocative become the individual aberrations from the norm. There are difficulties, already mentioned in Chapter V, about referring the bodies buried in cemeteries to the inhabitants of the town. But equations can be made, and we have at least three major recently published excavations – Roman cemeteries at Cirencester and Winchester, and a medieval graveyard at York – which have laid a fresh foundation for further demographic studies.

69 Roman lead coffin (a) and stone sarcophagus (b) from Ilchester (Peter Leach)

The burial rites mainly adopted in towns are for once in our favour. Although cremation was practised in the earliest centuries of town-life (first to second centuries), later periods use inhumation, where the whole body is buried and leaves more accessible pathology. In Roman times, when the cemeteries lay outside the town, the body might be placed in a stone or lead sarcophagus, which may be inscribed, or in a cist of roof-tiles or a coffin. Sometimes the body is encased in gypsum, as at Poundbury and York. Orientation of the grave is north/south or east/west, the latter becoming more prevalent in the Christian period. Burials may be accompanied by glass vessels or pottery. Sometimes a coin is found in the mouth, and quite commonly the head is cut off and placed between the legs. A particularly anomalous, and grand, burial was the double inhumation accompanied by swords and belt-fittings found *inside* the walls at Canterbury.

Trends within the choice of burial rite are not easy to observe. Neither east/west orientation nor the absence of grave goods is considered to be proof of

Christianity. Other Eastern religions, such as Mithraism were present from the first centuries AD, and it may have been their influence, or a general mood created in other religions under their influence, which encouraged the gradual adoption of east/west alignments. J. McDonald has made a convincing case for a change in outlook, towards hope for an after-life during the late second and third centuries AD, although pointing out that this need not be reflected in burial rites. A believer is always buried by someone else, not necessarily of his same cult, so that a lag in the conservative business of the undertaker is likely. In England, Poundbury and St Brides in London have been thought to be Christian cemeteries of the Roman period.

Archaeologists have watched the later Roman town carefully for signs of intrusive peoples, notably, of course, the Anglo-Saxon mercenaries who were to become the English. The main success story here is the Lankhills cemetery in Winchester whose excavator noticed at least three separate groups of graves, identifying them as the local Romano-British militia, a contingent from the Danube, and a small group (six graves) which are (possibly) Anglo-Saxon. Towards the end of the sequence (in the fifth century), there are many new

70 *Sequence of burial practices in the Cathedral Green cemetery, early medieval Hereford (Hereford Museum)*

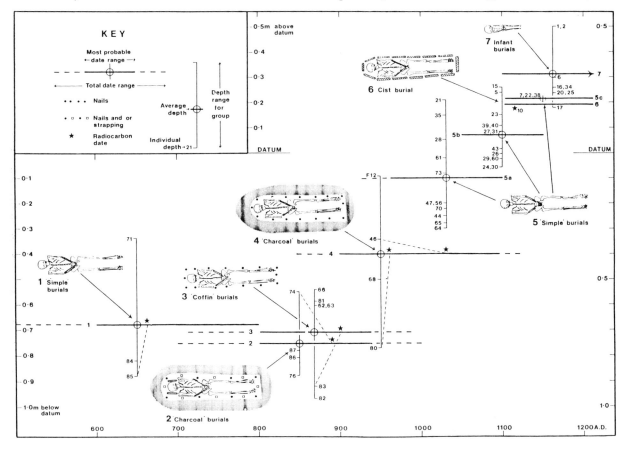

varieties of burial rite and after AD 370 a number are being buried with grandeur in special 'high status' areas.

Archaeologists are equally alert for the very latest inhabitants of the Roman towns and there are certainly signs that some of them met unconventional deaths. Bodies, apparently unburied, are sometimes discovered in and around the latest occupation layers, and some episodes are famous, such as the old man who took his life savings and crawled into the hypocaust of the baths at Wroxeter where he died. For John Wacher, these are victims not of rebellion or marauding Anglo-Saxons, but of one of the major epidemics which are known to have ravaged the late empire. He points out that these epidemics would have particularly affected the towns, and the idea receives support from later documented examples: Bocaccio writing about Florence during the Black Death, Samuel Pepys about London in 1665, or Maurice Pagnol about twentieth-century Marseilles. All report the flight to the country and the civic unrest that was left behind, and Pagnol graphically describes the obstinacy with which Christians continued to congregate in church to pray for help, and thereby gave each other the disease.

People eventually returned to Roman towns and buried their dead outside and inside them, sometimes within the graveyard of a designated church, although Martin Biddle's work at Winchester has put a more subtle gloss on this process. The sixth-century Saxon cemeteries which cluster around Winchester suggest that, even then, it exerted some attraction. Burials found inside the walls post-date the foundation of the Old Minster in AD 648, but are not within its graveyard. These were found at Lower Brook Street, in the area thought to have then been a middle-Saxon estate: a group of four or five burials, probably Christian, two with grave goods, one with a fine bead necklace and a set of silver rings. The cathedral cemeteries themselves otherwise offer the best sequences from the beginning of post-Roman occupation. Those from Winchester (the old Minster) and York will be the largest and probably most informative, when they appear in print; in the meantime, we have examples from Worcester, Hereford and Exeter. At Hereford, the seventh- to eighth-century burials are simple inhumations, but from the ninth century coffins are used, sometimes laid on a bed of charcoal. Burials in stone cists return in the eleventh century, or a single 'pilow stone' may be used, with the head and shoulders packed in clay.

The use of charcoal in burials is widespread, particularly in cathedral cemeteries of the ninth to twelfth centuries, and examples are known from Winchester, Oxford, Shrewsbury, Lincoln and York as well as in the three cities already mentioned. The practice lasted into the twelfth century in Scandinavia. The point of it is unclear, although it may have had its roots in the wish to preserve the body, and be awarded to people of special, perhaps especially holy, status. The reason for suggesting this is the strange sequence from beneath the Chapter House in Durham, where, as an alternative to charcoal burial, the bodies were laid on lime or pickled in salt. Durham, however, has every chance of being a special case, since its cathedral housed the revered remains of St Cuthbert, whose resistance to decay was something of an article of faith.

The practice of lining graves with stone or tiles and providing pillow stones, which essentially derived from Roman tradition, also continued late in London. At the cemetery of St Nicholas in the Shambles, which begins in the tenth/eleventh century, there were tombs built of mortared stone with a chalk and mortar floor, bodies encased in crushed chalk and mortar, and forty graves lined with stones or tiles. There were eight cases where a small stone had been placed in the mouth of the corpse, an echo of the Roman *obol*.

Many of the early medieval town cemeteries were disturbed when medieval redevelopment took place in the cathedral precinct. When the Normans built their grand replacement for the Old Minster at Winchester, the disturbed bones were gathered up and reburied in a charnel pit some 18.3m (60ft) across, with the skulls grouped at the west end in token of the Christian manner. Human remains were not always treated with such respect. The human bones found scattered in the town tip at Newcastle were more probably dug up by someone encroaching on an old cemetery, than the remains of a murder victim. The severed heads of Stafford (see Chapter VI) are thought to be punitive, since no other human bone was found.

The vast majority of graves excavated in towns are not individual or special, being simple inhumations aligned east/west, and, in the crowded Christian graveyards, often disturb the remains of their predecessors. Nevertheless, the richness of the pathological and demographic evidence that can be drawn from the skeletons is considerable. The discussion which follows compares some statistics of published groups from Roman Cirencester, early medieval Hereford (Castle Green) and medieval York (St Helen-on-the-Walls). They offer three windows on the people of their day, but it would be wrong to take the results as typical of the whole – nor would their archaeologists claim as much. The experience of one age is not going to be the experience of the next, so a cemetery in which more than twenty generations are buried, such as St Helen's, can hardly be treated as a single population.

Another important factor is class, which no doubt divided the population physically as well as economically. In theory, upper-class Christians lived sumptuously but could be buried humbly, beside the stunted bodies of the peasants of their parish. Estimates of life-expectancy can also be distorted by one or two outbreaks of the plague. If certain trends are read here, it is only so that they can be contradicted by future studies.

Throughout the last two millennia, people retained the capacity to live long and grow tall; reduced life expectancy and small stature are not endemic in earlier humans as is popularly supposed, but must be put down to deprivation of some kind. It would be interesting to compare the fourth-century population of Cirencester, most of whom had died in their fifties, with the earlier citizens of that same city who probably had a quite different standard of living. In early medieval Hereford, most people died between sixteen and forty-five, and in medieval York 56 per cent of women and 35.8 per cent of men had died by the age of thirty-five. However, over 9 per cent lived to be over sixty. The death of children shows a similar fluctuation. At Cirencester it was 17.4 per cent, in Hereford 30 per cent and at St Helens 27 per cent. These figures can be compared with those for Iron Age Owlesbury, 58 per cent, and the early medieval cemetery at Jarrow, 41 per cent. All the town cemeteries contained individual men who were 1.8m (6ft) tall, and a range in stature not so very different to ours. This is confirmed for the early medieval period by the sizes of shoes, found, for example, in the cobbler's shop at Durham. It used to be supposed that skeletons, particularly the form of the head, would betray racial characteristics, but work on the St Helen's cemetery has shown that it cannot be as simple as that; the races might become rapidly mixed, and the skull form may actually be dictated by other factors, such as diet. At the Roman cemetery of Trentholme Drive in the York *colonia*, the males were of varied skull-form (and more numerous, as at contemporary Cirencester), while the females were generally more similar to each other, having a long face and a moderately wide nose. If the men were predominantly former soldiers from different parts of the empire, and the women were native Britons, this might provide an explanation, if a facile one. These 'native' women resembled the Iron Age people buried at Wetwang, also in Yorkshire, but resembled also in some degree the inhabitants of Anglo-Scandinavian York (ninth-century). These are described as having large heads, long faces, and 'fairly low rectangular eyes'. One of the great

surprises of this work is to find that the most decisive change in facial appearance comes at the Norman conquest, a time when no large-scale immigration is anticipated. It seems that at Durham the named bishops before and after the Norman conquest are respectively long-headed and round-headed, and it is curiously common to find this difference between Anglo-Saxon and medieval bodies, even in cemeteries where no special social status is suspected. The new stock at St Helens is markedly round-headed with short faces, and matches that in the contemporary nunnery at Clementhorpe. These are puzzles which anatomical work in the next few decades may help to unravel.

The skeletons of buried people are not usually marked by the diseases that killed them, but the bones sometimes carry subtle traces of the suffering they bore in life. The Roman population at Cirencester carried much lead in its bones – 500 micrograms per gram (as compared with 50 micrograms per gram for ourselves) – but even such levels were not thought to be fatal. There was also evidence at Cirencester for a mystery disease, reminiscent of that which is supposed to have killed Herod: a periostitis of the skin, which would have made it exquisitely painful to the touch. There are a few other examples of disease which show in skeletal remains: people with gout in Roman Cirencester, leprosy from late Roman Dorchester, syphilis from medieval York and Chichester. Wounds are unexpectedly rare in the cemeteries reported, there being only eighteen cases among over 1000 burials at St Helen's. One of these was caused by an ear being cut off, and there were two cases of women who died of head wounds. Serious illness or malnutrition among children leaves traces in the form of 'Harris lines' marking the bone. Using these as a guide, it would appear that early and middle-Saxon populations suffered most, with examples ranging from 2.6 to 5.1 lines per bone in cemeteries at Caister-by-Yarmouth, Thornham and Burgh Castle, and there appears to have been a tendency to care more for boys at the expense of girls. At St Helen's in medieval York, the average was improved at 2.1, but still severe compared with Bronze Age people, such as those from Crichel or Shrewton.

Attempts to discover how unhealthy or healthy town life was, of course, do need comparison with rural populations of the same date and earlier. They need, too, anatomists of genius like the late Calvin Wells, whose skills as analyst and as raconteur brought so many long-dead individuals back to life. Something that emerges at present is that, although little evidence has been found in this group for malignant neoplasms (i.e. cancer), all the population suffered severely from osteoarthritis for which chronic stress is deemed to be a major factor

This is in some ways the result we are expecting from the onset of urban life – crowded conditions, an unhealthy diet and enforced competition, all the ingredients of stress. It is far from certain, however, that any of these factors were, for example, anything like as grievous as they are now. If we look at living conditions and the way they changed, we find that there were bad times and there were good, evidence for unbelievable squalor and evidence for regulated hygiene, and evidence for a wide choice of good food as well as for deprivation. The modern reader would do well to avoid using the word 'medieval' as a term of abuse. The average medieval peasant was probably more healthily fed than most of us, and the medieval merchant might be appalled at what is offered by a modern London Club by way of dinner.

The Romans set great store by drinking water, and went to great lengths to secure a pure, and presumably diuretic supply. This tradition was completely lost in England, and even in later medieval towns, with some exceptions such as Lichfield (where water was piped) and Exeter (where it came by aqueduct), water was drawn from wells and the taste largely disguised by making it into beer. The meat available throughout the period was beef, mutton, pork and poultry, with little change observable in the two principal published groups (London and Exeter) except for the increasing size of the animal and a tendency for the consumption of pork and mutton to increase with respect to beef in the Middle Ages. At Southampton, joint sizes decreased between the eleventh and thirteenth centuries, which might indicate a change in marketing practice, or a trend towards smaller groups of diners. Sea fish and shellfish, including oysters in profusion, were brought to inland towns. The shoemakers in Saxo-Norman Durham were dining off beef, pork, mutton, chicken, goose, grouse, capercailzie, cod, haddock, lobster, salmon, eel, cockles and mussels; and amongst the edible plants were hazelnuts, blackberries, raspberries, apples, plums and fat-hen (which can be cooked like spinach). The range available in Roman London and medieval Southampton was wider still. Locally cultivated grapes have been found in thirteenth-century Hereford, and in a Worcester latrine dated to the fourteenth century. The staple diet of the townsman was bread, sometimes very coarse bread, as implied by the ground-down teeth of a person buried in Norwich. In Anglo-Scandinavian York, a preponderance of oats has been detected in contrast to the Roman and medieval cities where wheat was more plentiful. One of the interesting changes which seems to be observable is in the availability of game

to ordinary citizens. In eighth-century Hamwih a wide range of wild animals, including, it would seem, crows, were eaten. Game animals, such as red deer, fallow deer and roe deer, and game birds such as partridge and woodcock increase in assemblages at Exeter towards the end of the Roman period; they are also available in early medieval Durham, but diminish rapidly in both Exeter and Durham from the eleventh century. This might be an indication of the effectiveness of the game laws, or at least an indication of the new class of people who formed the majority of the inhabitants at that time. It is more likely to be the former, since the range of wild vegetable foods also appears to be higher before, rather than after, the Norman conquest. The Anglo-Saxon townsmen would seem to have had the run of the countryside, assuming they did not actually retain rural interests. David Baker has argued that many medieval tenement holders in Bedford doubled as farmers, even if they too no longer had access to game. The rural flavour of medieval town life (and it was true of Roman urbanized places like Great Dunmow too) was enhanced by the small-holding that each tenement had, where vegetables and fruit could be grown, and pigs and poultry could be kept. A beehive was found in early medieval York. The new tenements at Winchelsea, although ultimately unsuccessful, must have been particularly desirable, laid out with ample gardens and orchards.

A healthy diet notwithstanding, some controversy has developed over how healthy the town was to inhabit. At this point it is worth recalling Don Brothwells's observations on the size of the problem of waste disposal. A hundred households will produce in one year, he estimates, 8100kg (8 tons) of wood ash, 36,500kg (36 tons) of human faeces (allowing 0.2 to 0.4kg [7 to 14oz] per person per day), 182,500 litres (40,150 gal) of urine (allowing 1 to 1.5 l [1¾ to 2½pt] per day), 14,600,000 (3,212,000 gal) of sullage (waste water from washing and washing-up), and 182,500kg (180 tons) of solid organic food waste. What became of it all? Visions of squalor, stink, rotting carcasses and excrement seem to be confirmed at certain times and were no doubt occasionally true at others. But how exposed were the inhabitants to such things – assuming, of course, that they found the exposure unpleasant? The problem is largely one of archaeological method, the problem of deciding which midden heaps, tanning pits and dead dogs were really open to view at the same time – the type of problem that has to be confronted in the last chapter.

In certain major towns, the Romans made provision for the disposal beyond the walls of all the principal sources of disease: main sewers for human excrement, town tips for organic rubbish and cemeteries for dead bodies. Early medieval people admitted all three within the walls, and in the case of excrement and rubbish, within the dwelling area itself. At York, environmental scientists have claimed that the Anglo-Scandinavian inhabitants were actually living on their own midden heaps, a dump of fly-blown rotting vegetables and flesh. In the later Middle Ages, some attempt was made to provide a service for the removal of sewage and garbage, and earth-closets and rubbish-pits were constructed for easy cleaning. By the sixteenth century, town-tips were provided, and pits both for rubbish and latrines became less common. Legal action still had to be invoked against tradesmen who buried entrails in pits sited in dangerous places, or, worse still, left them open. Litigation was also provoked by the overhanging garderobe, from which 'putredo cadit super capita hominum transeuntum' – a constant hazard.

On the face of it, therefore, the medieval town at least was a dirty and unhygienic place, compared with the Roman or modern, but this judgement might need some qualification. First, the Roman town had already lost its image of the clean white city in the third and fourth centuries. It is then possible to find streets thick with mud and animal bone as at Worcester, although they might subsequently be resurfaced. Secondly, the 'squalor' of rubbish disposal within medieval towns might be more apparent than real. The York evidence notwithstanding, the floors of houses have been found to be generally clean, only acquiring decayed vegetation *after* disuse. The midden heaps at Durham were sealed with wet sand and nobody lived on them. The cesspits and rubbish-pits of the later period are often found sealed with clay. Earth-closets are not, of themselves, unhygienic, especially when they are sited in a garden shed. Overhanging garderobes such as the one quoted above (from Ebbegate in Oxford in 1321) or that which discharged in Raven Meadows in fourteenth-century Shrewsbury, or the two pairs of garderobes discharging into the river Thames from the fifteenth-century manor house at Greenwich, were another matter. These must have constituted a nuisance to the user, no less than to the pedestrian, fisherman, or indeed the swimmer.

People did get ill, and sewage and rubbish must sometimes have been the cause. It will also be remembered that many Saxon and medieval towns were sited on marshy ground and this cannot have helped resistance against colds and rheumatism, not to mention malaria ('the ague') and arthritis (probably 'the palsy'). The principal remedies available were heat from the central hearth, and

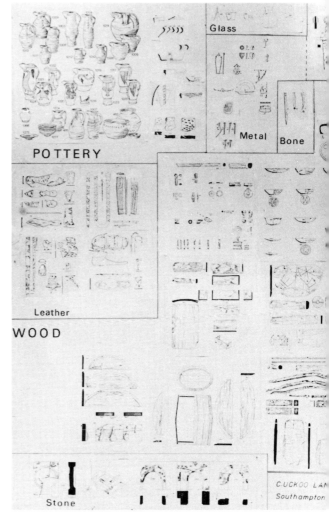

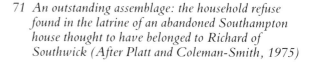

71 *An outstanding assemblage: the household refuse found in the latrine of an abandoned Southampton house thought to have belonged to Richard of Southwick (After Platt and Coleman-Smith, 1975)*

herbs. Here is a medieval recipe to cure dropsy, palsy, dysentry and pleurisy: 'Brew up fennel and cumin in a pot of brass and then decant into an earthenware cooking pot; seal the mouth with cloths and go to bed, placing the pot in the bedstraw at your feet. Lay a cloth against it as hot as you can bear. Repeat every night for a week.' Charcoal and peat were available for Roman heating, and the Romans had coal, but it would be dangerous to use in a hypocaust. Its use in open hearths did not return again until late medieval times; we must assume the medieval hearth to be full of logs; but the house not necessarily full of smoke. The use of cavity walls is known as early as the ninth century in York, and even wattle and daub is by no means ineffective as insulation With rush matting on the floor and heavy cloth hangings on the walls, the medieval town house could achieve warmth and comfort, even in winter.

If we get an unfavourable impression of what it was like to live in a medieval town, it is partly at least because documents and archaeology both leave us such a partial record. Fully furnished, such buildings as Butcher Row in Shrewsbury or the High House in Stafford would be veritable palaces; but we rarely find their furnishings or appurtenances. This is what makes finds like the famous pit at Cuckoo Lane, Southampton, or the Pottergate cellar at Norwich of such special value. The Cuckoo Lane pit (known as Pit 14), was actually a stone-lined latrine with a wooden floor, and had been used as such by the inhabitants (who were suffering from worms). Their diet had included figs, strawberries, plums, cherries, grapes, raspberries, hazelnuts and walnuts. Small pieces of cloth and fern fronds were no doubt used for the convenient purpose. In about 1300 the house was abandoned, and a mass of debris dumped in the latrine pit, which preserved it. It included parts of the house, such as a stone window sill, lead cames from the window and fragments of drains or ovens, and personal objects such as a sword handle, a ring-key, a leather belt with a bronze buckle, shoes, boots and sheaths, the seals of Richard of Southwick and Bernard of Vire, and a tumbler bell possibly from a set of children's reins. From the dining area came a mass of crockery, including jugs from Saintonge in France, a tin-glazed plate from Spain, a three-handled pitcher and fourteen cooking-pots. There were glass bottles and goblets, and, in wood, there were bowls, baskets, barrels, churns, boxes, a comb, two whistles, and eight tally sticks. But perhaps most impressive of all was the range of animals. In addition to the bones of the usual stock animals, there were those of red deer, donkey, dog, cat, rabbit, ferret and a barbary ape; amongst the birds there were goose, duck, teal, lapwing, curlew, woodcock, sparrowhawk; and amongst fish, conger eel, plaice, cod, red guarnard, snails, oyster, mussel, barnacle, limpet, cockle. This was a household where there were children, pets, and plenty to eat, as well as one member apparently obsessed by hunting, if not actually eating, anything that ran, flew or swam.

The Pottergate houses (nos. 21-55) burnt down in a fire which swept through Norwich on 25th April, 1507. The material which fell into a cellar, and was preserved there, again included parts of the house: oak framing, panels for wattle and daub, thatch, hinges, doorbolts, decorated window glass and a chimney crane. From the living area came a cauldron, a skillet, a frying pan and iron wool cards,

and amongst personal objects were a devotional medallion and a fragment of a terracotta mask, probably of a classical philosopher, thought to have been made in Italy about AD 1490.

These are the rare catastrophes which allow the capture of an individual ménage. For the most part we have to explore the variation of personal taste through a more generalised pattern of rubbish, in particular through pottery, which survives in nearly every type of terrain. Pottery is, moreover, essentially domestic in purpose and pottery preferences should have something to say about the way people lived their private lives. The range of vessels available in Roman Britain was large, specific and arrived suddenly, bringing with it a particular style of cuisine: a variety of smooth polished bowls and plates, which was the mass-produced *samian* tableware; mortaria for making and blending pastes of various kinds, pitchers for pouring wine and *amphorae* for carrying it. The vessel types were still produced at the end of the Roman period (for example in the Home Counties), and then disappeared together, presumably with the dining habits that went with them. The sparse post-Roman occupation of towns is accompanied by an equally sparse use of pottery for cooking and dining. Although some fifth- to sixth-century Roman pottery still reached the British Isles, it hardly did so on a scale on which cooks could depend. The expectation is that bronze cauldrons and drinking horns (of the type found at Sutton Hoo), wooden platters, and skewered kebabs (like those seen on the Bayeux tapestry) served the needs of the kitchen and hall in the rural manors, if not those of the villagers.

With the rebirth of the towns, the pottery industry is also suddenly reborn, with a full range of utensils: jars, bowls, lamps, pitchers and cisterns, but above all the cooking-pot with sagging base (presumably to sit on the embers) and sometimes signs of a lid. The Middle Ages is somehow indelibly associated with stew. If the size of the cooking-pot indicates the size of the household, they got steadily bigger between the tenth and fourteenth centuries. At this point they became markedly rarer, but it is known that large bronze cauldrons were again manufactured, such as that buried in a flood at Durham. The glazed pottery jug reigns from the twelfth to the fifteenth century, at which point it gives way to leather and pewter vessels (which are, however, much more rarely found).

The town-tip excavated in the castle ditch at Newcastle provides an excellent monitor of the evolving medieval taste in crockery. The record begins in the thirteenth century, with cooking-pots and jugs. Storage vessels arrived at the end of the century, and by the late fourteenth century cisterns,

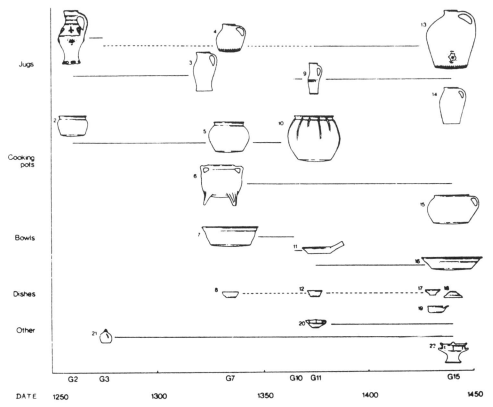

Trig Lane 1974–76: Diagram illustrating the life-span and evolution of the main Surrey Ware pottery forms

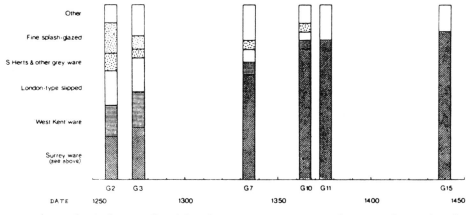

72 Pottery on the market in later medieval London (Museum of London)

frying pans, plates, bowls and mugs had been added to the dresser. In the late fifteenth century, there are also cups, chafing dishes, costrels and urinals. Window and vessel glass is deposited from the early sixteenth century, which is the time from which the variety of rubbish also increases dramatically: nails, a chain, a chisel, knife handles and old shoes and clothing. The Newcastle town-tip, then described as 'a dung hill', was closed down in 1643 and medieval town-life with it.

These vignettes should illustrate that early towns were not always quite such miserable places as we thought, and that real people lived in them. After the first efforts of Imperial Rome, the attempts at planned civilisation were few, brief and partial. The town-dweller learned to live with the self-centred tinkering of authority and the visitations of plague, flood, fire and economic depression with equal insouciance, resilience and ingenuity. After all, it was in the greatest medieval city of them all that the cockney was born, a peculiarly English type of citizen who has no doubt been developing his inimical brand of good-humoured scepticism since the days of Mercian supremacy.

VIII
Exploring cities: urban archaeologists in action

Nearly all the information used in this evocation of Roman, Anglo-Saxon and medieval town life, has, in one form or another, come out of the ground. It began as faint discolourations, and pieces of stone, metal and timber encased in mud, and ends as a story, some would say a fairly tall story, intended to enhance, perhaps even assist the lives of later members of society. But getting history out of the ground and onto the bookshelves is not as simple, or as comfortable, as taking a stroll to the Public Records Office. Digging is difficult and dangerous, particularly so in towns, where sites can be deep and anything from a loose tile to a jettisoned take-away meal is likely to land in them. The process has been compared to carrying out a surgical operation on a traffic island. And yet no type of archaeology has received more energy and invention over the past few decades. It has almost become a discipline in its own right, practised by a very special breed of scholar – the urban archaeologist. How and why did this come about?

The early exploration of ancient cities was an epic, played out by heroes. After his first season campaigning in the desert ruins of Assyria, Sir Austen Layard was given an honorary DCL by the University of Oxford, and after his second, he was made a Freeman of the City of London. His *Nineveh and its Remains*, published in 1849, was the first archaeological best-seller. In 1871, Schliemann, inspired by writings of Homer, began his search for the lost cities of the Trojan War. In 1889, Evans was excavating the buried civilisation of Minos, with its palace and frescos of bull-leaping boys and girls, and its faience 'snake goddess'. Wooley led the joint expedition to Ur in 1922, and in 1926 excavated the great cemetery there with its royal death-pit. Eridu, investigated by Sayyid Fuad Safar in 1946, gave signs of having had an urban community in 4000 BC and could lay claim to the title of the oldest city made by man.

These archaeological adventures in pursuit of the lost Homeric and biblical cities of the eastern Mediterranean were well-known to English readers of the newspapers and the *Illustrated London News*, and they kept the public imagination alight for nearly a century. They were also responsible for giving a particular flavour to the archaeological exploration of towns, which the ideas of the following half century failed to eradicate completely from the public mind. A primary virtue was an association with ancient history or legend, be it the eruption of Vesuvius, the Trojan war, Noah's flood, the destruction of Atlantis or the Arthurian utopia at Camelot. A second virtue was antiquity itself, and allied with it, dereliction. Petra, the 'rose red city half as old as time' (actually a religious precinct of the first and second centuries AD) is only one of those remote stage-sets of abandoned civilisation so attractive to the self-consciously overcivilised. Also expected of a successful dead culture is that it produce treasure, preferably of gold and mysterious of form. When Schliemann decorated his young Greek wife Sophie with the necklace found at Hissarlik (identified as Troy), he was performing a conscious act of worship on behalf of his contemporaries. A further characteristic of these expeditions was the dramatic way in which they were conducted: sondages cut by workmen, sometimes to extraordinary depths. That dug by Wooley beneath the death-pit at Ur descended over 12m (40ft), while at Kuyonjik the shaft was cut down an astonishing 28m (70ft), displaying in its section over 3000 years of demolished urban life.

In these circumstances, it is hardly surprising that the idea of digging cities was, and remains, almost inseparable in the popular imagination from the world of moonstones, camels, deep trenches and well-starched khaki shorts. To transfer this activity, which rightly belongs in deserts, to one's own country, is regarded by many Britons as somewhat unnecessary or distasteful, like playing football in the living room. Where it does happen, the old expectations are encountered, if on a reduced scale: the resolution of legends, great antiquity, great depth of deposit, mystery and treasure. A report in the *Observer* for the 10th July, 1949 described how a Ramsgate resident had been at work in the (eighteenth-century) Danehill grotto at Margate, photographing the mosaics and, as he put it, 'breaking down their symbolism'. He concluded that the grotto was the central chamber of a Cretan King's tomb dating from 2000 to 1500 BC. The newspaper report remarked dryly: 'It is of course news to Margate people – and many others – that Cretans were burying Kings in their Borough such a long time ago, but the Corporation was so impressed by this exposition that a Committee is being set up to pursue the investigation further'. It is not always misplaced civic pride, but sometimes misplaced expectation that assigns the highly individual discoveries underneath English towns to the far better known and better publicised city cultures of the ancient East.

The early archaeologists who explored English towns did in fact retain subconcious links with their nineteenth-century colleagues. The methodology employed was, so to say, in direct line of descent. Historical and anthropological objectives also evolved from that eastern experience; and, perhaps less to be expected, the English urban archaeologist often experienced the same kind of official scepticism and native hostility as did his desert forebears – this time at the hands of his own countrymen. Let no one complain. All archaeology is exploration, and every archaeological campaign an intellectually motivated expedition into unknown territory. For some it is an expedition from which they never really return. The world hidden beneath our feet is so vast, so varied, and so puzzling that only the very obstinate or arrogant manage to send back a few coherent despatches. The story of the exploration of the long sequence of human life buried beneath English towns is a story of struggle against prejudice, indifference and sentimentality. So if the archaeology of living cities has taken more than a century to gain a foothold in the intellectual life of the nation, that is not because it was predictable, or banal, but simply because it was unknown, and for many, barely credible.

In 1845, the same year that Layard began work at his *Nineveh*, the first meeting of the Royal Archaeological Institute was held at Winchester. This did not mark the first step in English urban archaeology as such – records had been kept of discoveries at Southampton since 1825, for example – but it was the beginning of a deliberate strategy to investigate the phenomenon of town life. Indeed these RAI meetings took on an almost anthropological air, as of intrepid academic delegates visiting a remote native community. The questionnaire prepared by J. Hunter for the Norwich meeting in 1847 demanded such information as 'What feasts, what wakes, what revels are observed?'; 'What have you observed peculiar in the amusements of the people?'; 'What have you observed remarkable in the dialect? Give a list of words in use among them [i.e. the inhabitants of Norwich] which are not in the dictionaries'. One hundred more years were to elapse before Grimes started work in the bombed City of London, and the systematic archaeological investigation of a town could be claimed to have begun. In the meantime, citizens very slowly became aware that they were living on debris of some kind, and usually turned to early history and topography in order to hazard a guess at what it might be. But it slowly became clear that this debris had a different, if complementary, story to tell about the town, and that this story could only be read with quite sophisticated techniques.

Early encounters underground did surprisingly little to stimulate the historical imagination. The Elizabethan topographer, John Stow, described the London Stone – a landmark for centuries – as 'pitched upright . . . fixed in the ground very deep . . . that if carts do run against it through negligence, the wheels be broken and the stone itself unshaken'. Not until 1975 was it realised that this 'stone' was the battered end of a buried pillar marking the entrance to the palace of the Roman Governor, which itself was eventually discovered beneath Cannon Street Station. Medieval builders broke into Roman sewers, and Victorian builders into medieval drains and cellars, although they were seldom recognised as such, giving rise to one of the more enduring elements of underground mythology – the secret passage. If the British citizen recognised the structures of his predecessors at all before the mid-twentieth century, he would generally accord them scant respect. 'For the last three centuries the old walls and towers appear to have been considered nothing but a nuisance, to be got rid of at the first convenient opportunity and the work has been very effectively done' complained W.T. Jones about Durham in 1923. Although he cited York and Chester as municipalities with a more enlightened attitude, the first century of urban archaeology, 1850 to 1950, was actually a period of wholesale destruction of ancient buildings and urban strata, one to which the *blitz* in many cases put the finishing touches. The RAI initiative, such as it was, bore little fruit, perhaps partly because the majority of archaeologists of talent were still first drawn to their calling by the magic of the abandoned ruin or earthwork. The British analogies to Babylon, Ur and Mohenjo-daro were not London, Winchester or Bristol, but the deserted cities of Roman Britannia, and it was in them that British urban archaeology really began. The first systematic excavations took place at Silchester in 1890, and in 1859 at Wroxeter where they have continued (on and off) until 1985. Here, with the occasional nostalgic glance at the sunlit *tells* of the east Mediterranean, the techniques of unravelling sequences of demolished stone buildings on British soil were slowly evolved.

Meanwhile, it took brave men to enter the gates of the living city, trowel in hand. Sir Mortimer Wheeler, with some of the earliest media coverage, worked at Verulamium, on the other side of the river from St Albans, and thereby did more than demonstrate the shifting nuclei of the British town. He brought the Roman town up through the floorboards and into the front room, setting a standard of public communication which few have since matched. His lesson – that anecdote is more welcome than homily, and that archaeology must be interesting before it can claim to be worthy – was generally forgotten, but the precedent was set. When Sheppard Frere began a series of revolutionary investigations at Canterbury and back at Verulamium, the Romans could expect a reasonably warm welcome from at least some of their successors.

The revelation of urban life through archaeology in England has a development which falls into four principal phases. The first, lasting for the 100 years before the end of the Second World War, saw the Victorian Imperial interest in exotic and ancient civilisations gradually transferred to the ruins of an earlier empire in the English countryside. The other three phases, occupying little more than a decade a piece since 1950 have seen an acceleration of activity unmatched by any other branch of archaeology at home or abroad.

The fresh initiative was principally powered by two ideas, not new of course, even to archaeology, but which had a devastating if belated effect on fieldwork. The first was that archaeological sequences wrote their own history, not merely for periods which have no written sources (pre-history) but for those which had plenty. At first sceptical, then condescending and finally respectful, historians now welcome the results of an excavation campaign on medieval, Tudor or eighteenth-century episodes, as on Roman. These results now have the status of a newly opened archive in which what is repetitious or predictable only serves to strengthen confidence in what is new. The second realisation was that people were still actively living on the evidence, building roads and cellars through it and transporting it away in skips during redevelopment operations. It would not be enough to study urban history at leisure; it would have to be fought for, and the task would fall largely to a single generation.

These ideas were by no means accepted immediately, and they are not even yet ubiquitous: but things have certainly changed. In the early days, excavators were prepared to shovel off thick medieval deposits to gain access to the Roman levels. By contrast, the recent volumes about Chichester include accounts of the diverse assemblages of nineteenth-century rubbish pits – the type of rubbish discarded by the great Victorian antiquaries themselves. In 1939, the Recorder of York could drive a tunnel through the walls of his city to provide access to pasture for his horses, so exposing the famous 'Anglian' tower. By 1981, not only town walls, but even dark brown layers of earth had earned, through their powers of revelation, the protection of the Government.

The first phase of post-war urban archaeology is exemplified above all by the work of W.F. Grimes in London. The campaign was initiated by the Society of Antiquaries in the bombed city and was carried out between 1947 and 1962. Grimes' discoveries were both marvellous and varied, encompassing in fifty-three excavations the whole period of London's exploitation before the Great Fire — a wide range of buildings and activities: the Roman fort at Cripplegate; the Temple of Mithras buried on the bank of the Walbrook beneath Queen Victoria Street; a Christian/Roman cemetery in Fleet Street; the London waterfront defined by excavation and bore-holes; Saxon huts discovered in Cannon Street, and the medieval Charterhouse adjacent to St Bartholomew's Hospital, whose church and water system were resurrected. Grimes' account of his work, published in 1968, remains the most accessible and articulate presentation of an urban campaign yet published, and ought to have been a best-seller, alongside Layard's *Nineveh* and Wooley's *Ur* But in the very year of its publication, Peter Marsden was still obliged to salvage the Roman provincial Governor's palace in six weeks.

In an epilogue to his book, Grimes has some hard things to say about the tragi-comedy of conducting scientific research below the pavements of the City of London, which will strike a sympathetic chord with many archaeologists working in towns during the 1960s and 1970s. He was not sparing in his criticism of the oppressive, even belligerent, ignorance of the British public and its even less culturally sensitive press. During nine days of feverish excavation to save the Mithraeum, or rather the knowledge of its existence, 30,000 visitors, of whose real interest Grimes was justifiably sceptical, contributed a total of £250. A press exposure subsequently raised a total of £6000 for the conservation of the building (estimated at £500,000) of which £300 was contributed by the London Corporation – that same Corporation which later paid £3000 for a silver gilt canister from the site by virtue of its rights over Treasure Trove. In 1959 a reconstruction of the Mithraeum was actually made in Queen Victoria Street 'in which professional advice was ignored and the results virtually meaningless'. But, in the same year, Britain was one of twenty-two nations which raised $34 million of archaeological resources to salvage the ancient sites of Nubia before their inundation when the Aswan Dam was constructed.

Grimes was perhaps the first to confront, almost single-handed, the special difficulties of digging under the feet of modern society: the complexity and vulnerability of the strata, the expense of its retrieval, the insensitivity of local authorities, speculators, or land owners, and above all the condescension or indifference of those for whom the work should have been most precious – the modern inhabitants of the town. Directors of urban campaigns were to be predominantly concerned in future years with creating acceptable conditions for research, and attempting to conduct a running defence of their activities through public relations. Their efforts were occasionally to be frustrated by some of the most inept press coverage in Europe, often, though regrettably not often enough, hilarious as well as inaccurate. If those days are now largely gone, it is thanks to pioneers whose archaeological skill and dedication to the public persevered through every type of obstruction. Pre-eminent among such pioneers was W.F. Grimes.

As the first London campaign drew to a close in 1962, a new type of archaeological research project was gathering momentum in Winchester. With a determination and insight that were soon to become celebrated, Martin Biddle succeeded in enlisting the support of the City Council, the Dean and Chapter, and central Government and gathered a set of targets, whose linking ideal echoed that of Fiorelli, working in Pompeii at the beginning of the first cycle of activity exactly 100 years previously: 'the object of our interest is the City itself . . .'.

Target areas were identified from a reading of the former topography of the city, as then known from documents, maps and casual discovery, and intervention was undertaken as opportunity and access allowed. No town ever presents a *tabula rasa* to the field archaeologist, but here perseverance led to the evolution of a coherent city-wide strategy. Tactics would come later, allowing priority to those parts of the deposit which were the most productive. In the justifiable conviction that it was the history of the early medieval town that was least understood, Biddle fought for and took advantage of opportuni-

ties to investigate at a number of nodal points: the Anglo-Saxon cathedral, the position of which had been predicted by Quirk in 1961, the Norman castle yard, and Wolvesey Palace. Beside these he set an extensive 'typical' area of the inner town, awaiting redevelopment at Lower Brook Street. The town was to be studied by the techniques of every appropriate discipline and among Biddle's early collaborators were the documentary historian Derek Keene, and the Danish prehistorian Birthe Kølbye.

In the ten years between 1962 and 1972, Winchester was given a historical geography and the most detailed statement of early English town life yet achieved. The city's Iron Age predecessor was located at Oram's Arbour; the Roman south-gate and its post-Roman destiny was examined; a Roman temple was discovered at Lower Brook Street, with a wooden effigy of a goddess (perhaps Epona) recovered from a nearby well; at Lankhills a late Roman cemetery was excavated, and evidence for individuals in the Anglo-Saxon period came from the cemeteries at Winnall. At the cathedral itself the nucleus of early Christian Winchester was brought to light at the shrine of St Swithun, and the Anglo-Saxon Old and New Minsters were resurrected. Complementary to the ecclesiastical complex of the minsters and their immediate predecessors were the vestiges of a wealthy middle-Saxon 'urban estate' at the Brooks. New historical perspectives were offered, not only for the exploitation of the city in the Dark Ages, but for its rebirth in the reign of King Alfred as an ecclesiastical and royal enclave contained by a planned grid of streets: the late Saxon planned town was born, a concept which was to have great influence on strategies developed elsewhere. The beginnings of organised commercial life were seen in evocative detail: rows of elongated properties (tenements) off a street frontage, from which goldsmiths, cobblers, carpenters and a great range of other medieval craftsmen traded.

Every excavation was carried out with the greatest precision and discipline, in the Wheeler tradition but not constrained by its methodology, so that Winchester in the late 1960s provided an unforgettable spectacle and a shop window for British archaeology which has had a lasting influence. The discoveries, and Biddle's provisional, but often far-reaching conclusions from them were published in a series of Interim Reports in the *Antiquaries Journal*, a series which not only had news-value at the time for sponsor and scholar alike, but the enduring benefit of allowing the development of strategy and method to be chronicled.

There were, of course, surprises, and the investigation as a whole carried certain emphases of research with which not all would now agree. But the campaign was a model academically and administratively, and set a standard and an inspiration for everything that was to follow. It is no coincidence that virtually every practising English urban archaeologist of the next decade, and a good many abroad, began their careers with Biddle on the sites at Winchester.

As the Winchester project was reaching its climax in the late 1960s, the stature of urban archaeology was never higher. The archaeological world, at least, was talking about towns; not, however, exclusively: it was also talking about hillforts and about the areas of prehistoric settlements being quarried away by gravel extraction or the construction of motorways. There was a growing, if belated, realisation of the extent of damage being inflicted on the archaeological record in both town and countryside, and new methods, new strategies, and more determined management policies were being discussed: in the Ancient Monuments Inspectorate, in the Royal Commission on Ancient Monuments, in the Universities – although principally in their Extra-Mural Departments – and above all among the new generation of urban excavators taking their coffee-breaks in Lower Brook Street or on Cathedral Green at Winchester.

Urban archaeology began its third post-war phase with considerable momentum and a greatly increased number of practitioners. In 1957 the new journal *Medieval Archaeology* had reported work in progress on six town sites; in 1970 the number was 23 (and by 1980 had risen to 40). The towns of England were being explored on an unprecedented scale. Three ideas dominated the strategy of the '70s, and blended to give that period its special research flavour: 'think big', 'think history', and 'think rescue'. These mysterious epithets are worth considering for a moment because of their profound effect on the type of results which came from this decade, and because of their rapid fall from grace at the end of it.

In 1969 among the papers appearing in the first volume of the new journal *World Archaeology* were two of special influence. Philip Barker's modestly entitled 'Some aspects of the excavation of timber buildings' reported his detection of ephemeral structures on the rubble of the demolished basilica at Wroxeter, and the Biddles' 'Metres, Areas and Robbing' which proposed methods for the resolution of that complex of compressed and mutilated urban strata to which Grimes and Frere had drawn attention ten years before. The messages of both papers were similar: the traces of wooden frame-buildings that had lost their timbers, of stone buildings that had lost their walls and foundations, of streets that had lost their paving, of floors that had

lost their flooring – all were observable given a large enough area. In 1964, Biddle, echoing Frere's innovations at *Verulamium*, demolished the baulks that ran across the Lower Brook Street site, and standing sections were retired as the principal evidence for sequence. Henceforth the interpretation was to rely on running sections and the three-dimensional survey of individual layers.

Not that such measures were really new: they had long been used in Scandinavia and were perhaps temporarily obscured in England by the dominance of the efficient 'Wheeler' system of standing boxes. But the blinkered heritage of urban archaeology was the sondage used in the ancient 'tel' settlements of the Middle East – the deep square pit or long trench designed to report a 'typical' sequence. Linked between town and town these sequences theoretically determined the relative antiquity of cities and indeed whole civilisations. Frere, Barker and Biddle showed that such methods were inappropriate for the heterogeneous English towns, and showed in the process what we were missing.

History, of course, demanded a clear statement of the geography of a town at a particular stage – Roman, Anglo-Saxon or medieval – and this is what no amount of sondages could provide. The town plan, the size and design of dwellings of the rich and poor, the changing economy – these were the targets of history. In his 'Archaeology and the History of the British town' published in *Antiquity* in 1968, Biddle left no doubt of his conviction that the purpose of archaeology in towns was to provide their history, and that the criteria for any archaeological excavation should be its historical relevance. Such relevance could only be apparent in advance from what history already knew, or from what it knew of, but said very little about. The paradox – that the location of archaeological evidence for unrecorded historical episodes was itself unrecorded – was to have repercussions later. For the moment, archaeologists sought guidance from the documentary record when deciding where to dig, and their targets were the urban communities and structures known to history or implied by it.

It was just as well that guidance of some kind was to hand, because the next few years were to see a proliferation of work in towns under a stimulus quite other than the academic thirst for knowledge. In 1963 Professor Sir Colin Buchanan's *Traffic in Towns* was published, adding to the growing awareness that the country had entered on a programme of urban renewal that would affect a great deal of traditional or historic architecture. Urban archaeologists also became aware, rather more slowly, that such a programme would affect no branch of knowledge more severely than their own: the deep foundations for high-rise residential blocks, multi-storey car parks and supermarkets, the ring roads and underpasses, all were causing the removal of those delicate strata which Biddle was bringing to life at Winchester, and which contractors still cheerfully referred to as 'unsuitable material', that is, unsuitable to take foundations.

If this realisation found the majority of the archaeological fraternity in a state of impenetrable and even scornful indifference, there were happily a few signs that communications were improving. In 1967 the Council for British Archaeology formed its Urban Research Committee, and in the same year Andrew and Wendy Selkirk's *Current Archaeology* began publication, bringing the import of the latest discoveries into the libraries and offices of both public and practitioner. In the atmosphere of rising concern, Philip Barker issued his famous paper 'Not waving, just drowning', and in 1970 *Rescue: a Trust for British Archaeology* was formed under Biddle's chairmanship. In 1972 the CBA published Carolyn Heighway's *Erosion of History*, which tabulated the research potential and vulnerability of historic towns in Britain. 'The seriousness of the present situation in urban archaeology cannot be overstated', wrote Martin Biddle in his preface: 'The most important towns of all historical periods will be lost to archaeology in twenty years, if not before.' It was this publication, in particular, which appeared to place the responsibility for urban archaeology, and the history that would come from it, on a single generation. Pressure brought by *Rescue*, in somewhat uneasy alliance with the more subtle, and eventually more effective, efforts of a by no means complacent or insensitive Ancient Monuments Inspectorate, produced increased financial means to meet the challenge. A militant (and largely untrained) new generation went out to rescue the urban history of England while there was still time. Some preliminary skirmishes had already taken place in the mid-60s, as in Hereford where one of the century's most brilliant excavators, Philip Rahtz, had rescued the first visible set of Anglo-Saxon town defences from the relief road. Similarly, Philip Barker had fought a one-man rearguard action for Worcester, and in 1970 had published one of the first syntheses to rely almost entirely on rescued archaeological evidence: 'The Origins of Worcester'. But the lessons of Verulamium and Winchester had not been lost on the new generation, many of whom had been Frere's or Biddle's volunteers: excavated areas must be large and historically relevant as well as under threat. It was vital to negotiate with the appropriate authorities the time and the space and the facilities needed for proper research by excavation. These negotiations had, at the same time, the far less

obvious effect of slowly awakening an awareness of the importance of archaeology in the conscience of Local Authorities, an investment which eventually came to maturity, early or late, all over the country.

A few field-workers considered the rescue of everything and anything as the only ethical and economical course; but to most it seemed that this could be a virtue only when negotiations had failed – which, it must be said, they often did. The successful negotiators were able to set up protective procedures in urban 'Units', often in direct collaboration with local councils. Most other Units were independent Trusts, apart from the one or two which were later grafted onto University departments. Many units covered counties or regions rather than single towns. All were dedicated to the retrieval of information that was otherwise to be lost, and all struggled with the same dilemma: the scale of destruction, the lack of money and trained staff, and the problem of priorities, in which the ideals of large areas, historical relevance, and an interdisciplinary approach were confronted with the real ethics of emergency.

To a great extent, the story of urban archaeology in the 1970s is the story of the achievements or failures of these Units. Those at Leicester and Stamford began work in 1966, and in 1969 the first 'Stamford-ware' late Saxon pottery kiln was discovered by Christine Mahany. Tom Hassall set up the Oxford Unit in 1967 and went on to map the historical topography of Oxford from some twenty-one excavations over the following thirteen years. It was mirrored by David Baker's compaign in Bedford which began in the same year. Assisted by a grant from the Gulbenkian Foundation, the Winchester Research Unit itself was established in 1968 with offices in Parchment Street. Systematic long-term investigation began in Chelmsford and Nottingham in 1969; in Exeter, Southampton and Waltham in 1971; Southwark, Poole and Taunton in 1972; Gloucester and Chesterfield in 1973, and Stafford and Wells in 1975. A thousand flowers had bloomed, in soil of great variety.

The campaign that perhaps adhered most accurately to the Winchester ideal was the Norwich Survey created in 1971 by an agreement between Norwich City Council, the Department of the Environment and the Centre of East Anglian Studies at the University of East Anglia. Its Director, Alan Carter, relentlessly pursued historical goals, combining expert excavations with the study of Norwich's 1000 historic buildings and 1500 shelf-feet of documents. The two Units which were to prove the most robust and strategically influential in the 1980s began work about the same time. The York Archaeological Trust, under the direction of Peter Addyman, was established in 1972. Although interdisciplinary, and dedicated to historical research, its manifesto took a pragmatic view on priorities: the needs of rescue were to be paramount and excavation at the Bedern, for example, extended only to strata destined to be destroyed by impending redevelopment. The new campaign in the City of London began in 1973, conducted by a special Department of Urban Archaeology within the Museum of London, under the direction of Brian Hobley. It was armed with a comprehensive planning document, *The Future of London's Past*, drawn up by Martin Biddle, Daphne Hudson and Carolyn Heighway and published by *Rescue*. In London, in particular, it was hoped to fill the principal historical lacuna – the gap between the Roman and medieval town – by judicious large-scale excavation guided by the sparse documentation; although as it turned out, this documentation was anything but reliable in guiding excavators to the site of middle-Saxon London. Archaeological enterprise at York and London would develop quite differently over the next fifteen years in the attempt to stay true to their academic objectives in the face of dramatic changes in the political situation.

Meanwhile, the creation of New Towns had offered special opportunities. Although Peterborough's archaeology was declared to have been largely destroyed in the nineteenth century, there and elsewhere Development Corporations supported long-term research programmes for the recovery of the old world. If partly inspired by the desire to give these new places a soul, they undoubtedly did more. Northampton produced one of the longest settlement sequences yet defined beneath an English town, while the superficially less promising Milton Keynes, with no documented ancestor, used the opportunity to retrieve an extensive medieval and earlier landscape.

All these differences in emphases given to the new campaigns of urban archaeology were reflections of the administrative arrangements that were possible at the time, as much as of the philosophy of the Unit directors. While it was true that conditions for serious research had generally improved since the days of the London Mithraeum, it was not true always or everywhere. The battle to implant professional teams of archaeologists in England's historic towns had to be fought over and over again, every town showing an individual brand of reticence or reluctance. Brian Philp's experiences at Dover give a startling example of how difficult the management of an urban excavation could still be. His rescue operations on the by-pass in 1971 brought to light a series of Roman forts (already predicted by Sir Mortimer Wheeler) among them the headquarters of the *Classis Britannica* (the Roman fleet based in the Channel). The walls still stood some 2.7m (9ft) high, and in spite of Philp's efforts their demolition in the course of road construction began, with the laying of a steel pipe through a bastion. However, by means of timely publicity, Philp obliged the authorities to stay their hand, and eventually commissioned his own surveyor to prove that the new road could be carried at split levels some 0.9m (3ft) and 1.8m (6ft) higher than planned, to save the fort, and the stratified evidence for its use, for the future. He was in action again in 1975 to save the Roman 'painted house', with its remarkable wallpaintings, which was discovered to lie on the line of the same by-pass. On this occasion, he raised some £72,000 to consolidate and display the building, the work being undertaken, for the sake of economy, by Philp's own archaeological Unit. This Unit epitomised for many the tireless struggle that was *rescue*, a militancy enshrined in the Unit's title: the 'CIB Rescue Corps', named from *Cohors I Baetasiorum*, the garrison of the Saxon shore fort at Reculver.

Inconvenient discoveries of this kind served to emphasise the richness of the legacy which remained underneath English towns, and archaeologists contrived to surprise and delight themselves and the public with their revelations throughout the '70s. The Roman metalworking establishment at Deansgate in Manchester was exposed in 1972, and the excavations were made into a film. The London basilica ('the largest Roman building north of the Alps') was planned from a G.P.O. engineers' tunnel 0.9m (3ft) wide, 1.2m (4ft) high and 305m (1000ft) long driven through it in 1977. Philip Rahtz and Ken Sheridan discovered an Anglo-Saxon timber horizontally-driven water-mill with its high quality steel bearing, beneath the streets of Offa's former capital at Tamworth. The section of Roman sewer at York, large enough for a man to crawl down, was all but indestructible to modern machinery. Perhaps most spectacular and significant of all were the sequences of massive timber waterfronts and riverside revetments recovered at London, with their preservation of leather, cloth, plants and dung. In 1974, after test excavations beneath Lloyd's Bank in Pavement, York, a group of natural scientists published a paper entitled 'York, an early medieval site', which demonstrated that in addition to the evocative range of artefacts only present in deposits having organic preservation, fragments of discarded plants and dead insects could be used to reconstruct the ambient conditions in astonishing detail. In 1979, the synthesis of a small preserved organic sequence at Durham was published, which incorporated the new range of biological evidence into the cultural story.

73 Philip Rahtz on site at Tamworth (Bob Meeson)

But in spite of these achievements, perhaps even because of them, the predominant feeling at the end of the decade was, on the whole, one of hopelessness. There seemed to be so much to know, so little that could be retrieved, and so little of that could be immediately understood. Respect for the evidence and its vulnerability, and its wide distribution beneath a thousand towns provoked a steady loss of confidence amongst practitioners. The public might enjoy unexpected discoveries, but archaeologists and planning authorities alike preferred accurate prediction. Large evocative structures would appear when inadequate archaeological provision had been made; or less frequently, large sums of money were spent excavating empty or already devastated urban spaces. Under English law, archaeological intervention could not be automatic and there would never be enough money to confront every threat, to rescue every Roman bath or medieval latrine, or to support the work of analysis needed to extract their

significance. Not every town could find a champion, let alone aspire to the Winchester ideal, and in very many, the gathering of data had become a desperate, self-validating end in itself. 'Research or rubbish collection?' was the question the Secretary of the Society of Antiquaries felt obliged to pose in print.

Urban archaeology badly needed a national research policy, national goals, national priorities and a nationally-based management. The Winchester philosophy had favoured the larger, well-documented historic towns – London, York, Lincoln, Oxford – but were these to be the only coherent expression of English urbanism? The role of other settlements, 'urban' or not, in Roman, Saxon and medieval society was not only unknown, but might be destined to remain so. Although the idea of 'importance' – that is, documented importance – contrived to dog discussions on priorities until the 1980s, steps were already being taken to plan the exploration of the urban corpus in quite a different way.

The 'implications report' produced for Tewkesbury in 1972 was another of the initiatives of

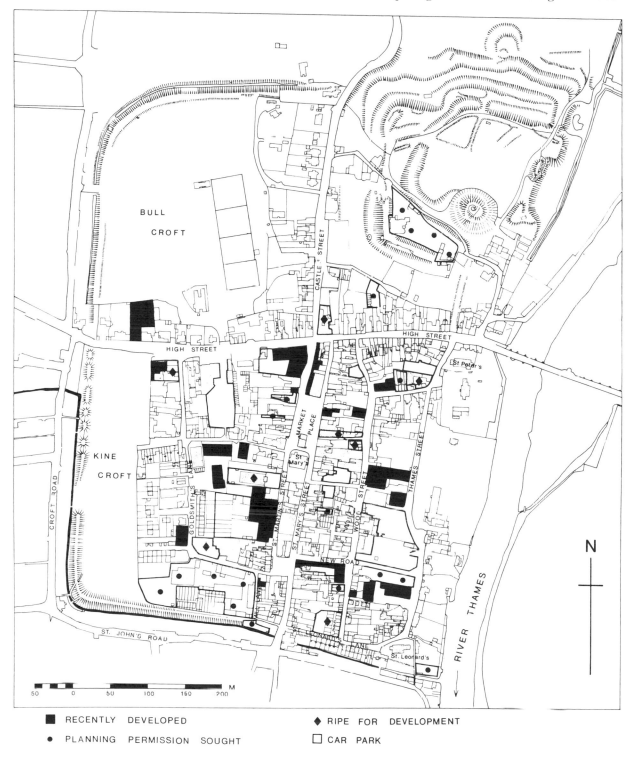

74 *Threats to the archaeological evidence buried under a town: Wallingford in 1973 (Simpson, 1973)*

the energetic half a dozen field archaeologists responsible for the rescue movement, and it led the way to the promotion of archaeology in a number of smaller towns which had no tradition and perhaps little expectation of an archaeological heritage. The views of the report-writers were not always welcome, nor were they always right, but they offered some kind of framework for places never visited by the Emperor Claudius or Alfred the Great, but which undoubtedly had something to contribute to what the French would call *le reseau urbain*. In 1974, Tom Hassall's Oxford Unit began a survey of all the towns of Oxfordshire, and the Committee for Rescue Archaeology in Avon, Gloucester and Somerset (CRAAGS, later to become the Western Archaeological Trust) undertook a similar survey of all the towns in their three counties. In the same year, following an assessment of their county, Suffolk Archaeological Unit decided to concentrate all its resources on middle-Saxon Ipswich – 'England's first town', as it was later styled. In 1975, the Welsh Urban Research Unit was set up under an agreement between the Welsh Office and University College, Cardiff, and the Ancient Monuments Inspectorate commissioned an urban survey of the West Midlands. Still in 1975, the Shrewsbury Archaeological Unit, earlier formed in the spirit of Winchester, Norwich or Oxford, became the first urban Unit to disband itself in favour of regional priorities. Two publications in the same year, *The Small Towns of Roman Britian* and *The Plans and Topography of Medieval Towns*, indicated the direction in which some strategic thinking was moving. Although attempts were made in 1976 to lighten the workload to manageable proportions by nominating 'towns of national importance', the drift of interest had already begun, away from the study of individual historic places and towards the archaeological study of urbanism using the whole urban corpus.

By 1978, Geoffrey Wainwright was counselling radical changes in the way towns were dug: 'We should currently be concerned with how little data we need to acquire from excavations to satisfy our conceptual framework . . . . We should be concerned with which conceptual framework would give us the most reliable, preferably replicable results.' In other words, the great mass of data already recovered must be digested, images of Roman, Saxon and medieval towns created, and then these images tested and improved by well-judged and economical intervention. Such a philosophy, with its implicit interest in understanding the processes rather than the tangible remains of urbanism, was a long way from Biddle's 'the object of study is the city itself', or of Barker's 'the purpose of excavation is to recover what is

there'. 1978 also saw the publication of the Shrewsbury site evaluation, which purported to predict and map the most fruitful archaeological deposits which remained. 'Site evaluations' followed for Worcester, Chester, and Stafford (1979), the latter being a publicly sponsored field campaign involving topographic survey, bore-holes, 'free sections' using disused cellars, trial excavations and a vegetation sequence of some 10,000 years derived from an adjacent peat bog. A well-judged intervention could henceforth involve the selection of sites of predicted archaeological quality.

By the end of the decade, as the campaigns at Oxford, Bedford and Norwich drew to a close, approaches to urban archaeology had, therefore, changed yet again. Development in historic centres, checked not so much by academic protest as by the economic winter provoked by the rise in oil prices, was to a certain extent under archaeological control. But the expertise demanded, and rightly so, in large-scale excavation required a substantial budget; the processing of hundredweights of pottery, timber, fauna and flora, now known to contribute to the detailed understanding of ancient town life, would cost even more. In most cases publication of the harvest gathered in the '60s and '70s was, and remains, a long way off and would demand prodigious efforts and great resources if its promise and ambitions were everywhere to be matched by comprehensible synthesis. No one denied that 6 tons of animal bone contributed an important potential source of evidence; but it might require 600 tons, well distributed, before the story of animal exploitation in a particular town could be accurately written. By 1980, the national rescue budget was no longer increasing; the boom was at an end.

Archaeological resolve has not weakened in the face of these immense logistic difficulties, but approaches are nevertheless changing again under the impact of an academic debate in which the theorist, the realist and the faint-hearted are not always easy to distinguish. By the early 1980s some were arguing for an economical sampling strategy based on site quality, whose goal was the understanding of urbanism itself. Others, particularly those working in the larger cities and in many cases integrated administratively with them, stood by the ideals of Winchester and turned to new sources of finance to fulfil them. In London, Brian Hobley's Department of Urban Archaeology succeeded in maintaining a large staff, conducting active programmes of site work and initiating the processing and study of an immense archive of excavated data, by gaining the support of property developers. W.F. Grimes would certainly be astonished by the sums dispensed on archaeology by London developers wishing to build, and build quickly. In York, the Trust turned to the public to support its work, and following the successful promotion of the Copper-gate excavations, using Magnus Magnusson as compere ('The most important archaeological excavation I have ever seen'), a £2.5 million underground display was constructed with the Vikings as its theme. Three months after opening in 1984, the *Jorvik Viking Centre* had already received half a million visitors.

It has never been enough, and never will be enough, for archaeologists to make discoveries, to fascinate, to entertain or to claim that their work is morally justifiable. Archaeology lives by its power of explanation, and the great moments of the last three decades have been when some aspect of the English town has suddenly become clear: A Roman drainage system; town planning in the reign of King Alfred; a twelfth-century water supply, or a tannery making parchment for illuminated manuscripts. The world underneath English towns is as enchanting as a trip to a foreign land, but this temporary enchantment turns to lifelong affection and interest only when the curious is explained. How near are we to making such explanations?

By 1981, 124 towns had experienced archaeological investigation of some kind and of these, forty-five had seen systematic campaigns lasting ten years or more. The major campaigns achieved the excavation of a few hectares of urban strata, at a cost of less than £10 million. From this minute fraction of the total still available a prodigious range of information has been extracted or saved from the bulldozer. The origins and development of places as diverse as Newcastle, Manchester, Thetford, Dover, Dunstable or Poole have been described; Roman, Saxon and medieval town-houses, sewers, workshops, defences, temples, churches and cemeteries have been unearthed and recorded with scientific diligence. A new field profession has been created which is dedicated to saving and making sense of this most unusual heritage to the highest standards. In 1983, archaeologists from all over Britain formed their own representative organisation, the Institute of Field Archaeologists. In 1984 that profession is living in reduced circumstances, and the most important of its functions, that of researching and explaining the data so far recovered, is also the most handicapped. The wealth of the information, its complexity and the fact that it is very largely still unpublished, means that it will be many years before the work of the last thirty years can be fairly judged.

It must certainly be thought foolish to attempt an assessment now, as I have tried to do in this book; but the dangers of public scepticism, disillusion and ennui are far greater than that of being thought a fool. At least this is some justification for putting aside reticence and prudence and taking a trip under the towns of England, leaving my betters to tidy the trail.

IX
A discourse on method

It is particularly over the last few decades, as we have seen, that archaeologists have entered and explored the peculiar underworld beneath the modern city. They have come back talking of Roman grandeur, Anglo-Saxon planners, the squalor of Viking suburbs, of horticulture, iron smelting and sewage disposal, and of burial practice, social classes and contagious diseases. They have encountered the individual town-dweller in a variety of conditions, and seen the trappings of political systems in his diet and crafts. Is it really all just imagination, fathered on luck?

To some extent it was, and always will be. Digging must find the unexpected or there would be little point in doing it. Indeed, some modern workers feel that any type of preconception is unnecessary, even dangerous: our duty is to recover what is there and place it objectively on the record. We are the archivists of our era: systematic, scientific and impartial. But others feel that information recovered in this way stands a good chance of meaning nothing, since it is not powered by the urge to understand; our duty is not only to take photographs but to create images. The profession currently risks polarisation from the confrontation of these, rather artificial, attitudes. My own feeling is that no scientist is truly objective in the sense of being a passive observer and recorder, and that to have facts is not the same as to have knowledge. An archaeological record is not wholly independent of the way we choose to define it, and dumb data might just as well stay beneath the ground, like the treasures of Beowulf, 'as useless to man as it was before'. A vocal meaning is what makes it all worthwhile, and the pursuit of meaning requires targets, strategies, and methods.

When all is said and done, the towns of England are just a set of settlements in a landscape, each with its own assets and personality. It is perfectly valid to examine the whole of one of them to try and understand the evolving structure of this most complex artefact. It is equally valid to examine parts of all, to try and understand the system to which they belong. To do either successfully (not to mention economically), it is essential to know as much as possible in advance, about everything. Thanks to the work of a gallery of pioneers – Grimes, Frere, Biddle, to name only the greatest – we do know something about how urban deposits are put together and how they can be understood. To make use of this knowledge is not giving way to dangerous bias; it is a fundamental act of common sense: 'we see further because we stand on their shoulders'. What we see does, however, lead us off in a new direction.

It will already have been noticed that the urban corpus is very unevenly distributed both in quality and quantity, so that in devising any plan for its retrieval, for lifting it, so to speak, from beneath the boots of our fellow countrymen, we cannot simply divide England into administrative areas and start digging. Where there were no towns, and even in places where there were, the evidence for town life might not be there. We must pursue it where it lies, trapped in the crevices provided by man or nature. In general, the archaeological study of urbanism divides into a number of attributes, many of which have emerged already: town planning, the vestiges of authority, military works, church organisation, the networks of craft and commerce. But each of these attributes requires a slightly different set of data, and the sources for these data are variously distributed. Each town-site conceals an individual set of archaeological assets, a personality lying deep beneath that historical reputation which attracted us in the first place.

A research design must take account of this personality and its variety; the urban corpus will not respond to interrogation under torture – it must be wooed and coaxed into clarity and eloquence. A simple division in the corpus already exists: that between towns (particularly new towns) that have been deserted, and those which lasted long. The former, being unencumbered before and after the event, give us our best chance to observe town

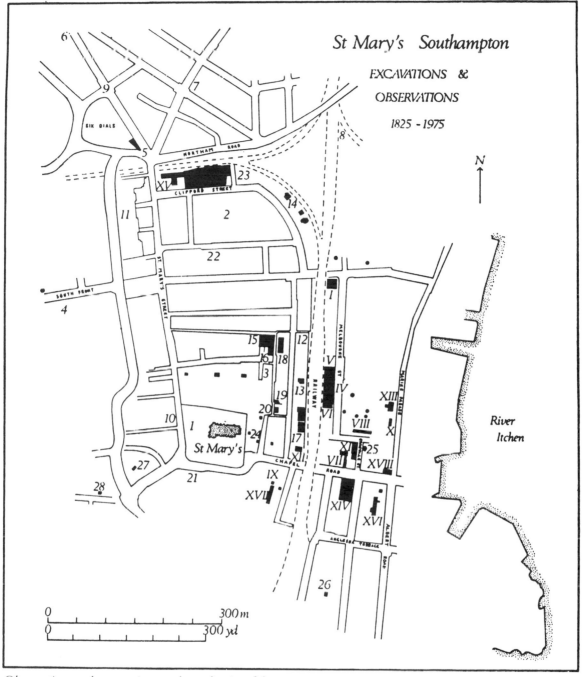

75 *Observations and excavations made on the site of the early medieval trading site at* Hamwih, *Southampton, since 1825. Sites with Arabic numerals were done before 1972; those with Roman numerals are the S.A.R.C. sites. Sites without numbers are where no archaeological excavations took place, although observations were made during building work. Thanks to 150 years of persistent recording and the recent campaign of large-scale investigation, this outstanding settlement is beginning to be understood (Southampton Museum)*

planning in its most exposed form. Ancient town plans are notoriously difficult to see beneath modern built-up areas – even major campaigns like Winchester, York and Tours in France can only talk of a small percentage of the whole examined, not nearly enough to be certain of an overall scheme. Deserted, or *single-period towns*, on the other hand, can be more easily mapped, and are, moreover, susceptible to remote sensing. They are indeed perhaps the most susceptible of all buried sites to

113

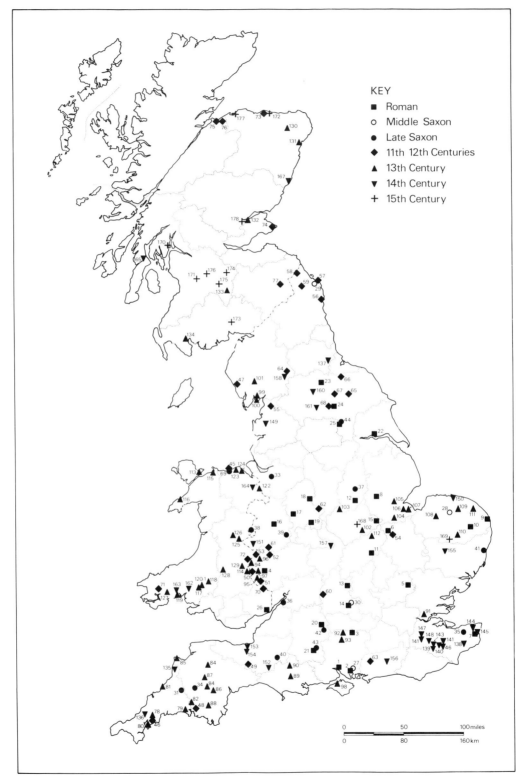

KEY
■ Roman
○ Middle Saxon
● Late Saxon
◆ 11th 12th Centuries
▲ 13th Century
▼ 14th Century
+ 15th Century

76 *'Single-period towns' in Britain. These places were, according to documents and archaeological evidence so far collected, occupied for only a few centuries of the* *whole urban continuum, and should thus be legible accounts for their particular periods, without too much interference from later development (see Appendix)*

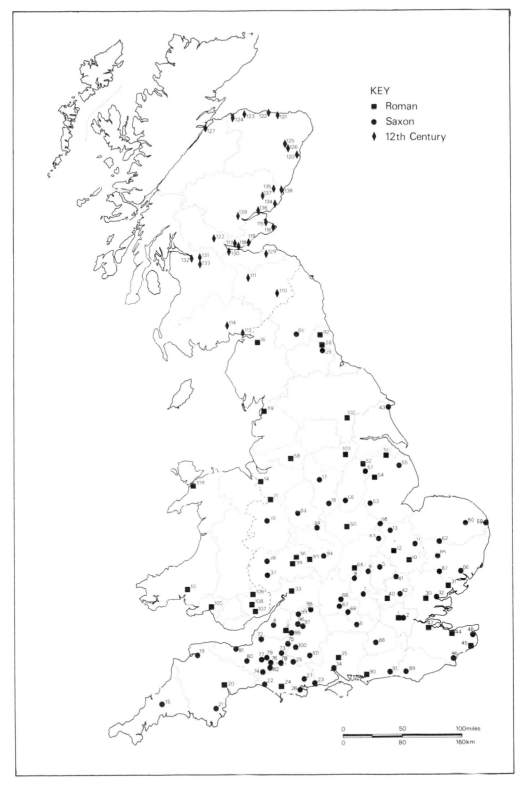

77 *'Multi-period towns' in Britain. These places are
thought on present evidence to have been continually
occupied since their foundation (see Appendix)*

non-destructive methods of mapping, because of their bold lines and robust construction. If it is town plans we are after, we do not need to dig the whole of Silchester or Winchelsea or Chirbury; aerial photography, field walking, geophysical survey, and radar can do the job for us, and uncertainties can be validated by quite small-scale interventions. The single-period town in England is a special subset of the urban corpus, exposing the innovations of town planners from the Roman Conquest to AD 1500, and from Bitterne to Fyvie (*Fig. 76*).

However, the majority of urban questions cannot be answered in this way. Such unsuccessful places, *ipso facto*, did not always have time to develop a hinterland or to take more than a temporary and artificial role in an urban network. The *multi-period town*, another subset of the urban corpus, offers a more direct monitor for the last two millennia in the natural regions of England. We *could* classify these multi-period towns according to their documented function – city, *municipium*, borough, port, county

town, market and so forth; we could, but we won't, because those classifications are not what the archaeologist needs for a research strategy. What is needed is rather a classification in terms of the evidence available, so that he can map that evidence, protect it, or go out and get it. The distribution of multi-period towns by foundation date (as currently known) is a measure of successful urbanisation, and provides a template to guide exploration of the urban system (*Fig. 77*).

In addition to the town as an artefact, it is necessary to study the context in which it functioned. The assumption made is that each town had an area of influence, or *hinterland*; this is, naturally, an over-simplification, but one which at least promotes a manageable study. If one had to choose a town of particular archaeological merit for which to study a Roman hinterland, it might be Wroxeter, for its apparent isolation from rivals, its distance from the sea and its modern accessibility, theoretically allowing all the settlements which depended on it, or served it, to be more easily found. A different case could be argued for the south, especially in the modern areas of dense population, on the grounds that we currently rely on rescue to see anything, and rescue creates opportunities where the population is currently most dense. In this

78 *An Anglo-Saxon hinterland for Worcester, drawn by Della Hooke. Dr Hooke's description of the landscape, drawn from place names and other sources, locates fields, woods and meadows since vanished (Carver, 1980)*

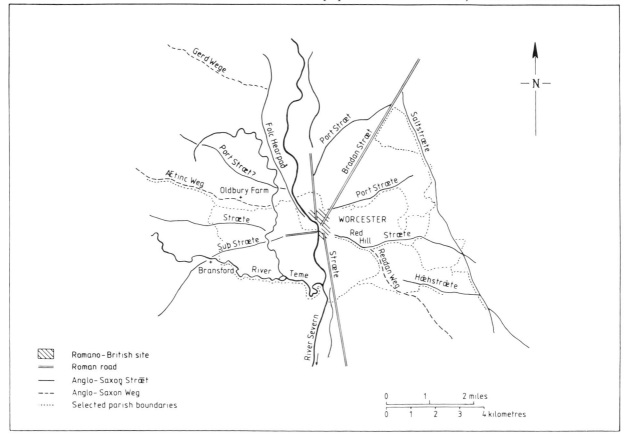

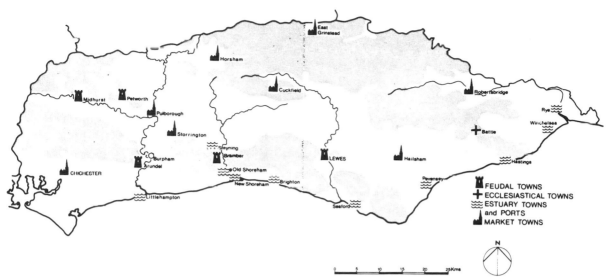

79 *Medieval urban functions in Sussex (D. Freke)*

hypothetical approach to a hypothetical concept we need not expect to be too rigid. The only important criterion for the study of an urban hinterland is that it should be inland; the sea being its own open-ended hinterland, distracts the role of a town from its region.

The Saxon and medieval towns, as has already been seen, were intensely regional in character. One way of isolating suitable medieval zones for treatment is to find groups of adjacent places which were urbanised at the same time. Ipswich and Bury, Winchester and Hamwih, Worcester and Droitwich are some of the early interdependent couples. Contiguous families of new towns date from the tenth century in Somerset, the twelfth century in Scotland, the thirteenth century in Wales, the fourteenth century in Kent and the fifteenth century in Argyll. Although Wales and Scotland are not direct subjects of this book, their potential for urban study emerges quite naturally from the accompanying maps. Each of these families (and there are, of course, other candidates) could be used to illustrate the ebb and flow of 'civilisation' in a region. The members of these families, being contemporary and adjacent, also provide small bounded hinterlands, or rather a place where the existence of such interdependent groups could be tested. But, being small, and themselves interdependent, the family group could turn out to have a molecular structure of its own; the proper region for the Saxon towns of Somerset, for example, could be Somerset itself, served by a structured network of small *burhs*, some of which may have had special functions. A more naked

medieval hinterland is again provided by Shropshire, dominated for ten centuries by its capital city of Shrewsbury. Here the potential for exploring a large region with a hierarchy of settlements is clearly high; within this region lies a central place destined to illustrate, in sequence, what rural England expected of its town, and similar claims could be made for Norwich, York, Carlisle or Northampton. In the Home Counties, cluttered by ambitious foundations and battered and chopped by the high price of real estate, it may be more difficult to see the wood for the trees.

These paper-exercises suggest a way of designing archaeological access to the huge urban corpus. But they are only a beginning – and not a very reliable one for the excavator. A few contemporary groups and dominant centres have been defined where the broader urban questions could be answered – always assuming that the evidence is still there, and this is the rub. It is one thing to identify systems on a map, quite another to go and pull them out of the ground. Archaeological management has always been torn between two ways of designing research: the one to select a town, study it and excavate it thoroughly and use it to illustrate the typical, from which to argue generalities; the other to nibble at a whole family of towns, deem each nibble typical, and to use the set of nibbles to determine the system. It is clear that we need both: some complete examples to determine attributes such as planning and social distribution within a town, and numerous samples from over the urban corpus in order to construct the underlying system. But the question remains: how can we be sure that the evidence is there, tangible if muddy, and know where it lies? We are about to try and answer the site visitor's most famous question:

117

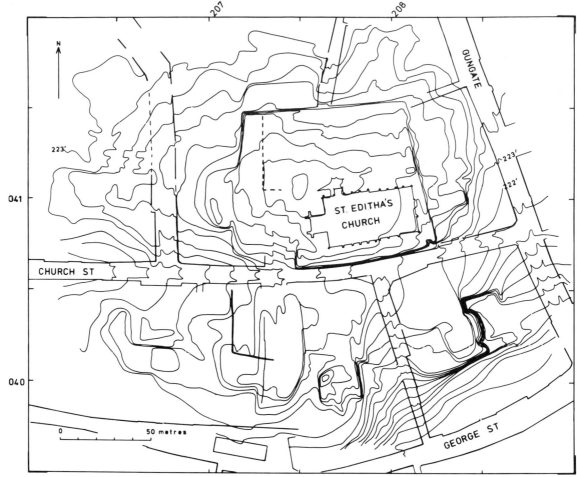

80 Aerial contour survey for Tamworth, showing the raised platform around St Editha's Church indicating the probable site of Offa's palace, discovered by Bob Meeson (R. Meeson)

'How did you know where to dig?'.

The process of *site evaluation* in living sites, not unlike prospecting for precious minerals, involves three stages: mapping, zonation and testing. The normal methods of remote mapping, which work well on open or abandoned sites, such as fieldwalking or aerial photography, are generally prohibited by built-up areas – except on rare occasions. In France, Renimel has used prospection by resistivity on car parks covered in tarmac, spraying them first with water to increase conductivity. A graveyard could theoretically be surveyed in three dimensions using soil-sounding radar. Bob Meeson has used (stereo) aerial photography to produce a contour plan of Tamworth; it was this that revealed the terraced platform around St Editha's church on which Offa's palace probably stood.

In compensation for this general opacity to instru-

ments, long-lived towns have a particular asset of their own: their rich documentation. This is broadly of two kinds: documents made by contemporaries about themselves, and records made by those who have later been underground, for whatever reason, and reported what they saw. Into the former category fall the English series of early maps, of which those by John Speed (*c.* 1610) are the best known. They often retain what is, in effect, the medieval street plan, and, together with the efforts of later cartographers, allow the nucleus of the early town to be located within its eighteenth-, nineteenth- and twentieth-century expansions. As an adjunct to this mapping, the relics of early buildings themselves can

81 A map of Stafford dated to about AD 1600, now in the William Salt Library. The town wall is partly of stone and partly timber palisade, and an enclosure is labelled 'castle built by Edward the Elder'. The burh was actually built by his sister Aethelflaeda, and more probably occupied the central area around the church. A modern archaeologist's map is shown for comparison. (William Salt Library and Birmingham University Field Archaeology Unit)

118

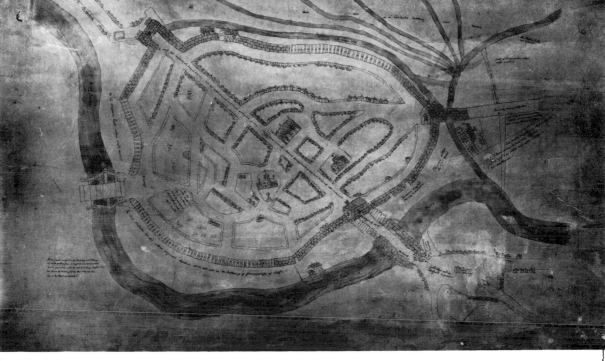

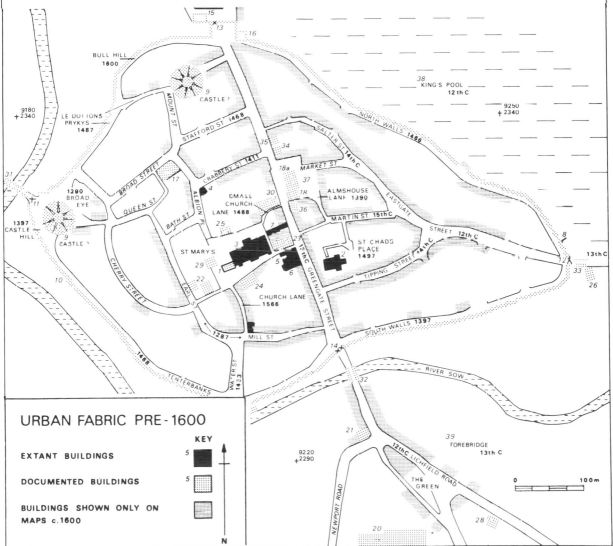

URBAN FABRIC PRE-1600

KEY

EXTANT BUILDINGS   5 ■

DOCUMENTED BUILDINGS   5 ▦

BUILDINGS SHOWN ONLY ON
MAPS c.1600 ▦

N

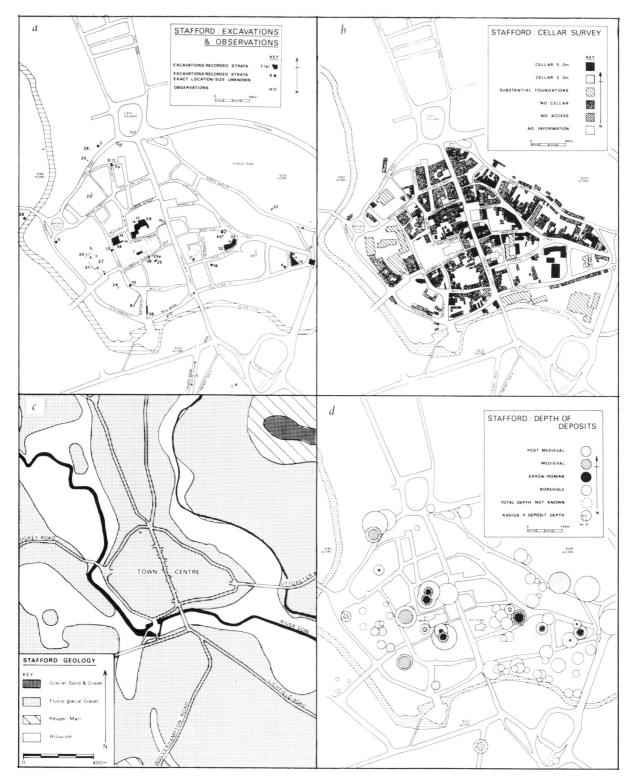

82 *Four contributions to the evaluation of the archaeological site of Stafford town compiled by Jenny Glazebrook. The objective is to map the natural site available for settlement (c), and to predict the quality location and accessibility of archaeological strata (d) (Birmingham University Field Archaeology Unit)*

be located, sometimes as pieces of timber-framing or stone cellars concealed by modern facades.

The information that emerges from the written documents is often of direct relevance to archaeological reconnaissance. Documents can imply the existence of certain structures and locate them accurately – Quirk's prediction of the site of the Old Minster at Winchester being a famous example. They can also provide notice of the earliest occurrence of named streets; it was this that led to the hypothesis of the new thirteenth-century suburb at Shrewsbury. They can also be used to map a probable location of trades which occur as bynames (*Simon the Bellmaker*) or street names (*Coppergate*), if not mentioned in their own right. Perhaps the greatest achievement in documentary mapping to

date is that provided by the Winton Domesday, recently published as *Winchester Studies*, Volume I. Altogether it is possible, at least in the better documented medieval towns, to map the streets, tenements, castles and ecclesiastical precincts back to the twelfth century, and even beyond, without putting a spade into the ground.

This leaves about two-thirds of the total occupation period, and a sizeable proportion of the urban activities, which are invisible in contemporary documents. This, strictly archaeological, evidence can be mapped in another way, also using documents, but this time the reports, sketches, newspaper cuttings and scrapbooks of those who had at some time made casual observation of ruins and strata. In some towns, for example Southampton, antiquarian observations were made from the early nineteenth century, and were characterised occasionally by remarkable insight. Antiquarian language may be somewhat recondite, but it is not difficult to extract from it the facts we need. These facts are, broadly, the characteristics of the natural subsoil, the depth of the deposit and the date of any material recognised. Add to these observations the data from modern boreholes, pipe-trenches and demolitions of various kinds and we

83 *Pollen diagram compiled by Sue Colledge from the King's Pool, now a peat deposit crossed by the Stafford ring-road. Pollen collecting in the Marsh gives a record of the surrounding vegetation over some 10,000 years. Stafford, it seems, was first exploited in the late Roman period when the growing of grain increased, and at the time of the Norman takeover there was an increase in the production of hops or hemp (Birmingham University Archaeological Laboratory)*

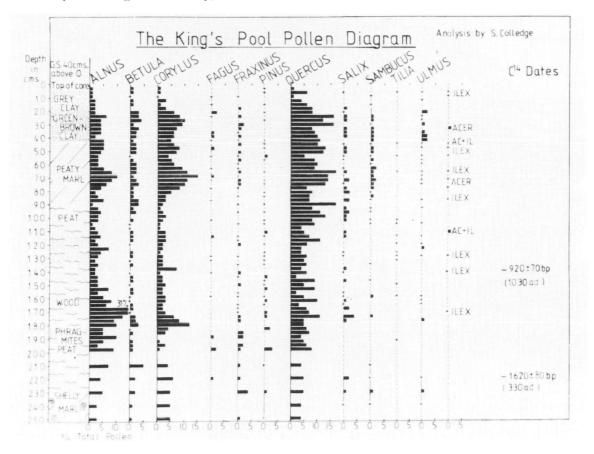

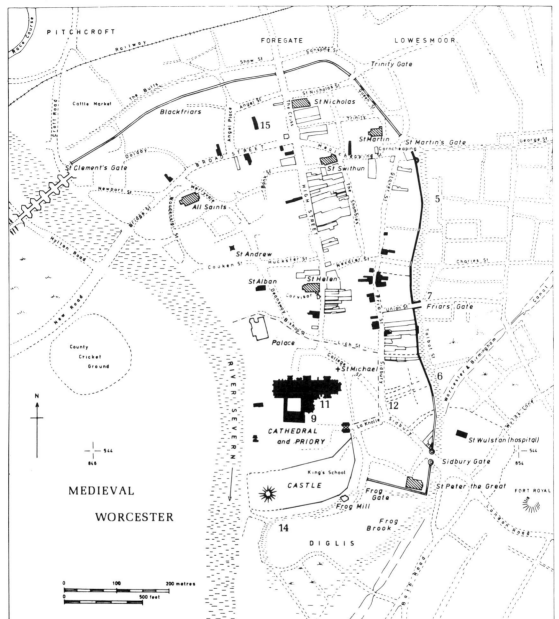

84 Medieval Worcester, mapped from documents, street names, buildings and archaeological excavations (M.O.H. Carver)

have a set of soundings from which the quality and content of the strata can be predicted. At Worcester, for example, where over 200 such observations were collated, it was possible to reconstruct the original topography of the site, before it was terraced, infilled and built up through 2000 years of occupation. Individual observations were of particular value; one manuscript told of the Norman *motte*, removed in the nineteenth century, and gave its plan and elevation. Another reported the removal of an ancient ford and the raising of the ground surface beside it by the dumping of thousands of tons of dredging. This type of strata-prediction offers a number of important factors for archaeological planning: first, a map of the probable extent of settlement, Roman, Saxon and medieval, from the distribution of pottery and other finds; second, an estimate of the surviving depth of the deposits and their probable derivation – whether deep and informative sequences, or modern dumping, and third, an idea of the underlying drainage pattern and natural subsoil, intimating the places where particular classes of archaeological materials are likely to be captured and preserved. Taken together,

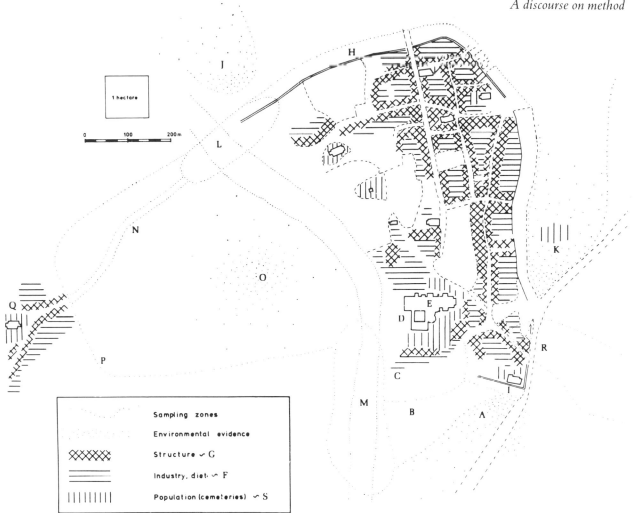

85 Sampling strategy for medieval Worcester, based on
the types of archaeological deposit and their predicted
survival (M.O.H. Carver)

86 Cellars used for strata-testing at Worcester
(M.O.H. Carver)

the three types of map-making allow the reconnaissance to proceed to the next stage – zonation – which provides in effect a blue-print showing the probable layout of the town, and where the archaeological evidence has best survived. Certain zones will suggest themselves for the retrieval of certain types of information: pollen for the vegetation sequence from a pond or adjacent bog; the cemeteries for information about the physical characteristics of people; the town-tips for preference of crockery, and so on.

Test excavation is the third stage, designed to confirm and improve the zonation, and is usually necessary, both because information from the documentation is inadequate or absent, and because it is important to get a view of the strata at first hand to understand what the earlier observers meant. Testing can usually be done economically, by removing cellar walls and inspecting the deposits they had cut through, but there will always be times and places where it is necessary to cut a fresh trench. It has to be remembered that these are still reconnaissance exercises, not substitutes for excavation. The test-section offers the depth, and the quality of the artificial and natural strata, and little more. Attempts to carry interpretation further will usually fail since urban strata have a subtlety and complexity which can only be resolved in large areas. This method of testing does rather beg the

question of what is meant by 'quality', since one man's sequence is another man's tip. 'Quality' as used here tries not to discriminate between the needs of historians of particular periods or classes of monument – that is for another stage in the research design; it is merely intended as a measure of archaeological legibility: how much comprehensible information, from whatever activities, of whatever period, does the deposit contain?

The ability to read layers and understand them really depends on three things: their state of preservation, their spacing and their status (in other words, how they were originally formed). If preservation is poor, the potential for interpreting the whole assemblage, objects of wood as well as objects of stone, is diminished. If the sequence is too sparse, obviously nothing much happened there; if it is too cluttered, the edges of pits and foundations become difficult to see and the assemblages get mixed up. If a deep deposit belongs to a rampart, its layers have less to say about town life than, say, a deep rich deposit of rubbish; its information is largely contained in its shape. All these deposit-types can be inferred from a cut section.

The purpose of site evaluation is therefore to predict where certain types of information now lie, and its results can be immediately exploited by those intending to explore a particular town, or to conserve it for exploration in the future. If we have a model for the original shape of the site, a map of the Roman, Saxon and medieval settlements that developed there, and an estimate of the quality of

87 Overstretching a test: interpretation of a section before and after its controlled excavation (M.O.H. Carver)

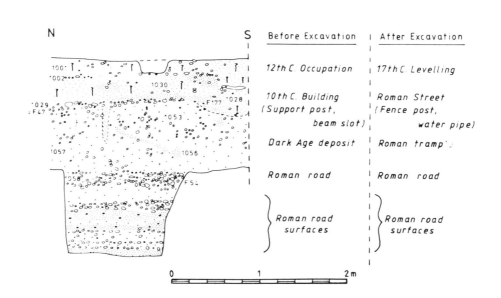

Test Pit in Cellar I — Interpretation

	Before Excavation	After Excavation
	12th C. Occupation	17th C. Levelling
	10th C. Building (Support post, beam slot)	Roman Street (Fence post, water pipe)
	Dark Age deposit	Roman tramp'
	Roman road	Roman road
	Roman road surfaces	Roman road surfaces

0   1   2 m

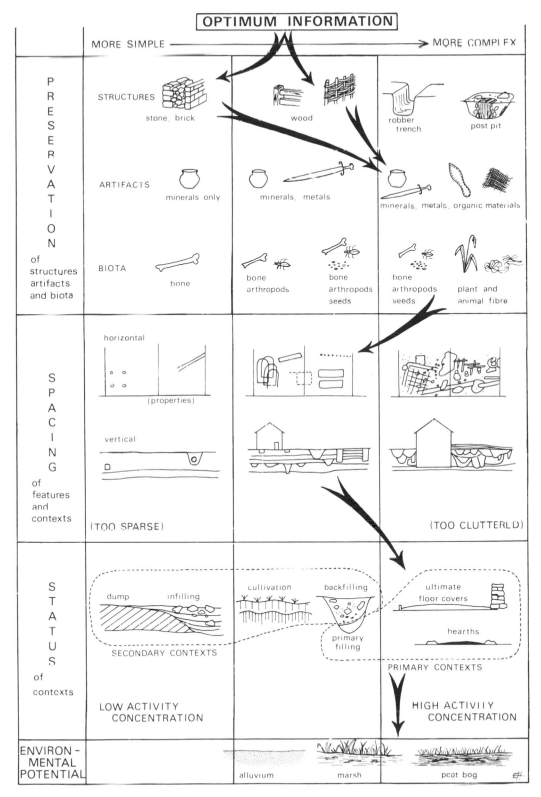

88 *Defining archaeological quality. A 'good site' follows the arrows (M.O.H. Carver)*

information that remains, and where it is, we have in effect a schedule of assets, usable by archaeologists and planning authorities alike.

This use is important enough, if we are to leave any urban archaeology for the next millennium to do, but there is yet another reward of evaluation which affects not so much the research in a particular town, but research into the phenomenon of urbanism as a whole. Assuming that towns come in many different shapes and sizes, it is clear that their capacity to capture and conserve strata into this century is also very varied. Peterborough has lost much of its archaeological evidence; the strata depth at Aylesbury is between 1 and 1.5m (3 and 5ft); at the Salwarpe in Droitwich it lies up to 5m (16ft) thick. Parts of the deposit under Truro were waterlogged for centuries, and at Great Yarmouth and St Ives have been buried by wind-blown sand. The anaerobic deposits captured in buried valleys at York and London are justly famous. Towns on high soft subsoil like Shrewsbury and Langport have been terraced down by builders seeking firm foundations, from the thirteenth century or earlier, tending to remove the traces of their predecessors. Towns with a buried stream running through the centre, like the

London Walbrook, tend to infill and capture earlier strata in a waterlogged state of high preservation. Towns built on flat ground, may unconsciously or deliberately rise to avoid flooding or to provide cultivated land, as in seventeenth-century Stafford. The construction of a large town wall, particularly one using the robust circuit of the legionary fortress such as that at Chester, has a 'belting effect' on later generations, whose debris rises within it like a cake in a cake-tin. Systematic comparison of strata-preservation between towns has not yet been attempted in England (which is why *Fig. 90* gives some results for France), but if it were it would provide a new basis for a national research strategy. The principle of 'maximum yield' would lead us to overlay on the area-studies already discussed, a programme of retrieval based on archaeological legibility. It might favour the timber-framed houses of one town, the Saxo-Norman tenements of another, and the Roman temples of yet another.

It goes without saying that no one aspect of the *research strategy* must be allowed to exclude totally all the others. A national plan for the exploration of English urbanism, when finally drawn up, will include factors of strata-preservation, accessibility and documentary prediction, and the programme to emerge will be a balance between them. But it is safe to say that the resulting strategy will be very

89 Depth of deposits recorded in the City of London (Biddle and Hudson, 1973)

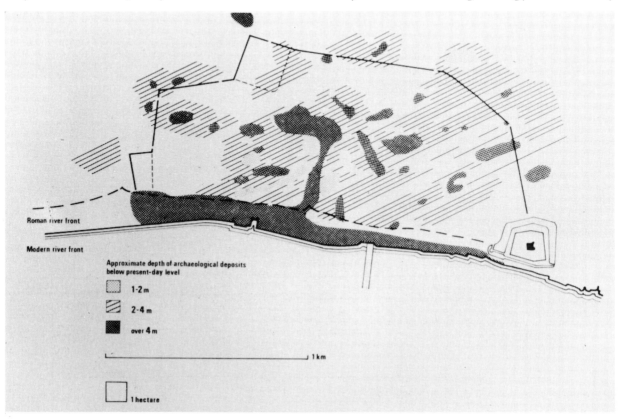

Roman river front

Modern river front

Approximate depth of archaeological deposits below present-day level

1-2 m

2-4 m

over 4 m

1 km

1 hectare

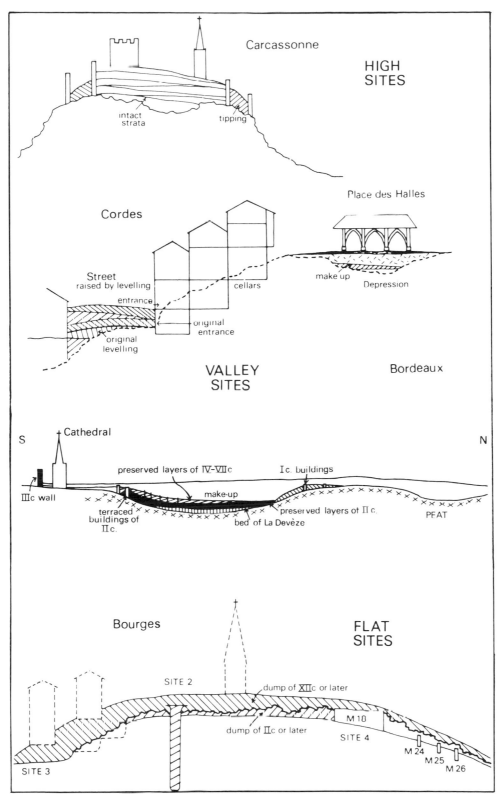

90 Different urban deposits compared: some French examples (Carver, 1983b)

different from the one we have now. We have the methods, and we have the documentation, and very easily could do the groundwork on which to base a programme of research. Our reluctance to do this sets us apart from some other countries of Europe. Perhaps it is the English sense of fair play, the wish to give our quarry a chance, which favours in urban archaeology the maintenance of a certain serendipity.

Serendipitous or not, the real results come not from prediction but from the act of retrieval itself. Euphemisms like 'retrieval', 'examination', 'investigation' and 'intervention' are currently used by archaeologists because the word 'digging' carries with it violent connotations of flying earth, which offends their scientific sensitivity. Of course it is digging, and sometimes the earth does fly, but in general we are talking about the slow unpicking of a set of interleaved episodes, and the work is done with spade, trowel, spoon, and spatula, by carefully trained excavators. Whatever the visitor might think of their appearance, theirs remains the crucial skill of urban archaeology.

The size of the area to be excavated will depend on a number of practical factors: the land accessible, the predicted size of the spoil heap (if one is obliged to live with it), the space required for a public viewing platform, and the depth and condition of the deposit. If deep, a major part of the available resources will have to be dedicated to holding up the sides of the excavation with steel shuttering, as at Coppergate (York) or Billingsgate (London). If the deposits contain running water, continuous pumping will be essential; a large area can be successfully kept workable in this way, even adjacent to a river, as P. Fasham demonstrated at Reading Abbey. Within these constraints, the excavator will try and achieve some coincidence between the area available and the research targets as defined by site evaluation. The coincidence will very rarely be perfect and an area can seldom be so large as to contain all of anything. Perhaps the site of St Helen-on-the-Walls in York approached the optimum, in this case for a medieval church and its cemetery. Nearly always we are obliged to extract parts of the continuum in both space and time; every site has artificial edges, and the contiguous areas will one day be recovered by somebody else, to be rejoined with what has been recorded, like severed internal organs after surgery. For this, if for no other reason, archaeologists are obsessed by accurate survey, far more accurate, for example, than a modern map maker, who would not normally require tolerances of less than 0.01 per cent. The same considerations have led to the steady development of standardised recording systems, where every element of strata is numbered and

described using a vocabulary which other professionals will understand. It has been a long time coming and has not been so easy to do, given the variety of pits, soils and stone surfaces that are encountered. That it is now possible is another sign of the achievements of the last twenty-five years.

In the same way as the site was chosen by virtue of a research design which gave it a predicted yield, so sectors and phases will often emerge within the site itself in which the yield is special, and special retrieval demanded. This is a somewhat contentious statement, liable to bring down on me the wrath of the 'objective' school of excavation, and I feel I owe them at least an explanation. Archaeological strata are not homogenous but hierarchical. At the crudest level major differences are defined: a wall, a pit; but within the pit are layers, which form a subset of the pit; within each layer are finds, soils, seeds and insects' wings; within the soils are minerals, within the minerals, chemical elements and compounds and so on. What is actually seen and recovered therefore depends on the level of definition applied: the number of layers in a pit might be one (brown), or four (light brown, dark brown . . .), or forty-four (on the sorting of small stones), or 404 (on post-depositional chemical horizons). Similarly, if the animal bones are picked out and put into a tray, certain animals like frogs are likely to 'escape' because their bones are too small to see; the use of a 1mm sieve will retrieve the frogs, but not the insects; a 0.5mm sieve the insects but not the pollen. 'Total excavation', as it appeared to develop after (but not because of) the publication of Philip Barker's *Techniques of Archaeological Excavation*, is therefore a somewhat meaningless concept; excavation can only be total if you take the whole site home with you, and even then decisions will still have to be made, one day, as to what constitutes the evidence for an event.

The reality of excavation is that a *sampling system* is always applied to it, from the moment a site is chosen, to the moment the last pot-sherd rattles into the tray. Rather than pretend it is unnecessary (because everything is done to perfection), it would seem more sensible to design it, control it and declare it right from the start. A rather basic system which seems to have worked fairly well in a few places uses 'recovery levels' (*Fig. 92*). It divides the possible applied effort into a series of grades, within each of which the acts of digging and observation, the type of records made and the quantity of material recovered are, as far as possible, consistent. They comprise, if you will, a series of gears by which a director can drive the excavation. It should be appreciated that this system is not merely intended to save money (although it may well have that effect). The decisions

91 *Excavation in progress at Ludlow in 1984. These excavations, on the site of a Carmelite Friary, were carried out by a professional team under Annette Roe,* *solely with the support of funds raised locally by public subscription (Birmingham University Field Archaeology Unit)*

Level	COMPONENT	ASSEMBLAGE	CONTEXT	FEATURE	STRUCTURE	LANDSCAPE	e.g.
A	(not recovered)	Surface finds PLOT 2-D	Inferred by sensor OUTLINE PLAN	Inferred by sensor OUTLINE PLAN	Inferred by sensor OUTLINE PLAN	Inferred by sensor	Field Walking
B	(not recovered)	Large finds RECORD EXAMPLES KEEP EXAMPLES	Defined by shovel DESCRIBE	Defined by shovel SHORT DESCRIPTION OUTLINE PLAN	as feature	PLOT STRUCTURES on OS	19th-C Houses
C	(not recovered)	All visible finds RECORD ALL KEEP EXAMPLES	Defined by coarse trowel DESCRIPTION (Munsell for mortars and natural)	Defined by coarse trowel FULL DESCRIPTION DETAILED PLAN	Defined by coarse trowel EXCAVATE AS ONE PHOTOGRAPH AS ONE	1:100 PLAN PROFILE	16th-C Pits
D	SAMPLE SIEVING of spoil offsite (spoil not kept)	All visible finds PLOT 2-D and KEEP ALL	Defined by fine trowel DESCRIPTION (incl. Munsell) PLAN 1:20	Defined by fine trowel FULL DESCRIPTION DETAILED PLAN 1:20 (colour coded) CONTOUR PHOTOGRAPH (B/W)	Defined by fine trowel EXCAVATE AS ONE: PHOTOGRAPH by PHASE	1:100 PLAN CONTOUR SURVEY	Timber trace building
E	TOTAL SIEVING of spoil on site for presence of specified material and KEEP SPOIL	All visible finds PLOT 3-D and KEEP ALL	Defined minutely DESCRIPTION (incl. Munsell) PLAN (natural colour) 1:10 or 1:5 CONTOUR	Defined minutely FULL DESCRIPTION PLAN (colour) 1:10 or 1:5 CONTOUR PHOTOGRAPH	Defined minutely EXCAVATE AS ONE: PHOTOGRAPH by PHASE	(as LEVEL D) CONTOUR SURVEY	Skeleton
F	MICRO-SIEVING of soil block in laboratory	(as component)	(as LEVEL E) and LIFT AS BLOCK	(as LEVEL E)	(as LEVEL E)	(as LEVEL D)	Storage Pit Fill

92 *Information recovery levels used to control the rate and intensity of data retrieved on excavations (M.O.H. Carver)*

it embodies are inherent in every excavation; all the system does is to make them explicit.

A director will almost certainly apply these 'recovery levels' in ways that depend on the present state of knowledge. Thus she will probably machine off the top 0.5m (20in) of the site, which contains demolished houses which were standing until last year (and whose plans are recorded on a number of maps and legal documents), perhaps keeping samples of bricks for comparative purposes (level A). She may then go on to shovel out the twenty-five seventeenth- and eighteenth-century pits that appear, giving them accurate plans and keeping the larger fragments of pottery and bone for a crude monitor of markets and livestock at that time (level B). The brown soil that then covers the site is searched for signs of agricultural or ephemeral buildings with a trowel, and all macroscopic fragments of pottery, etc. are recovered for analytical purposes (level C). Beneath the brown soil lies the tenement sequence of the tenth to thirteenth centuries, each episode of which is carefully defined and recorded, all macroscopic material plotted and gathered, and specific deposits, such as cess-pits, sampled (level D). Beneath this lies the dark earth, the interface between the Roman and late Saxon town. So important is this period for the understanding of urbanism, that the surface is carefully examined again and again, and every bucketful of earth sieved for minute signs of human and animal life (level E). Within the dark earth lie two entangled skeletons with a scatter of gold braid and a crushed spread of metal fragments. This small patch of earth is consolidated with a polymer, boxed and lifted to be transported away for three-dimensional dissection in the laboratory (level F). By the time the stubs of demolished Roman buildings begin to emerge with their attendant mantle of rubble it is time to return again to level D.

This hypothetical itinerary will change its

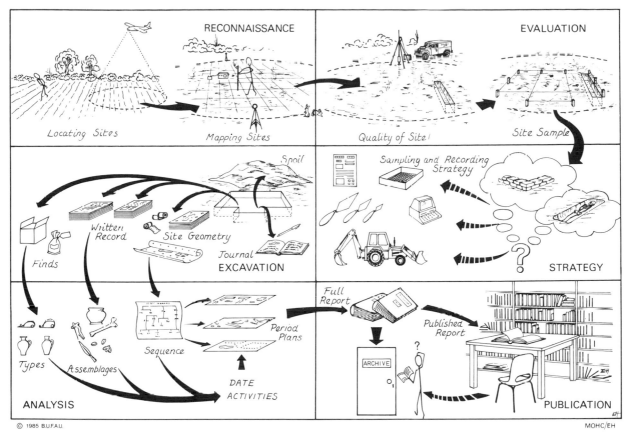

RECONNAISSANCE

Locating Sites   *Mapping Sites*

EVALUATION

Quality of Site   *Site Sample*

Spoil

Written Record   *Site Geometry*

Journal

Finds

EXCAVATION

Sampling and Recording Strategy

STRATEGY

Types   *Assemblages*

Sequence

Period Plans

DATE ACTIVITIES

ANALYSIS

Full Report

Published Report

ARCHIVE

PUBLICATION

© 1985 B.U.F.A.U.   MOHC/EH

93 Field research procedure (M.O.H. Carver, drawn by Liz Hooper)

character as research objectives change, and is flexible enough to do so. In the meantime, it has a useful application within the site itself, since it allows groups of material to be compared which were recovered in the same way. The 'assemblage', that group of diverse debris which is recovered together, is not the easiest thing to interpret and perhaps is more deserving of new methodology than any other aspect of our work. The meaning is difficult enough to extract when the group is large and well preserved, as in the examples mentioned in Chapter 7; it becomes more difficult still, when the material was not in fact deposited together in the first place. Urban excavation is the recovery of a long sequence of depositions each resulting from an individual circumstance, each arrived from an individual provenance. A pottery vessel may be abandoned in a burning house, dropped into a latrine, broken on the floor, and dumped in a rubbish pit, trampled into the muddy courtyard or street, dug into a construction trench, mixed up with builder's mortar, or spread upon the garden with the midden. Needless to say, several of these events can occur consecutively after, sometimes long after, the first loss of the artefact by

its owner. It is the busy, mobile, underground after-life of objects, which makes the interpretation of urban sequences such a challenge. As a first step to unravelling the assemblage, deposits can be hypothetically divided into 'primary' groups, which are assembled by their users, and 'secondary' groups, assembled by the various post-depositional disturbances to which each has been subjected. The multitude of 'secondary deposits' which abound in urban sites are mainly characterised by residual, that is anachronistic, finds of pottery, and, we must assume, contain also equally anachronistic animal bones and seeds dug up from earlier periods. Occasionally the group, when excavated, is found to be equally distorted by material arriving, through worm action or other types of post-depositional mixing, from later periods. The truth is, of course, that given the way people live, a 'primary' deposit, which preserves in cameo the activities carried out on the spot, is fairly rare in settlements. We can hope for a savage flood, such as that which overwhelmed the fourteenth-century inhabitants of New Elvet in Durham; or a fire, such as that which preserved the contents of a granary in Roman York, or those of the Pottergate cellar in sixteenth-century Norwich. Or we can pray that the inhabitants will lay down and tread in their refuse as regularly as the days of the

131

week. But, as we have seen, such practices are seldom followed. To make sense of an urban sequence is not, therefore, as simple as Chapter I's site-tour perhaps implied; it is a whole art in itself which begins largely when the excavation has finished, and takes much longer than digging. The purpose of this programme of analysis is, ultimately, to make history.

The site that the excavators eventually return to the developers has been turned into a large set of records: *written*, which include descriptions of every layer found and of its position in the sequence; *drawn*, which include maps and plans of every layer and every interpreted man-made feature; *photographic*, to illustrate the conditions of the excavation (and the excavators) as well as the details of the findings; and *material*: boxes of pottery, corroded iron packed in silica gel, human and animal bones, samples of charcoal for radio–carbon dating, timber for dendro-

chronology, and dark soils for the identification of seeds, pollen, insects, cess and chemical residues. The analysis of all these records can be broken down into a number of stages, although some can happen simultaneously if sufficient funds and staff are available. The first task is to prepare all the records for an archive, so that before any interpretation is put on their overall import, they are safe and accessible for other generations to study. The technology employed for the archive is currently as varied as the recording systems which feed it. Those who employed computers to collect and collate the paper-record as it emerged from the ground, find it relatively easy to print out the appropriate lists and indexes, as provided by the database management system. Many people now use microfiche to store these lists and indexes, whether originating from print-outs or typescript. Many old-fashioned systems used notebooks, finds and plans of diverse sizes packed in tobacco tins and cardboard boxes. This traditional type of archive often solved its own storage problems by getting progressively smaller as it was rammed into evermore constricted spaces in the study or attic, or under the bed. Many such unsystematic records were simply lost.

Assuming an adequate set of records, the next

*94 Stratification diagram showing the sequence of layers and features from the earliest (*bottom*) to the latest times (*top*), at Saddler Street, Durham. The 'lives' of features are represented by vertical arrows, and the diagram identifies structures which were in existence at the same time (Carver, 1979b)*

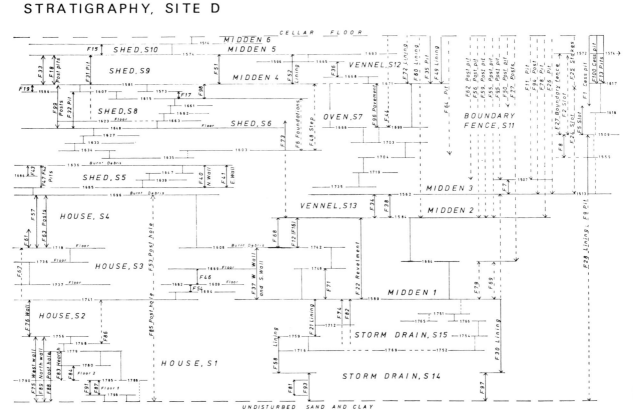

DURHAM CITY, SADDLER STREET 1974
STRATIGRAPHY, SITE D

stage is to decide how far research on all this material should be undertaken for the benefit of people living and working now, and how much of it could wait for regional studies or more advantageous funding. This is not an easy decision, and again tends to divide the archaeologists into 'totalitarian' and 'selective' schools, but it may be that a compromise can be found in what follows. A certain basic analytical routine is considered essential if the recorded site is to exist in a comprehensible form. Fresh targets can often be met as the objectives of research evolve, and hopefully the records will support them. The analytical routine divides into five simple stages: first, reconstruct a sequence; second, establish what activities were present; third, establish which activities occurred together; fourth, date them, and fifth, reconstruct the whole story in a form which can be easily understood.

The *stratification diagram* (*Fig. 94*) shows how a sequence can be modelled for a site where layers and features were recorded separately. Horizontal lines show the position of each layer in time, relative to the others, on the principle that later layers lie on top of earlier ones. The vertical lines are the features – pits, ditches, post-sockets and so forth – and arrows at the ends of each line show the limits of their possible existence – their life. This ordering is not unequivocal, since not every feature and layer can relate to every other, and there will be an ambiguity of position where two episodes of deposition were not in physical contact.

The less specific the stratification was on site, the more uncertainties will be exhibited by this 'stratification diagram'. At a later stage, contemporary activities can be earmarked and dated and the diagram adjusted, but before doing this, the activities themselves must be isolated.

The source for the interpretation for an activity is partly the *assemblage* – for example a group of pottery and burnt grain – and partly the situation in which it was found – for example in an oven. Using methods of scientific identification, the purpose of the assemblage can be distinguished in startling detail: the seeds of plants for consumption or for sleeping on; the animal bones, which might imply food (beef, mutton, fish) or pets (dogs, cats,) or vermin (rats, mice) or lovers of special conditions (frogs). Insects, too, need special ambient conditions and their 'death assemblages' indicate whether a layer was outside or inside, wet or dry, or contained rotting meat or compost. Residues of various kinds can be identified and distinguished, such as slag (smelting or smithing), frit (glassmaking or pottery glazing), bone offcuts (butchery or handle making or making glue), or burnt clay (for ovens, hearths, kilns or a burnt-down house covered in daub). The detective

work that has been done by natural scientists in recent years, particularly those working at York, shows such great skill and potential, that there would seem at present to be no limit to the reconstruction of activities captured as primary deposits on archaeological sites.

Pre-eminent for the interpretation must be the artefacts which alone can provide the cultural link with the contemporary world, and still constitute the most accurate method of dating. Every artefact, from a flint axe to a bicycle, contains within it attributes of fabric, form and style which indicate with greater or lesser clarity, where it was made, when, what for and by what group of people. Much of our analytical energy goes on pottery, since it is virtually ubiquitous and therefore a fine cultural and chronological indicator. But there is another reason too. Since pottery tends to occur virtually throughout the period in which towns were occupied, it can be used as a way of monitoring the character of the strata themselves. The method is relatively simple. The quantities of each type of pottery present in each layer are tabulated against the order in which the layers were deposited, which can be obtained from the stratification diagram. This gives a *seriation table*, a statement (in effect) of how the population of different types of pottery varied through time. The types of pottery are put in their order of date of manufacture, as so far known – Roman on the left and nineteenth-century on the right. The layers are also put in their best order of deposition, the earliest at the bottom and the latest at the top. Both orders can then be adjusted within the limits imposed by the known date of manufacture or the known stratification, to get the best diagonal, since in the nature of things, later pottery should arrive later in the system (*Fig. 95*).

The seriation table has some interesting properties. The presence of many different types of pottery in a layer, for example, shows that the layer contains much residual material, so is a 'secondary' deposit and is not much good for fine-grained biological analysis. The presence of small quantities of large numbers of different pottery types ('in high diversity') shows that a layer was a plough soil. A smoothly rising edge to the diagonal shows a gradual and continuous sequence of occupation; while a vertical edge (or 'cliff') indicates that there had been a rapid development, with a whole lot of new features dug at the same time. A jagged or indented edge shows that those layers belonged to a secondary dump, such as a rampart or a ground-clearing operation.

The full potential of this particular analysis has yet to be developed. Its most significant service so far, and the one which seems to earn it a place in the

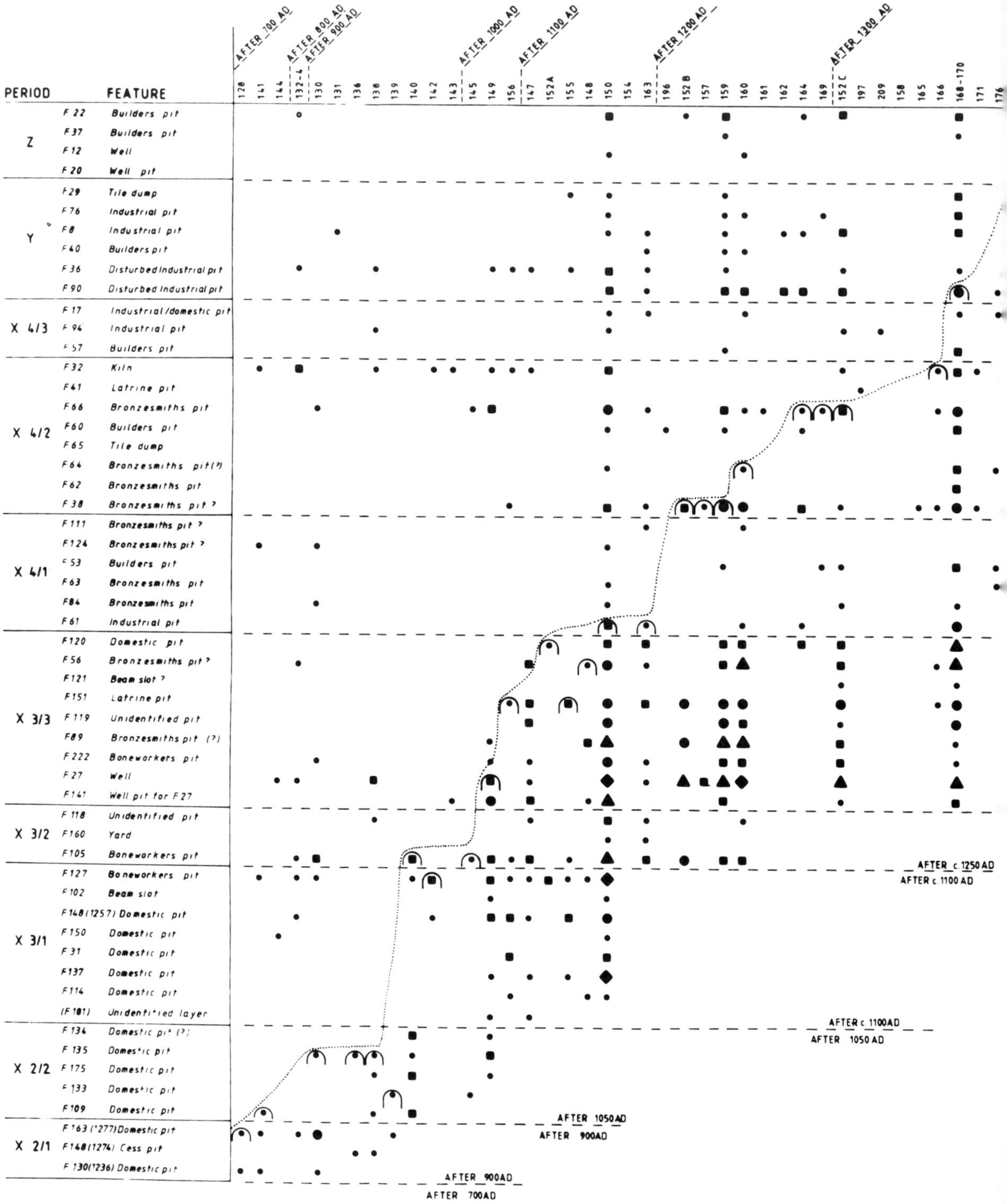
AFTER 700 AD
AFTER 800 AD
AFTER 900 AD
AFTER 1000 AD
AFTER 1100 AD
AFTER 1200 AD
AFTER 1300 AD
PERIOD
FEATURE
128 141 144 132-4 130 131 136 138 139 140 142 143 145 149 156 147 152A 155 148 150 154 163 196 152B 157 159 160 161 162 164 169 152C 197 209 158 165 166 168-170 171 176
Z
F 22 Builders pit
F 37 Builders pit
F 12 Well
F 20 Well pit
Y
F 29 Tile dump
F 76 Industrial pit
F 8 Industrial pit
F 40 Builders pit
F 36 Disturbed Industrial pit
F 90 Disturbed Industrial pit
X 4/3
F 17 Industrial/domestic pit
F 94 Industrial pit
F 57 Builders pit
X 4/2
F 32 Kiln
F 41 Latrine pit
F 66 Bronzesmiths pit
F 60 Builders pit
F 65 Tile dump
F 64 Bronzesmiths pit(?)
F 62 Bronzesmiths pit
F 38 Bronzesmiths pit ?
X 4/1
F 111 Bronzesmiths pit ?
F 124 Bronzesmiths pit ?
F 53 Builders pit
F 63 Bronzesmiths pit
F 84 Bronzesmiths pit
F 61 Industrial pit
X 3/3
F 120 Domestic pit
F 56 Bronzesmiths pit ?
F 121 Beam slot ?
F 151 Latrine pit
F 119 Unidentified pit
F 89 Bronzesmiths pit (?)
F 222 Boneworkers pit
F 27 Well
F 141 Well pit for F 27
X 3/2
F 118 Unidentified pit
F 160 Yard
F 105 Boneworkers pit
X 3/1
F 127 Boneworkers pit
F 102 Beam slot
F 148 (1257) Domestic pit
F 150 Domestic pit
F 31 Domestic pit
F 137 Domestic pit
F 114 Domestic pit
(F 101) Unidentified layer
X 2/2
F 134 Domestic pit (?)
F 135 Domestic pit
F 175 Domestic pit
F 133 Domestic pit
F 109 Domestic pit
X 2/1
F 163 (1277) Domestic pit
F 148 (1274) Cess pit
F 130 (1236) Domestic pit
AFTER c. 1250 AD
AFTER c. 1100 AD
AFTER c. 1100 AD
AFTER 1050 AD
AFTER 1050 AD
AFTER 900 AD
AFTER 900 AD
AFTER 700 AD

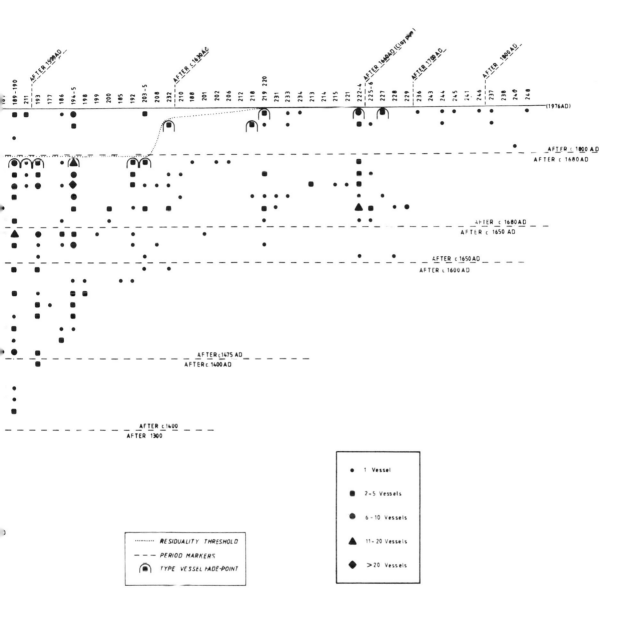

95 *Seriation of pottery types at Sidbury, Worcester. The x-axis shows the types of pottery in their suggested order of appearance, while the y-axis gives the feature numbers (mainly pits) in an order suggested by stratification. The order of both axes is adjusted to give the best diagonal, and the result is a model, showing the types of pottery in use in particular periods. Such diagrams may also show a number of other characteristics, such as episodes of dumping, of gradual growth, of levelling and of horticulture (Carver, 1980)*

135

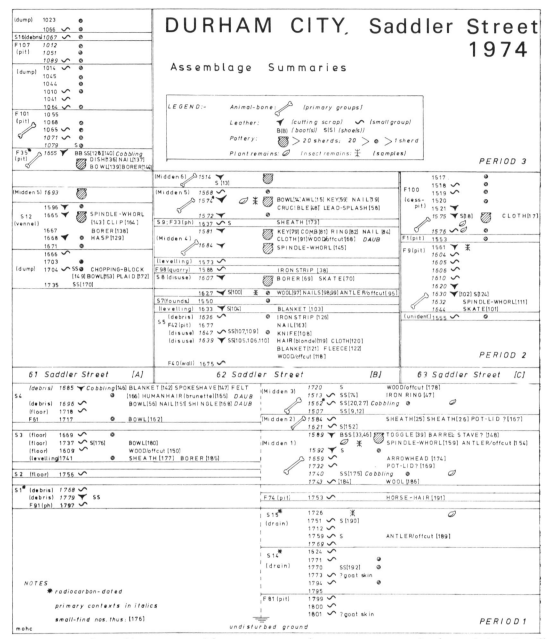

DURHAM CITY, Saddler Street 1974

Assemblage Summaries

LEGEND:— Animal-bone: *(primary groups)*
Leather: ▼ *(cutting scrap)* ∿ *(small group)*
B(B) *(boot(s))* S(S) *(shoe(s))*
Pottery: ▨ >20 sherds; 20 > ⊘ >1 sherd
Plant remains: ⊘ Insect remains: ✳ *(samples)*

PERIOD 3

61 Saddler Street [A]   62 Saddler Street [B]   63 Saddler Street [C]

PERIOD 2

PERIOD 1

NOTES
✳ radiocarbon-dated
primary contexts in italics
small-find nos. thus: [176]

mohc

undisturbed ground

96 *A synoptic view of assemblages recovered from a well-stratified sequence in Durham (Carver, 1979b)*

standard routine, is to show which layers and features could be contemporary, or at least be very close to each other in date, and which of these could be primary – material simultaneously deposited by the inhabitants and diagnostic of their living conditions and lifestyle. This is the information fed back to the stratification diagram and the assemblages, to produce an ordered account of events. Our next task is to date them.

The *dating* given by pottery and coins, although

made more representative by seriation, is still not as accurate as we would like for the Roman, Saxon and medieval periods. Unfortunately, the error range inherent in radio-carbon and other non-artefactual methods is just as great, up to ± 120 years. Here is one reason (among many) why archaeologists are reluctant to couple their site sequences too closely to historical events. Very occasionally the historical record can provide a date for an archaeological event – the Great Fire of London which created an unmistakable black layer in 1666 is one rare example. But normally, the archaeological sequence can rarely pinpoint a structure or activity more closely in time

Period	Earliest Date of Event	29 SIDBURY (TENEMENT C)	25 SIDBURY (TENEMENT B)	23 SIDBURY (TENEMENT A)
	1920 AD	Site Frontage Levelled		
Z	1920 AD — 1700 AD	? Residential	Shop/Residential	Shop/Residential
Y	1700 AD — 1680 AD	?	Residential	Residential
	c. 1680 AD	Site Frontage Levelled; Rear quarried		
X 4/3	1650 AD — 1600 AD	? (Tiling)	Residential (Horses)	?
X 4/2	1600 AD — 1475 AD	BRONZESMITH	BRONZESMITH	BRONZESMITH (Bellmaker)
X 4/1	1475 AD — 1400 AD	BRONZESMITH	BRONZESMITH	?
	14th C.	Site Frontage levelled and lowered; City wall built at rear		
X 3/3	1300 AD — 1300 AD	BONE/BRONZE-WORKER	?	BONE/BRONZE-WORKER
	c. 1300 AD	Site Frontage levelled and lowered		
X 3/2	1250 AD — 1250 AD	Residential	BONEWORKER	BONEWORKER
	c. 1250 AD	Site Frontage levelled and lowered		
X 3/1	1100 AD — 1100 AD	Residential	BONEWORKER	Residential
	c. 1100 AD	Site Frontage levelled and lowered		
X 2/2	1100 AD — 1100 AD	Residential	Residential	Residential
	c. 1050	Levelling and lowering		
X 2/1	900 AD — 900 AD	Residential	Residential	Residential
		Desertion		
X 1	c. 3rd C. AD	STREET, used by cattle, etc.		
W	c. 2nd C. AD	ROAD, used by iron smelters.		

97 Site model for the sequence of activities in three
adjacent tenements at Worcester (Carver, 1980)

than: 'the end of the first century AD', 'after 370 (from a coin)', 'post-Roman', 'Saxo-Norman', 'early twelfth-century', 'pre-dissolution'. Such epithets are at least honest, if irritating.

What every site can usually offer the historian is an account of the broadly dated sequence of events and a picture of certain periods. The sequence may be presented in words or pictures, but the end result is the same: to give a story, or *'site model'* as it is more appropriately called (Fig. 96, 97). The professional literature is full of such stories, which, however unsympathetically they are sometimes presented, comprise the source book for local historians and students of urbanism alike. Likewise, the recreation of the site at certain periods, by word-picture or reconstruction-drawing, is what puts flesh back on the dry bones of the structures and assemblages refined by analysis. If only we were better at it!

The problem, of course, as has no doubt been evident throughout this book, is to know who you are talking to. Archaeologists are obliged to address, at certain times, their sponsors, their colleagues, the public, professional town planners, engineers and contractors, students, the press, lawyers, bishops and workers on Manpower Services Schemes – to name but a few; obliged to address them and to bring the site and its meaning alive both for the sceptical expert and the credulous majority. In all this demanding and diverse communication, urban archaeologists have probably failed to make such impression on the public at large; but they should, I believe, be forgiven for having put needs of their own discipline first. The evidence is so plentiful and so vulnerable, and its potential has grown so rapidly in the hands of excavators and natural scientists that there has been little time to develop effective systems for exchanging ideas – little time indeed to do more than the most basic research before it is time to move on to the next crisis and the next unheated hostel.

Academic publications are now beginning to appear which will broaden and deepen our understanding of town life, well beyond the range of such superficial surveys as the present essay. Some scholars have staked out the subject matter for the study of individual towns in advance, as at Winchester, York and Lincoln. Others are pursuing thematic targets, like regional cultures or Roman trade networks. Others . . . but why say more? Urban archaeology is decidedly alive and is, or should be, an integrated field of research, ranging in its application from site evaluation to the analysis of slag, from the Claudian invasion to the dissolution of the monasteries, from temples to churches, from palaces to hovels, and filled with all manner of people, from busy artisans to children playing – a most exciting, exacting and necessary study.

Topic headings for some major urban projects

WINCHESTER STUDIES

The topography of medieval Winchester

Pre-Roman and Roman Winchester

The Old and New Minsters

The Brooks and other town sites of medieval Winchester

Winchester Castle and Wolvesey Palace

Crafts and industries

The Winchester mint and other medieval numismatic studies

Human and animal biology

Botanical and environmental studies

The origins and development of Winchester

THE ARCHAEOLOGY OF YORK

AY1 Sources for York history to AD 1100

AY2 Historical sources for York archaeology after AD 1100

AY3 The legionary fortress

AY4 The colonia

AY5 The Roman cemeteries

AY6 Roman extra-mural settlement and roads

AY7 Anglian York

AY8 Anglo-Scandinavian York

AY9 The medieval walled city south-west of the Ouse

AY10 The medieval walled city north-east of the Ouse

AY11 The medieval suburbs

AY12 The medieval cemeteries

AY13 Early modern York

AY14 The past environment of York

AY15 The animal bone

AY16 The pottery

AY17 The small finds

AY18 The coins

AY19 Principles and methods

LINCOLN VOLUMES

I   Prehistoric discoveries

II   The Roman military occupation of Lincoln

III   The upper Roman city

IV   The lower Roman city

V   The environs of Roman Lincoln

VI   The cemeteries of Roman Lincoln

VII   The defences of Roman and medieval Lincoln

VIII   Lincoln c. AD 450–c. AD 850

IX   Lincoln in the Anglo-Scandinavian period

X   Medieval Lincoln: the upper city

XI   Medieval Lincoln: the lower city

XII   Medieval Lincoln: the suburbs

XIII   Early modern Lincoln

XIV   Medieval cemeteries

XV   Artefacts

XVI   Roman pottery

XVII   Post-Roman pottery

XVIII   Environmental studies

Appendix

GROUP 1 : SINGLE PERIOD TOWN SITES
(*Fig. 76*)

CRITERIA for inclusion in this list are (1) Towns showing zero population growth and zero development in Heighway 1972, and (2) towns registered as non-urban or having a population of less than 1 person per hectare in HMSO 1981 (England and Wales only), and (3) towns occupied in specific period or periods, following Heighway 1972.

Old counties named.   ★Site not now occupied

A. Roman
1. Hampshire: ★Bitterne (*Clausentum*)
2.   ★Portchester
3. Berkshire: ★Silchester
4. Herefordshire: ★Kenchester
                              (*Magnis*)
5. Hertfordshire: Braughing Station
6. Huntingdonshire: The Castles
                              (*Durobrivae*)
7. Kent: Richborough
8. Lincolnshire: Ancaster (*Causennae*)
9. Norfolk: Caister-on-Sea
10.   Caistor-St. Edmunds
11. Northamptonshire: Irchester
12. Nottinghamshire: Castle Hill
                              (*Margidunum*)
13. Oxfordshire: Alchester
14.   Dorchester
15. Rutland: Great Casterton
16. Shropshire: ★Wroxeter
17. Staffordshire: Gnosall
18.   Rocester
19.   Wall (*Letocetum*)
20. Wiltshire: Blackfield (*Cunetio*)
21.   ★Old Sarum
22. Yorkshire: Brough-on-Humber
                              (*Petuaria*)
23.   Catterick
                              (*Cataractonium*)
24.   Aldborough
                              (*Isurium Brigantium*)
25.   Tadcaster (*Calcaria*)
26. Monmouthshire: Caerwent

B. Middle Saxon
27. Hampshire: ★Portchester ?
28. Norfolk: ★North Elmham ?
29. Northumberland: Bamburgh ?
30. Oxfordshire: Dorchester ?

C. Late Saxon
31. Cornwall: Launceston St. Stephens
32. (Deleted from map)
33. Cheshire: Eddisbury
34. Devon: Lydford
35. Kent: Fordwich
36. Gloucestershire: Berkeley
37. Nottinghamshire: Southwell
38. Shropshire: Chirbury ?
39.   Quatford ?
40. Somerset: ★South Cadbury
41. Suffolk: Dunwich
42. Wiltshire: Bedwyn
43.   ★Old Sarum
44. Yorkshire: Tadcaster
45. Flint: ★Rhuddlan I

D. 11th/12th C
46. Cornwall: Tregoney
47. Cumberland: Ravenglass
48. Devon: Plympton Earle
49. Dorset: Corfe
50. (Herefordshire): Castle Clifford
51.   Ewias Harold
52.   Richard's Castle
53.   Stapleton

54. Cambridgeshire: Yaxley
55. Lancashire: Hornby
56. Northumberland: Alnmouth
57.   Bamburgh
58.   Norham
59.   Wooler
60. Oxfordshire: Burford
61. Shropshire: Ludlow
62. Staffordshire: Tutbury
63. Sussex: Midhurst
64. (Westmorland): Brough
65. Yorkshire: Helmsley
66.   Stokesley
67.   Thirsk
68.   Boroughbridge
69. Flint: Rhuddlan II
70. Monmouth: Skenfrith
71. Pembrokeshire: Wiston
72. Radnor: Old Radnor
73. Banffshire: Cullen
74. Fife: Crail
75. Nairn: Nairn
76.   Auldearn
77. Roxburgh: ★Old Roxburgh

E. 13th C

78. Cornwall: Grampound
79.   St. Germans
80.   St. Mawes
81.   Tintagel
82. Devon: Bere Alston
83.   Chagford
84.   Chumleigh
85.   Hartland
86.   North Bovey
87.   North Taunton
88.   South Brent
89. Dorset: Milton Abbas
90.   Sturminster Newton
91. Essex: Horndon-on-the-hill
92. Hants: Kingsclere
93.   Overton
94. (Herefordshire): Huntington
95.   Longton
              (Ewias Lacey)

96.   Pembridge
97.   Preston-on-
              Wye
98. Isle of Wight: Newtown
              (Franchville)
99. Lancashire: Cartmel
100.   Flookburgh
101.   Hawkshead
102. Leicestershire: Hallaton
103.   Kegworth
104. Lincolnshire: Crowland
105.   Donington
106.   Holbeach
107.   Long Sutton
108. Norfolk: Castle Acre
109.   Cawston
110.   New Buckenham
111.   Worstead
112. Northamptonshire: Weldon
113. Anglesey: Beaumaris
114. Brecknockshire: Hay-on-Wye
115. Caernarvonshire: Conway
116.   Nevin
117. Carmarthenshire: Dryslwyn
118.   Llangadog
119.   Laugharne
120.   Newton-by-
              Dinefor
121.   Old Dynevor
122. Denbighshire: Holt
123. Flintshire: Dyserth
124.   New Mostyn
125. Montgomery: Dolforwyn
126.   Caerswys
127. Pembrokeshire: Templeton
128. Radnorhsire: Cefnllys
129.   Painscastle
130. Aberd: ★Fyvie
131.   Newburgh
132. Fife: Newburgh
133. Lanarkshire: Crawford
134. Wigtown: Wigtown

F. 14th C

135. Cornwall: Kilkhampton

136.   Michell
137. Durh: Sedgefield
138. Kent: Elham
139.   Goudhurst
140.   Headcorn
141.   Ightham
142.   Lenham
143.   Marden
144.   Minster-in-Thanet
145.   Richborough
146.   Smarden
147.   Wrotham
148.   Yalding
149. Lancashire: Garstang
150. Norfolk: Cley-next-the-sea
151. Shropshire: Clun
152. Somerset: Montacute
153.   Stogursey
154.   Stowey
155. Suffolk: Ixworth
156.   Storrington
157. Warwickshire: Brinklow
158. Westmorland: Kirkby Stephen
159. Yorkshire: Seamer
160.   Middleham
161.   Pateley Bridge
162. Carmarthenshire: Abergwili
163.   St. Clears
164. Flint: Hope
165. Argyle: Tarbert
166. Dumfries: Sanquhar
167. Kincard: Inverbervie

G. 15th C

168. Leicestershire: Billesdon
169. Norfolk: East Harding
170. Argyll: Kilmun
171. Ayr: Newmilns
172. Banffshire: Fordyce
173. Dumfries: Torthorwald
174. Lanarkshire: Carnwath
175.   Douglas
176.   Strathaven
177. Moray: Kinloss
178. Perth. Abernethy

GROUP 2: LONG-LIVED CENTRAL PLACES
(*Fig. 77*)

Towns on sites continuously or nearly continuously occupied since before the Norman Conquest.

R – Roman   S – Saxon   N – not now urban

The figures give the population pressure in persons per hectare in 1981 (HMSO 1981).

1. City of London	21.5	R
2. Southwark (G.L.)	73.5	S
3. Bath (Avon)	27.8	R
4. Bristol (Avon)	35.4	S
5. Bedford (Bed)	30.5	S
6. Reading (Berks)	33.6	S
7. Aylesbury (Bucks)	33.1	S
8. Buckingham (Bucks)	3.1	S
9. Newport Pagnell (Bucks)	7.8	S
10. Cambridge (Camb)	22.2	R
11. Ely (Camb)	1.7	S
12. Huntingdon and Godmanchester (Camb)	6.1	R
13. Peterborough (Camb) (incl. Newton)	26.0	S
14. Chester (Ches)	30.9	R
15. Bodmin (Corn)	9.1	S
16. Carlisle (Cumb)	29.0	R
17. Bakewell (Derbys)	3.2	S
18. Derby (Derbys)	27.6	S
19. Barnstaple (Dev)	20.8	S
20. Exeter (Dev)	21.8	R
21. Totnes (Dev)	9.8	S
22. Bridport (Dors)	22.2	S
23. Christchurch (Dors)	17.1	S
24. Dorchester (Dors)	20.8	R
25. Shaftesbury (Dors)	11.4	S
26. Wareham (Dors)	16.1	S
27. Wimborne Minster (Dors)	20.9	S
28. Chester le Street (Durh)	19.1	R
29. Durham (Durh)	14.3	S
30. Chelmsford (Ess)	30.1	R
31. Colchester (Ess)	16.9	R
32. Maldon (Ess)	7.8	S
33. Gloucester (Glouc)	6.9	R
34. Southampton (Hants)	4.8	S
35. Winchester (Hants)	19.4	R
36. Droitwich (H/W)	21.8	R
37. Hereford (H/W)	23.4	S
38. Leominster (H/W)	2.6	S
39. Worcester (H/W)	30.0	R
40. St. Albans (Herts)	24.5	R
41. Ashwell (Herts)	N	S
42. Hertford (Herts)	13.6	S
43. Bridlington (Humbers)	12.7	S
44. Canterbury (Kent)	17.7	R
45. Dover (Kent)	21.6	R
46. New Romney (Kent)	7.4	S
47. Rochester (Kent)	31.5	R
48. Sandwich (Kent)	4.9	S
49. Lancaster (Lancs)	22.4	R
50. Leicester (Leics)	38.1	R
51. Caistor (Lincs)	N	R
52. Gainsborough (Lincs)	7.3	R
53. Grantham (Lincs)	19.2	S
54. Lincoln (Lincs)	21.5	R
55. Louth (Lincs)	11.7	S
56. Stamford (Lincs)	20.8	S
57. Torksey (Lincs)	N	S
58. Manchester (Met Dist)	38.7	R
59. Great Yarmouth (Norf)	31.9	S
60. Norwich (Norfolk)	31.4	S
61. Thetford (Norf)	6.8	S
62. Northampton (North)	26.4	S
63. Oundle (North)	3.6	S
64. Towcester (North)	N	R
65. Hexham (Northumb)	4.0	S
66. Nottingham (Notts)	36.5	S
67. Abingdon (Ox)	32.0	S
68. Oxford (Ox)	27.7	S
69. Wallingford (Ox)	20.5	S
70. Shrewsbury (Shrops)	15.7	S
71. Whitchurch (Shrops)	N	R
72. Axbridge (Som)	N	S
73. Bruton (Som)	N	S
74. Crewkerne (Som)	10.2	S
75. Frome (Som)	30.1	S
76. Ilchester (Som)	N	S
77. Langport (Som)	N	S
78. Milborne Port (Som)	N	S
79. Somerton (Som)	N	S
80. Taunton (Som)	33.0	S
81. Watchet (Som)	15.3	S
82. Yeovil (Som)	28.3	S
83. Stafford (Staffs)	27.0	S
84. Tamworth (Staffs)	20.8	S
85. Bury St Edmunds (Suff)	19.5	S
86. Ipswich (Suff)	29.9	S
87. Sudbury (Suff)	13.3	S
88. Guildford (Surr)	19.1	S
89. Lewes (E. Suss)	17.1	S
90. Chichester (W. Suss)	20.8	R
91. Steyning (W. Suss)	N	S
92. Newcastle on Tyne (T/W)	42.9	R
93. Alcester (Warks)	N	R
94. Warwick (Warks)	10.7	S
95. Bradford on Avon (Wilts)	10.1	S
96. Chippenham (Wilts)	26.0	S
97. Calne (Wilts)	19.9	S
98. Cricklade (Wilts)	N	S
99. Malmesbury (Wilts)	27.4	S
100. Warminster (Wilts)	6.6	S
101. Wilton (Wilts)	3.7	S
102. York (N. Yorks)	33.9	R
103. Doncaster (S. Yorks)	24.1	R
104. Carmarthen (Dyfed)	5.9	R
105. Neath (W. Glam)	15.1	R
106. Abergavenny (Gwent)	9.7	R
107. Caerleon (Gwent)	5.7	R
108. Usk (Gwent)	7.2	R
109. Caernarvon (Gwynedd)	10.6	R

Scotland (12th C foundations)

110. Jedburgh	125. Inverurie
111. Peebles	126. Kintore
112. Stirling	127. Inverness
113. Annan	128. Edinburgh
114. Dumfries	129. Haddington
115. St. Andrew's	130. Linlithgow
116. Crail	131. Glasgow
117. Dunfermline	132. Renfrew
118. Inverkeithing	133. Rutherglen
119. Kinghorn	134. Arbroath
120. Aberdeen	135. Brechin
121. Banff	136. Dundee
122. Cullen	137. Forfar
123. Elgin	138. Montrose
124. Torres	139. Perth

Abbreviations

Ant. J.	*The Antiquaries Journal* (Journal of the Society of Antiquaries of London)
Arch. J.	*Archaeological Journal* (Journal of the Royal Archaeological Institute)
AY	The Archaeology of York (York Archaeological Trust)
BAR Brit.	British Archaeological Reports, British Series
BAR Int.	British Archaeological Reports, International Series
Brit.	*Britannia*
CA	*Current Archaeology*
CBA	Council for British Archaeology
EM	Early medieval (fifth to eleventh centuries AD)
FA	*The Field Archaeologist* (Journal of the Institute of Field Archaeologists)
IFA	The Institute of Field Archaeologists
IA	Iron Age (eighth to first centuries BC)
J. Arch. Sci.	*Journal of Archaeological Science*
JBAA	*Journal of the British Archaeological Association*
JRS	*Journal of Roman Studies*
LA	*The London Archaeologist*
M	Medieval (eleventh to sixteenth centuries AD)
Med. Arch.	*Medieval Archaeology* (Journal of the Society of Medieval Archaeology)
ND	No date of publication given
RARET	*Recent Archaeological Research in English Towns* ed. J. Scholfield and D. Palliser (CBA, 1981)
RN	*Rescue News* (Journal of Rescue, A Trust for British Archaeology)
TLMAS	Transactions of the London and Middlesex Archaeological Society

Bibliographical gazetteer

TOPICS

Anglo-Saxon buildings
Addyman 1972a, 1972b; Addyman and Leigh 1973; Hope-Taylor 1962, 1977; Radford 1957a; Carver 1986

Anglo-Saxon industry
Jope 1964; Loyn 1961; Macgregor 1978, 1984; Radley 1971; Wilson 1976

Anglo-Saxon towns
Biddle 1974b; Biddle 1975c; Biddle 1976a; Biddle and Hill 1971; Brooks 1971; Cam 1963; Chadwick 1905; Davison 1968; Freke 1977; Haslam 1984; Hassall and Hill 1970; Hill 1981; Loyn 1962, 1971; Radford 1970, 1973b, 1978; Tait 1936; Vince 1985; Whitelock 1952

Environmental archaeology in towns
Brothwell 1982; Hall and Kenward 1982; Kenward 1978; Kenward *et al.* 1978; Olsen 1982

General Development of towns
Alexander 1972; Barley 1982; Bruel 1975; Duby 1980; Everitt 1973; Hassall 1977; Hilton 1978; Hodges 1982; Morris 1979; Roberts 1981; Robson 1979

Medieval churches
Rodwell 1983, 1984; Baker, N.J. 1980

Medieval industry
Crossley 1981; Salzman 1923; Unwin 1904; Wymer 1949

Medieval towns
Beresford and Hirst 1971; Keene 1982; Platt 1976; Platt 1978; Salusbury-Jones 1975; Salzman 1923, 1967

Methods in site evaluation
Biddle and Hudson 1973; Biek 1958, 1978, 1979; Carver 1978, 1980, 1983b; Hall 1978; Mason 1976; Meeson 1979, Renimel (Boussuet 1980)

Methods of analysing animal remains
Armitage 1982; Coy 1982; Jones A.K.G. 1982a, 1982b; Maltby 1979; Rackham 1982; Ryder 1969; Schmid 1972

Methods of analysing human remains
Brothwell 1972; Dawes and Magilton 1980; McWhirr 1982

Methods of analysing insect remains
Jones A.K.G. 1982a; Kenward 1978, 1982; Kenward and Williams 1979

Methods of analysing plant remains
Green 1982; Grieg 1981, 1982; Keepax 1977; Morgan 1982: Willcox 1977

Methods of building reconstruction
Drury 1982; Innocent 1906; Salzman 1976

Methods of documentary survey
Barley 1974; Beresford 1973; Biddle 1975b; Dyos 1968; Hill 1969; Martin and McIntyre 1972; Rogers and Rowley 1974; Whitelock 1955

Methods of excavation
Barker 1969; Barker 1977; FA 1, 2 and 3; Fasham 1984

Methods of stratigraphic analysis
Carver 1979a, 1979b, 1980, 1983a, 1983c; Crummy and Terry 1979; Durham 1977; Harris 1979; Rathje 1974, 1979

Post-Roman continuity
Barley and Hanson 1968; Biddle 1968; Frere 1966; Gould 1972; Hope-Taylor 1977; Jones A.H.M. 1966; Jones G.D.B. 1974; Rahtz 1970; Rahtz and Fowler 1972; Rodwell 1984

Romano-British buildings
Blagg 1983; Collingwood and Richmond 1969; Ward 1911; Heighway and Parker 1982

Romano-British industry
Strong and Brown 1976; Duby 1980; Wacher 1966, 1975

Romano-British towns
Collingwood and Richmond 1969; Corder 1955; Esmonde Cleary 1979; Frere 1966, 1967, 1975; Hobley 1983; Hodder and Hassall 1971; Hodder and Millet 1980; Maloney and Hobley 1983; Millet 1975; Rivet 1964, 1966; Rodwell and Rowley 1975; Somner 1984; Todd 1970; Wacher 1966, 1975

Shipping and waterfronts
Milne and Hobley 1981

Strategy and methods of archaeological survey
Aldsworth and Freke 1976 (Sussex); Astill 1985 (Small towns); Beresford and St Joseph 1958; Biddle 1968; Biddle 1974a; Carter 1978; Carver 1980, 1981b, 1983b; Clack and Gosling 1976 (the north); Clack and Haselgrove 1981; DUA 1975 (London); Grimes 1968 (London); Hassall 1974 (Oxford); Hawkes 1982 (Kent); Heighway 1972; Hughes 1976 (Hampshire); Jope 1956

(Oxford); Leach 1981 (the north); *Norwich Survey* 1980; O'Connell 1977 (Surrey); Rahtz 1974; RCHM 1960, 1972; Raper 1972 (Pompeii); Rodwell 1975 (Oxfordshire); Sheppard 1980 (Cornwall); Tatton-Brown 1982 (Kent); Wainwright 1978; Wade 1978; Ward 1968

Town planning and spatial organisation
Barley 1974; Beresford 1967; Biddle 1975c; Biddle and Hill 1971; Colvin 1958; Crummy 1979, 1982; Keene 1975; 1979; Raper 1972; Rodwell 1984; Walthew 1978

TOWNS

ABINGDON, Oxon.
Archaeology at: Rodwell 1975. *Roman settlement:* Rodwell and Rowley 1975. *Seventh-century abbey* and *EM settlement:* RARET. *Abbey:* Biddle, Lambrick and Myres 1968

ALCHESTER, Oxon.
Archaeology at: Rodwell 1975. *Roman settlement:* Rodwell and Rowley 1975. *Roman drainage operations:* RARET. *Roman tablet-weaving:* Strong and Brown 1976, 73

ANDOVER, Hants.
Archaeology at: Champion 1973

AYLESBURY, Bucks.
EM settlement: Farley 1974

BATH, Avon.
Roman settlement at: Cunliffe 1969; Rodwell and Rowley 1975. *Roman spring:* Cunliffe 1980. *EM defences:* O'Leary 1981

BEDFORD, Beds.
Archaeology at: RARET; Baker 1972, 1974, 1979; Baker and Hassall 1974. *EM settlement, English burh and Danish burh:* Baker 1979. *Economic decline in fourteenth to fifteenth centuries:* Baker 1979, 295. *M Castle.* RARET; Hassall, 1977. *Houses:* Baker 1979, 256, 294. *Lime-kilns* Baker 1979, fig. 30 *Baking and brewing:* Baker 1979, 127-36. *Fishmonger (?):* Baker 1979, 287. *Craftsmen and farmers:* Baker 1979, 288. *Pottery imports:* Baker 1979, 179

BEVERLEY, Yorks.
EM collegiate buildings: RARET; *M bridge:* RARET

BIRMINGHAM, W. Mids.
M moated site: Watts 1977

BITTERNE, Hants.
Stone robbing: Platt and Coleman-Smith 1975 (I), 24

BOLSOVER, Derbys.
M castle and settlement: RARET

BOURNE, Lincs.
EM and M settlements: RARET. *M pottery industry:* RARET

BRAINTREE, Herts.
IA, Roman, EM, M settlements: RARET. *Roman settlement and houses:* RARET

BRANCASTER, Norfolk
Roman settlement: RARET; Somner 1984, fig. 3

BRISTOL, Avon.
EM settlement: Ponsford 1981. *M defences:* RARET; Hassall 1977. *Bridge:* RARET. *Waterfront and dock.* RARET. *Houses and tenements:* RARET. *Halls of the Templars (?):* RARET. *Greyfriars:* RARET; *Med. Arch.* 18 (1974) 190. *Industries (cloth, iron, bronze, bone-working):* RARET. *Pottery, exports and imports:* RARET

BROUGH-ON-HUMBER, Yorks.
Roman defences: Frere 1975, 14

BUCKINGHAM, Bucks.
EM burh: RARET

BURY ST EDMUNDS, Suffolk
Town plan; Smith 1951

BUXTON, Derbys.
Roman and post-medieval spa: RARET. *Arnemetia's spring:* RARET

CANTERBURY, Kent
IA, Roman and EM settlements: RARET; Wacher 1975, 178-95; CAT 1982; Tatton-Brown 1982; Frere 1962b. *IA road:* RARET. *Roman crenellation:* CA 62 (1978) 78-83. *Baths:* RARET. *Temple:* RARET. *Theatre:* Frere 1970. *Double-burial:* RARET. *Pottery kilns:* RARET; Wacher 1975, 19. *Baker's shop:* Wacher 1975, 192. *EM exploitation:* Tatton-Brown 1982; Hawkes 1982, 75. *Cellars:* RARET; Tatton-Brown 1982, 83; *Med. Arch.* 24 (1980) 227, Plate XIIB; *Med. Arch.* 25 (1981) 172. *M defences:* Hassall 1977. *Poor Priests Hospital:* RARET. *St Augustine's Abbey:* Saunders 1978. *Church and cemetery of St Mary Breidin:* RARET. *Almonry Chapel at Christchurch:* RARET. *Unit founded:* Tatton-Brown 1982, 79

CARLISLE, Cumbria
Archaeology at: McCarthy 1980, 1981. *Roman settlement:* RARET. *Neolithic agriculture under:* CA 68 (1979), 272. *Roman gate:* McCarthy 1980, 8. *Roman vicus at Old Carlisle:* Rodwell and Rowley 1975; Somner 1984. *Roman wheel:* Brit. 13 (1982), Plate III

CHELMSFORD, Essex
Archaeology at: RARET; Rodwell and Rowley 1975. *Topography:* CA 41 (1974) 69. *IA agriculture under:* RARET. *Roman and twelfth-century settlements:* RARET. *Roman mansion, temple, religious precinct, houses:* RARET; Rodwell and Rowley 1975

CHESTER, Ches.
IA, Roman and Saxon settlements: RARET; Webster 1951. *Site evaluation:* Mason 1976. *Rubbish disposal:* Mason 1976. *Topography:* Milne and Hobley 1981, 106. *Roman principia:* Hassall 1977. *EM 'Chester ware':* Webster 1951. *Street frontage:* RARET. *M tannery, M pottery imports:* RARET. *The Rows:* Lawson and Smith 1958

CHESTERFIELD, Derbys.
Archaeology at: RARET. *M first-floor hall:* RARET

CHICHESTER, Hants.
Archaeology at: Down and Rule 1971, 1974. *IA settlement*

and Roman town: RARET. *IA palace and garden:* Cunliffe 1971. *Gravel foundation to planned Roman town: Brit.* 11 (1980) 397; Frere 1975, 14. *Late Roman iron-working:* RARET. *Roman extra-mural cemetery and church of S. Pancras:* Biddle, pers. comm. M *houses, bell-founding, pottery industry:* RARET. M *syphilis:* Brothwell 1982, 128

CHRISTCHURCH, Hants.
EM *settlement and late Saxon burh:* CA 58 (1977), 343; Jarvis 1981

CIRENCESTER, Glos.
Archaeology at: McWhirr 1976. *Bagendon:* Wacher 1975, 30. *Roman diversion of R. Churn:* Frere 1975, 12. *Roman road with ruts:* McWhirr 1982, fig. 4. *Late Roman cemetery: Sunday Times* 28.11.82; McWhirr 1982. *Roman farm in insula xii:* RARET; *Roman interval tower, townhouses:* Hassall 1977. *Roman town unencumbered until 1971:* CA 29 (1971). M *Hospital:* Hassall 1977; *Med. Arch.* 21 (1977), 223-24

COLCHESTER, Essex
IA *settlement:* RARET. *Roman defences:* RARET. *Roman barracks, theatre, temple complex at Gosbecks:* Frere 1975, 9. *Roman pottery industry, cemetery, martyrium:* RARET. *Roman glass manufacture:* Strong and Brown 1976, 116. *Roman legionary fortress and colonia:* Crummy 1977. *Roman imported dates:* Crummy 1977. *Sub-Roman huts:* Hassall 1977. *Clearance and robbing of Roman town:* Crummy 1981. *Saxon town planning:* Crummy 1977, 1979a. *Temple of Claudius and Norman Castle:* Crummy 1981, 47. M *houses, pottery industries:* RARET: *Med. Arch.* 17 (1973) 168. *Roman hare: Brit.* 11 (1980), Plate XXVII

COLYTON, Lincs.
Shrunken medieval settlement: RARET

COVENTRY, W. Mids.
M *tenements, houses, metal-working and cultivation:* RARET

CRICKLEWADE, Wilts.
Roman and EM *settlements:* RARET. *Late Saxon defences:* Radford 1973

DERBY, Derby
EM *settlement:* RARET

DONCASTER, S. Yorks.
Roman, EM *and Norman defences:* RARET

DORCHESTER-ON-THAMES, Oxon.
Archaeology at: Rodwell 1975. *Roman settlement at* Rodwell and Rowley 1975. *Roman cemetery:* Hassall 1977. *Sub-Roman huts:* Hassall 1977; Frere 1962a. *Early Saxon settlements:* Rowley 1974

DORCHESTER, Dorset
Roman public baths, defences, street sequences, houses, ovens, smithy: RARET. *Roman rubbish disposal:* RARET. *Roman aqueduct:* Frere 1975, 11. *Roman Christian church and pagan temple at Maiden Castle:* Wheeler 1943. *Roman Christian cemetery at Poundbury:* Frere 1975, 11

DOVER, Kent
Rescue work at: CA 38 (1973); CA (1976). *Roman fort:* CA 38 (1973). *Painted house:* Hassall 1977; CA 57 (1976)

DROITWICH, Her. and Wor.
IA, *Roman and* M *salt works:* RARET; Freezer ND. *Roman villa and post-Roman mansion:* RARET

DUNSTABLE, Som.
Archaeology at: RARET. *Roman and* M *settlements:* RARET. *Dominican Friars:* RARET

DURHAM, Co. Durham
Archaeology at: Clack and Gosling 1976. EM *settlement:* Carver 1981c. *Saxo-Norman tenements, boundary fences, midden heaps, houses, leather-working, fish:* Carver 1979b. *Burials of* EM *Bishops:* Carver 1981c. M *river wall:* Carver 1974. *Demolition of* M *walls:* Jones W.T. 1923

EXETER, Devon
Roman, EM *and* M *settlements:* RARET. *Roman defences, basilica:* RARET. *Roman town-house:* Frere 1975, 12. *Roman baths:* CA 39 (1973). EM *cemetery, church, belltower:* RARET EM *dry-stone houses:* Hassall 1977. M *Cathedral, Church of St Edmund on Exe bridge:* RARET. *Roman,* EM, M *animal exploitation and husbandry:* Maltby 1979. M *aqueducts: Med. Arch.* 28 (1984) 213-15

FARNHAM, Surrey
Roman market town (?): Millett 1975. *Roman pottery:* RARET. M *settlement:* RARET

GLASTONBURY, Som.
EM *and* M *monastic town:* RARET; Radford 1955, 1957, 1961, 1968

GODMANCHESTER, Cambs.
Roman settlement: Rodwell and Rowley 1975. *Roman temple:* Hassall 1977. M *blacksmith:* Crossley 1981, fig. 25

GLOUCESTER, Glos.
Archaeology at: RARET. *Field Unit:* RARET. *Roman legionary fortress and colonia:* Hassall 1977. *Roman barracks, forum, equestrian statue, courtyard house:* Frere 1975, 9. EM *town:* Heighway 1984. EM *minster at St Oswald's, bell-founding:* Heighway 1980. EM *houses:* Heighway *et al.* 1979. *Water-front:* Heighway and Garrod 1981. *Roman tilery:* Heighway and Parker 1982

GRANTHAM, Lincs.
Franciscan Friary: Hassall 1977

GREAT DUNMOW, Essex
Roman settlement: Rodwell and Rowley 1975; RARET

GREAT YARMOUTH, Nor.
M *fisherman's houses, fishing industry, imported pottery and querns:* RARET

GREENWICH, Outer London
M *manor house sewage system:* Dixon 1971

GUILDFORD, Surrey
Dominican Friary: Alexander and Poulton 1979

HALIFAX, W. Yorks.
Peoples' park: Doe 1974, 65

HAMWIH *see* Southampton

HARWICH, Essex
 M *waterfront:* RARET

HEMEL HEMPSTEAD, Herts.
 Roman stepped swimming pool: CA 1 (1967) 9

HEREFORD, Her. and Wor
 Archaeology at: RARET. EM *defences:* Rahtz 1968; Shoesmith 1982. EM *town planning:* Shoesmith 1982, 88. EM *cemetery of Cathedral Green:* Shoesmith 1980. EM *corduroy causeway:* Shoesmith 1982. EM *suburb south of R. Wye:* Radford 1978, 149. EM *mortar-mixers (?):* Shoesmith 1982, 100. EM *imported pottery:* Shoesmith 1982. M *grape-cultivation: Shoesmith 1982, 104.* M *smithing, bell-founding, button-making, stake-ringed oven, butchery, saw-pit, imported pottery:* Shoesmith 1982, 58, 100, 101, 234. *Disposal of castle mound:* Shoesmith 1982, 60

HEYBRIDGE, Essex
 Roman settlement and Saxon huts: Drury and Wickender 1982

HORNCASTLE, Lincs.
 Roman and EM *settlements:* RARET

ILCHESTER, Som.
 Archaeology at: Leach 1982. *Roman settlement:* Leach 1982; Frere 1975, 11. *Roman houses:* RARET. *Man and dog buried together:* CA 50 (1975) 83

IPSWICH, Suffolk
 Archaeology at: Wade 1978; RARET. EM *settlement:* Wade 1978. *Imported pottery and glass:* RARET. EM *herring industry:* Jones A.K.G., 1982b. 84. EM *skating accident:* Wade 1981, 130

KELVEDON, Essex
 Roman settlement: Rodwell and Rowley 1975. *Roman mansion, water supply, pottery industry, metal and bone-working:* RARET

KINGS LYNN, Nor.
 Archaeology at: Clarke and Carter 1981. M *waterfront tenements:* Clarke and Carter 1981. M *timber wharf:* CA 1 (1967) 13. M *tenement boundaries: Med. Arch.* 9 (1965) 196; *Med. Arch.* 11 (1967) 294. *Tenements divided:* Clarke and Carter 1981

KINGSTON-UPON-HULL, Humbers.
 M *defences:* Hassall 1977. M *tile manufacture:* Salzman 1923, 180.

LAMBETH, Inner London
 Early settlement at: Imber 1979

LEATHERHEAD, Surrey
 M *settlement, declined:* RARET

LEICESTER, Leics.
 Archaeology at: RARET. *Roman town:* Wacher 1975. *Roman graffiti:* JRS 54 (1964) 182. M *Austin Friary:* Mellor

LICHFIELD, Staffs.
 Archaeology at: Carver 1982a; Bassett 1982. EM *and twelfth-century settlement:* Carver 1982a; Bassett 1982.

Post-Roman structures by cathedral: Carver 1982b. *Early Christianity at:* Gould 1972. M *water supply:* Gould 1976

LINCOLN, Lincs.
 Roman, EM *and* M *settlements:* RARET. *Roman town:* Wacher 1975. *Roman new town:* Wacher 1975, 21. *Colonia defences:* Hassall 1977. *Fourth-century gate:* Hassall 1977. *Roman gate at Newport:* CA 26 (1971). *Roman fountain:* Thompson 1956. *Sub-Roman huts:* Hassall 1977. *Roman and* EM *buildings:* RARET; Perring 1981. EM *copper, glass, bone, antler, lead-working:* RARET; Mann 1982; *Roman ? and* EM *church at St Paul-in-the-Bail:* RARET; Gilmour 1979; *with fourth-century burials:* Biddle pers. comm. EM *church at St Mark's Wigford:* RARET. EM *pottery industry:* RARET. EM *Syrian and Chinese imports:* RARET; Adams 1979; EM *pottery exported to Birka:* Biddle, pers. comm. M *buildings:* RARET. *Undated wharves:* RARET

LONDON
 Archaeology at, 1947-62: Grimes 1965. *Archaeology at, 1962-73:* Biddle and Hudson 1973; DUA 1975, Scholfield, and Dyson 1980. *London Unit founded:* CA 41 (1974) 164. *Roman,* EM *and* M *settlement:* RARET. *Site evaluation:* Grimes 1968. 4; Biddle and Hudson 1973; Milne and Hobley 1981. *Roman defences:* RARET; Maloney and Hobley 1983. *The London Stone:* Marsden 1975, 65. *Roman provincial governor's palace:* Marsden 1975; CA 8 (1968), 215; Frere 1975, 13. *Roman basilica and forum:* CA 8 (1968) 215; CA 59 (1977) 370. *Roman triumphal arch:* Blaggs 1983. *Roman baths at Huggin Hill and Cheapside:* Marsden 1976. *Roman timber water-storage tank:* Marsden 1976, fig. 16. *Roman town bridge:* Milne 1982. *Roman town house with baths:* Frere 1975, 9. *Roman shops at Fenchurch Street:* RARET. *Roman pottery industry:* Marsh and Tyers 1976. *Roman gold-working:* Marsden 1975. *Roman baker:* Wacher 1966, 79. *Roman seed-grain imported from Mediterranean:* RARET. *Roman exotic plants:* Wilcox 1977; Scholfield and Dyson 1980. *Roman ship with building-stone from Kent:* Frere 1975, 13. *Roman ship with cargo of Samian:* Marsden 1981, 10. *Roman ships working from London:* Marsden 1981. 11. *Silver canister from east Mediterranean:* Grimes 1968, 115. *Roman imports from Germany and east Mediterranean:* Marsden 1981. 10. *Roman mithraeum:* Grimes 1968. EM *settlement:* RARET. *Viking London:* Wheeler 1927. *Saxon London:* Wheeler 1935. *Post-Roman stake-holes at* GPO *site:* Scholfield and Dyson 1980, 37. *Middle-Saxon settlement by the Strand:* Biddle 1984; Vince 1984. *Offa's palace at Cripplegate:* Scholfield and Dyson 1980. *Eighth-century wharf at New Fresh Wharf:* Hassall 1977. EM *church and cemetery at St Brides:* Grimes 1968, 182. EM *church at St Martin-in-the-Fields:* Biddle, pers. comm. EM *church at St Alban's, Cripplegate:* Grimes 1968. *Saxon cellared building in Milk Street:* Scholfield and Dyson 1980. 38; *Med. Arch.* 22 (1978), plate XXIIB. *Late Saxon house at* GPO *site:* LA 2.15 (1976), 400; Scholfield and Dyson 1980, 39. EM *ships:* Marsden 1981. *Tenth-century imports:* RARET. M *settlement:* RARET. M *castle (Baynards): Med. Arch.* 17 (1973), 164; Scholfield and Dyson 1980, 56. M *preferred pottery:* Milne and Milne 1982. M *imported pottery:* RARET; Milne and Milne 1982. M *imported cattle:*

Armitage 1982. *Walking turkeys:* Sutcliffe 1978, 8. *Meat supply:* Armitage 1982, 96. M *ships:* McGrail 1981. M *waterfront tenements:* Schofield 1981. *River front reclamation:* Milne 1981. M *horn-glazed lanthorns:* Armitage 1982, 102. M *pregnant girl:* CA 65 (1979), 1976–79. M *church and cemetery at St Nicholas Shambles:* RARET. The *London waterfront:* CA 45 (1974, 304; Milne and Hobley 1981; Milne 1981; Schofield 1981; Milne and Milne 1978

LYDFORD, Devon
EM *and* M *settlement and castle:* Addyman and Saunders, forthcoming

MALDON, Essex
EM *settlement and late Saxon burh:* RARET. M *port: RN* 16.3 (1978)

MANCHESTER
Roman fort at Deansgate, metalled road, iron smelting and smithing: Jones, G.D.B. 1974; EM *exploitation:* Jones G.D.B. 1974, 165–71 (Bu'lock 1974)

MILTON KEYNES, Bucks.
Archaeology at: Mynard 1984. *Unit founded:* CA 71 (1980), 375. M *settlements:* CA 71 (980), 375

NEWBURY, Berks.
M *houses, smithing, weaving and imported pottery:* RARET

NEWCASTLE-UPON-TYNE, Tyne and Wear
Archaeology at: Clack and Gosling 1976. M *town rubbish tip:* Harbottle and Ellison 1981. M *imports:* Harbottle and Ellison 1981, 98. M. *human bone in rubbish tip:* Harbottle and Ellison 1981. M *Blackfriars:* Harbottle 1977

NEWENDEN, Kent
Late Saxon settlement (?): Davison 1972. M *marshbound castle:* RARET

NORTHAMPTON, Northants.
Archaeology at: RARET; Williams and Bamford 1979. *Unit founded:* Williams 1979. *Prehistoric, Roman* EM *and* M *settlements:* RARET; Williams 1982; Williams and Bamford 1979. EM *halls at St Peter Street:* Williams et al 1985. EM *mortar-mixers:* RARET; Williams 1979. EM *iron, copper and silver-working:* RARET. M *tanning:* Williams 1982. M *malt-roasting ovens:* CA 46 (1975), 348. M *decline:* Williams 1982, 31. *Sixteenth-century town tip:* Williams 1979, 225

NORTH ELMHAM, Nor.
EM *planned settlement:* Wade–Martins 1980

NORWICH, Nor.
Archaeology at: Jope 1952a; Norwich Survey 1980; Carter 1978. RAI *meeting at:* Proc. Arch. Inst. (1847) 69–98. *Unit founded:* CA 48 (1975), 8. EM *and* M *settlements:* RARET; Carter 1978. EM *settlements:* Carter 1984. EM *church and cemetery below Bailey:* RARET. EM *pottery industry:* RARET. EM/M *church of St Benedits:* RARET. M *houses:* CA 48 (1975), 8–15. M *cess-pits:* CA 68 (1979). M *bronze and horn working, iron-extraction:* RARET. M *imports:* RARET. M *worn teeth:* RARET. *Sixteenth-century*

assemblage from Pottergate: CA 48 (1975), 8–15. *Documents and standing buildings:* CA 48 (1975)

NOTTINGHAM, Notts.
Archaeology at: RARET. IA, *Roman,* EM *(Saxon and Danish), and* M *settlements:* RARET; Barley and Straw 1969. EM *defences:* RARET. EM *hall:* Biddle, pers. comm. EM *buildings:* RARET. EM/M *grain drying and malting:* RARET. *The Nottingham Caves:* CA 59 (1977), 358, 366; CA 69 (1979), 300. *Open space:* RARET. M *town wall:* Barley 1955. M *bronze and horn working:* RARET

OXFORD, Oxon.
Archaeology at: Hassall 1972, 1974, 1975; Benson 1966; Rodwell 1975. *Roman pottery dryer and kiln:* Hassall 1972, 8. EM *building under All Saints:* Hassall 1975, plate III. EM *building in Castle Bailey:* Hassall 1973, 284, 1976. EM *pits under castle:* Jope 1952b. EM *causeway across Thames:* Durham 1977, 176–80. EM *charcoal burials at St Frideswides:* RARET. EM *church at All Saints:* RARET. EM *hinterland:* Jope 1956. M *street sequence:* Hassall 1971b, 9; CA 24 (1971), 27. M *double defensive wall:* RARET. M *castle well:* Hassall 1971a, 8. M *culvert under Greyfriars:* Hassall 1970, plate III. M *building at St Aldates:* CA 24 (1971), 25. *Greyfriars:* RARET. *Blackfriars:* RARET

PETERBOROUGH, Cambs.
Archaeology lost at: RARET

PLYMOUTH, Devon
M *quay: Med. Arch.* 13 (1969), 263–4; Milne and Hobley 1981, 144. M *imports:* RARET

POOLE, Dorset
Archaeology at: RARET. *Seventh-century oysterage:* RARET. *Twelfth-century settlement:* RARET. M *quay:* Milne and Hobley 1981, 145

PORCHESTER, Hants.
Archaeology at: Cunliffe 1966, 1967, 1970, 1972. *Roman,* EM *and* M *settlement:* Cunliffe, *ibid. Well, first- to seventh-century AD:* CA 30 (1971), 191

RECULVER, Kent
EM *trading station:* Tatton-Brown, 1982

REIGATE, Surrey
EM *settlement, Norman castle, medieval town:* RARET

RAMSBURY, Wilts.
EM *iron working:* Haslam 1980

ROMSEY, Hants.
Roman iron working: RARET. EM *church and cemetery:* RARET

ST ALBANS, Herts.
Archaeology at: Frere 1960, 1964a, 1964b, 1983. IA/*Roman continuity:* Frere 1975, 1983, 16. *Roman town:* Wacher 1975. *Roman shops:* Frere 1975. *Roman sewer:* Frere 1975, 16. *Roman water-pipe in Insula XXXVII/2:* Frere 1975, 16. EM *sequence at cathedral:* Biddle, pers. comm.

ST IVES, Cornwall
Archaeology at: Sheppard 1980, 8

SAFFRON WALDEN, Essex
Archaeology at: Basset, 1982

SANDWICH, Kent
EM trading station: Tatton-Brown 1982. *Carmelite Priory:*
Hassall 1977

SHEFFIELD, S. Yorks.
Archaeology at: RARET

SHREWSBURY, Shrops.
Archaeology at: Carver 1978. *Unit founded and disbanded:*
Carver and Wills 1974; RARET. *EM settlement:* Carver
1978, 1983a. *EM cemeteries and charcoal burials:* Carver
1978; 1983a. *M tenements:* RARET. *M town houses:* Carver
1983a; Baker 1983. *M pottery preferences:* Carver 1983a.
M earth-fast floor-joists: Baker 1983

SILCHESTER, Hants.
Roman town: Wacher 1975. *Roman shops, silver-working,*
smithing and carpentry: Strong and Brown 1976, 12, 146.
IA settlement at, medieval use of amphitheatre: Fulford 1985

SOUTH CADBURY, Som.
Saxon defences: Radford 1978, 147; Alcock 1972

SPALDING, Lincs.
Roman settlement and post-Roman flooding: RARET

SOUTHAMPTON, Hants.
Archaeology at: Addyman and Hill 1968, 1969; SARC
1975; Holdsworth, 1976. *Roman, EM and M settlements:*
RARET. *EM town and ports:* Biddle 1975b, 450. *EM trading*
station: Hodges 1981, 93. *EM defensive ditch:* RARET. *EM*
street: SARC 1975; RARET. *EM tanning:* RARET. *EM imported*
pottery: Hodges 1981. *EM game animals:* Coy 1982, 110.
M quarrying for Roman tile: Platt and Coleman-Smith I
1975, 24. *M houses:* Platt and Coleman-Smith I 1975:
24-32. *Devon slate used in twelfth century:* Platt and
Coleman-Smith I 1975. *Richard of Southwick's pit:* Platt
and Coleman-Smith I 1975, 293. *M butchery and meat:*
Platt and Coleman-Smith I 1975, 32. *M furrier (?) at*
Cuckoo-Lane: see Richard of Southwick's pit. *M bone-*
working at Winkle street: Platt and Coleman-Smith I
1975, 24. *Distribution of classes in sixteenth century:* Platt
and Coleman-Smith I 1975, 20

SOUTHWARK, Inner London
Archaeology at: RARET. *Roman settlement and drainage*
operations: RARET. *Roman houses, bronze, iron and leather*
working: RARET. *Roman brushwood water channel:* LA 2. 11
(1975), 287. *Dark earth at:* Brothwell 1982, 127. *M metal-*
working: RARET. *Sixteenth- to seventeenth-century tanning*
and bone (dice) manufacture: RARET

STAINES, Surrey
Roman, EM and M settlement: RARET. *Roman pottery*
industry: RARET. *M brewing and fulling:* RARET

STAFFORD, Staffs.
Archaeology at: Carver 1981a. *EM and M settlements:*
Carver 1981a, forthcoming. *EM pottery, bread*
manufacture, butchery: Carver 1981a. *EM rubbish tip:*
Carver 1981a

STAMFORD, Lincs.
Archaeology at: RARET. *EM (Anglian, Viking and late*
Saxon) settlements: Mahany 1969; Mahany et 1982.
Danish defended area: Radford 1978. *EM pottery*
manufacture and iron-working: Mahany 1969; Mahany et
al 1982. *M cellar, garderobe, malting kiln, chemistry:* RARET;
Mahany et al 1982. *Norman quarry pits:* Mahany et al
1982. *Castle:* Hassall 1977.
M buildings: Rogers 1970. *EM (Saxon) enclosure and M*
castle: Med. Arch. 21 (1977), 235-7

STEYNING, W. Sussex
EM settlement: RARET

STRATFORD-UPON-AVON, Warks.
Roman, EM and M settlements: RARET

SUTTON COLDFIELD, W. Mids.
Prehistoric, Roman and M settlement, peat deposits: RARET

TAMWORTH, Staffs.
Archaeology at: RARET; Rahtz 1977; Meeson 1979. *EM*
and M settlements: Rahtz 1977; Meeson 1979. *EM defences:*
Radford 1978, 144; Gould 1967, 1968. *EM mill:* CA 29
(1971), 166; Rahtz and Sheridan 1971; Crossley 1981;
(date) CA 72 (1981) 62. *EM houses:* RARET. *EM palace:*
RARET. *EM imported querns:* RARET. *M town:* Meeson 1979

TAUNTON, Som.
Archaeology at: Leach 1984. *EM and M settlements:* Leach
1984. *Priory barn:* Leach 1984

TEWKESBURY, Glos.
Archaeology at: RARET. *Implications report:* Miles and
Fowler 1972; CA 32 (1972), 252

THETFORD, Nor.
Archaeolgy at: Dunmore and Carr 1976. *EM burh:* Barley
1964; Davison 1967; Dunmore and Carr 1976. *EM*
pottery industry: RARET

TORKSEY, Lincs.
EM (Danish, Saxon) and M settlements: RARET. *EM pottery*
industry: RARET

TOWCESTER, Northants.
Late Roman road: RARET

TRURO, Cornwall
Archaeology at: Sheppard 1980, 25

WALLINGFORD, Oxon.
Archaeology at: RARET. *Implications report:* Simpson
1973. *EM defences:* Durham 1973. *Castle:* Brooks 1965.
Cob building in castle bailey: RARET

WALTHAM ABBEY, Essex
Archaeology at: RARET. *Roman, EM (Saxon, Viking) and M*
settlements: RARET

WAREHAM, Dorset
Prehistoric and EM settlements: RARET; Hinton and
Hodges 1977. *EM burh and defences:* RARET; Hinton and
Hodges 1977; RCHM 1959; Radford 1970

WARWICK, Warks.
Neolithic, EM and M settlements: RARET

WELLS, Som.
  Archaeology at: RARET. *EM town plan:* RARET. *EM and M minsters:* Rodwell 1980. *M water system:* RARET. *Roman mausoleum, EM and M chapels: Med. Arch.* 25 (1981), 177

WEYMOUTH, Dorset
  M port and land reclamation: RARET

WHITCHURCH, Shrops.
  Roman mutton-curing: Jones, G.B.D. 1975, 101–6

WIMBORNE, Dorset
  EM Monastery and M town: RARET

WINCHCOMBE, Glos.
  EM royal burial place: Bassett 1985

WINCHELSEA, E. Sussex
  Thirteenth-century planned town: RARET; Freke 1977. *M gardens:* RARET. *M cellar:* Freke *et al.* 1977. *M house:* RARET. *M imported roof slates:* RARET. *Buried harbour:* Morris 1979, Fig. 4. 46

WINCHESTER, Hants.
  Archaeology at: RARET; Cunliffe 1964; Biddle, 1964, 1965, 1966, 1967, 1969a, 1969b, 1970, 1972, 1975a; Hassall 1977. *Archaeological Institute meeting: Proc. Arch. Inst.* 1 (1845), XL. *Research Unit set up: CA* 9 (1968), 221. *Prehistoric, Roman, EM and M settlements:* RARET. *Roman-Saxon street sequence at Southgate:* Biddle 1975a; Frere 1975, 14. *Roman bone-working at Crowder Terrace:* RARET. *Roman shops on Mildenhall Road:* RARET. *Roman cemetery at Lankhills:* RARET; Clarke 1979. *Post-Roman continued use of Roman cemeteries:* Frere 1975, 15. *Middle-Saxon estates and late Saxon burh:* Biddle 1975b, 451–8. *Late Saxon streets:* Biddle 1975b, 450. *Saxon building under St Mary in Tanner Street:* Hassall 1977, 11. *EM (late Saxon) planned town:* Biddle and Hill 1971. *EM pottery industry:* RARET; Biddle and Barclay 1974. *Prediction of EM Old Minster:* Quirk 1957, 1961. *EM Old Minster:* Biddle and Quirk 1962; Biddle 1964, 1965, 1966, 1967, 1969, 1970. *EM church at St Mary in Tanner Street:* Biddle 1969a. *M dye house and cloth-finishing: CA 6 (1968), 159. M metal-working: CA 6 (1968), 159. Norman charnel pit at Minster: CA* (1970), 248. *EM/M street sequences:* Keene 1982, 28. *EM/M street sequences:* Keene 1982, 28. *EM/M hinterland:* Biddle 1975b, 451; 1975c.

WORCESTER, Her. and Wor.
  Archaeology at: RARET; Barker 1969; Carver 1980. *Site Evaluation:* Carver 1980. *Roman metalled road at Sidbury:* Carvery 1980. *Roman causeways:* RARET. *Roman iron-smelting:* Barker 1969. *EM pits:* Carver 1980. *Norman castle:* Carver 1980. *M tenements:* Carver 1980. *M latrines:* Carver 1980; Greig 1981. *M grape cultivation:* Greig 1981

WROXETER, Shrops.
  Roman manufacture of glass and bronze repoussée work: Stong and Brown, 1976, 116, 39. *Late Roman, post-Roman settlement on basilica:* Barker 1971, 1973; Frere 1975, 17. *Planning method: CA* 39 (1973), 116. *Roman settlement:* Wacher 1975

YORK, N. Yorks.
  Archaeology at: Addyman 1973, 1974, 1981; Andrews 1984. *Settlement at:* RARET; Hall 1978. *Roman defences:* RARET. *Roman interval tower:* Sumpter and Coll 1977. *Roman/M multangular tower:* Hall 1978, 32. *Roman riverside roads at Skeldergate:* RARET. *Roman waterfront crane:* RCHM 1960, 64. *Roman sewers in Church street:* Buckland 1976, Whitwell 1976. *Roman timber-lined wells at Skeldergate:* RARET; Carver *et al.* 1978. *Roman houses:* RARET. *Roman use of peat fuel:* RARET. *Roman pottery preferences:* RARET. *Roman counterfeit coining:* RARET. *Anglian fish-processing plant:* Kenward 1978, 64. *Roman granary:* Kenward and Williams 1979. *Roman principia building:* Hassall 1977. *Roman houses:* RARET. *Post-Roman flooding/silting:* Hall 1978. *Anglian tower rediscovered: CA* 17 (1969), 162–7; *Med. Arch.* 16 (1972) 167. *Roman buildings surviving in ninth century:* Hassall 1977. *Roman/EM sequence, EM (Anglian and Viking) houses and pavements:* RARET. *Under York Minster:* Hope-Taylor 1971. *EM absence of pottery:* RARET. *EM tanning, leather-working, cobbling, bone-, antler-, jet-working, spinning, weaving:* RARET; Radley 1971, Dolley 1978; Macgregor 1978, 1984. *EM bone skates:* Macgregor 1978, 1984. *EM imported cowrie shell from Red Sea, silk, counterfeit dirhams from Samarkand, Scandinavian amber and whetstones, pottery:* RARET; Macgregor 1978. *Imported mulberry:* Brothwell 1982, 128. *EM bean storage, chickens, shellfish, walnut:* Kenward 1978, 61–64. *EM beehive at Coppergate: CA* 58 (1977). *EM churches at St Mary's Castlegate and All Saints pavement:* RARET. *EM/M church and cemetery at St Helen-on-the-Walls:* Magilton 1980; Dawes 1980. *EM shoes and clothes:* Macgregor 1978. *EM Irish moneyer:* Dolley 1978. *EM (Frisian) comb and boot:* Macgregor 1978, 37. *EM robbing of Roman stone:* Carver *et al.* 1978. *M houses:* RARET; *CA* 58 (1977). *M ladder:* RARET. *M tiled baking hearths: CA* 58 (1977). *M folding candlestick:* Crossley 1981, fig. 64. *M bell-founding, pewter and pottery manufacture:* RARET; Macgregor 1978. *M Carmelite Church of St Mary in the Horsefair:* RARET. *Franciscan Friary:* RARET. *College of Vicars Choral at the Bedern:* RARET. *M syphilis:* Brothwell 1982, 128. *Seal of Snarr the Toll Collector:* Macgregor 1978. *Norman desertion:* Hall 1978. *M tenement width:* Hall 1978. *Post-medieval horticulture:* RARET. *Post-medieval parchment at Walmgate:* RARET. *Environment of York:* Kenward *et al.* 1978. *Rubbish disposal in York:* RARET. *Topographic infilling:* Kenward *et al.* 1978, 68. *Death of Jeffry Radley: CA* 26 (1971), 58. *For Coppergate Excavations see now R.A. Hall The Viking Dig* (London, 1984).

Sources

Adams, L. 1979 'Early Islamic pottery from Flaxengate, Lincoln', *Med. Arch.* 23: 218-19

Addyman, P.V. 1972a 'The Anglo-Saxon house: a new review', *Anglo-Saxon England* 1: 273-307

— 1972b 'Anglo-Saxon houses at Chalton, Hampshire', *Med. Arch.* 16: 13-31

1973 *Rescue archaeology in York* (Middlesborough Teeside Museums and Art Galleries Service. Fourth Elgee Memorial Lecture)

— 1974 'York' in Rahtz: 153-63

— 1981 'The York Archaeological Trust's recent excavations in York: The means and the end' in P. Clack and S. Haselgrove. *Approaches to the Urban Past:* 29-36

Addyman, P.V. and Black, V.E. 1984 *Archaeological Papers from York presented to M.W. Barley* (York Archaeological Trust)

Addyman, P.V. and Hill, D. 1968 'Saxon Southampton: a review of the evidence. Part I: History, location, date and character of the town', *Proceedings of the Hampshire Field Club*, xxvi: 61-93

— 1969 'Saxon Southampton: a review of the evidence. Part II: Industry, trade and everyday life', *Proceedings of the Hampshire Field Club* xxvii, 61-69

Addyman, P.V. and Leigh, D. 1973 'The Anglo-Saxon village at Chalton, Hampshire: second interim report', *Med. Arch* 17: 1-25

Addyman, P.V. and Saunders, A.D. forthcoming *Lydford, Devon: castle, fort and town* (Royal Archaeological Institute Monograph)

Alcock, L. 1972 *By South Cadbury is Far Camelot: the Excavation of Cadbury Castle 1966-70* (London)

Aldsworth, F. and Freke, D. 1976 *Historic towns in Sussex: an archaeological survey* (London)

Alexander, J.A. 1972 'The beginnings of urban life in Europe', *Man, Settlement and Urbanism* (eds. P.J. Ucko, R. Tringham and G.W. Dimbleby), London: 843-50

Alexander, M. and Poulton, R. 1979 *Guildford Dominican Friary: recent excavations* (Guildford Museum)

Andrews, G. 1984 'Archaeology in York: an assessment' in Addyman and Black: 173-208

Armitage, P.L. 1982 'Studies on the remains of domestic livestock from Roman, medieval and early Modern London: objects and methods' in Hall and Kenward: 94-106

Astill, G.G. 1985 'Archaeology and the smaller medieval town' *Urban History Yearbook:* 46-53

Baker, D. *et al.* 1970 'Excavations in St. John's St, Bedford' *Bed. Arch. Jnl* 5: 67-100

Baker, D 1972 'Bedford Castle'; some preliminary results from rescue excavation', *Chateau Gaillard* 6: 15-22

Baker, D.B. and Hassall, J.M. 1974 'Bedford: Aspects of Town Origins and Development', *Bed. Arch. Jnl.* 9: 75-94

Baker, D.B. *et al.* 1974 'Excavations in the area of Mill St, Bedford, 1971', *Bed. Arch. Jnl.* 9: 99-128

Baker, D.B. *et. al.* 1979 'Excavations in Bedford, 1967-1977', *Bed. Arch. Jnl.* 13

Baker, N.J. 1980 'Churches, parishes and medieval topography' in Carver 1980: 31-38

Baker, N.J. 1983 'Excavation at Riggs Hall, Shrewsbury' in Carver 1983

Barker, P.A. 1961 'Excavations on the Town Wall at Roushill Shrewsbury *Med. Arch.* 5: 181-210

— 1969-9 'The origins of Worcester: and interim survey', *Transactions of the Worcestershire Archaeological Society*, 3rd series, 2: 1-116

— 1969 'Some aspects of the excavation of timber buildings', *World Archaeology* 1: 220-33

— 1971 *Excavations on the site of the Baths basilica at Wroxeter 1966-1971* (Birmingham)

— 1973 *Excavations on the site of the Baths basilica at Wroxeter (Viroconium Cornoviorum) 1966-1973. An interim report.* (Birmingham)

— 1977 *Techniques of Archaeological Excavation* (London)

Barley, M.W. 1955 'Nottingham Town Wall: Park Row Excavations, 1964' *Transactions of the Thoroton Society* 69: 50-65

— 1964 'The medieval borough of Torksey: excavations 1960-2', *Ant. J.* 44: 165-87

— 1974 *A guide to British Topographical Collections*

— (ed.) 1976 *The Plans and Topography of Medieval Towns in England and Wales* (CBA Res. Rep. 14)

— (ed.) 1982 *European Towns: their Archaeology and early History*, (London)

Barley, M.W. and Hanson, R.P.C. (ed.) 1968 *Christianity in Britain 300-700* (Leicester)

Barley, M.W. and Straw, I.F. 1969 'Nottingham', *Historic Towns*, ed. M.D. Lobel, (London and Oxford)

Bassett, S.R. 1982a 'Medieval Lichfield: a topographical review' *Trans. S. Staffs Arch. and Hist. Soc.* 22: 93-121

— 1982b *Saffron Waldon: Excavations and Research* (Saffron Walden) (CBA Res. Rep. 45)

— 1985 'A probable Mercian royal Mausoleum at Winchcombe, Gloucestershire', *Ant. J.* 65: 82-100

Benson, D. 1966 *City of Oxford Redevelopment: archaeological implications*

Beresford, M. 1967 *New Towns of the Middle Ages* (London)

— 1973 *English medieval boroughs: a handlist* (Newton Abbot)

Beresford, M. and Hurst, J.G. (eds.) 1971 *Deserted Medieval Villages* (London)

Beresford, M. and St. Joseph, J.K.S. 1958 *Medieval England: an aerial survey* (Cambridge)

Biddle, M. 1964 'Excavations at Winchester 1963' *Ant. J.* 44: 188-219

— 1965 'Excavations at Winchester 1962-3. Third interim report', *Ant. J.* 45: 230-64

— 1966 'Excavations at Winchester 1965', *Ant. J.* 46: 308-32

— 1967 'Excavations at Winchester, 1966' *Ant. J.* 47: 251-79

— 1968 'Archaeology and the history of British towns', *Antiquity* 109-16

— 1969a *Excavations near Winchester Cathedral 1961-8* (Winchester)

— 1969b 'Excavations at Winchester, 1968. Seventh interim report' *Ant. J.* 49: 295-329

— 1970 'Excavations at Winchester 1969. Eighth interim report', *Ant. J.* 50: 277-326

— 1972 'Excavations at Winchester 1970. Ninth interim report', *Ant. J.* 52: 93-131

— 1973 'Winchester: the development of an early capital', *Vor-und Frühformen der europaischen Stadt im Mittelalter* (ed. H. Jankun, W. Schlesinger and H. Steur), Göttingen (Abhandlungen der Wissenschaften: Philologisch-Historische Klasse, 3 Folge, Nr. 83): 229-61

— 1974a 'The future of the Urban past' in Rahtz: 95-112

— 1974b 'The development of the Anglo-Saxon town', *Settimane di studio del centro italiano degli studi sull'alto medioevo 21: Topografia urbana e vita cittadina*: 203-31

— 1975a 'Excavations at Winchester 1971. Tenth and final interim', *Ant. J.* 55: 96-126, 395-337

— (ed.) 1975b F. Barlow, M. Biddle, O von Feilitzen and D.J. Keene, *Winchester in the Early Middle Ages. An edition and discussion of the Winton Domesday* (Oxford)

— 1975c 'Hampshire and the origins of Wessex' in G. de Sieveking (ed.) *Problems in Social and Economic Archaeology* (London

— 1976 'Towns' in Wilson D.M. (ed.) 99-150

— 1984 'London on the Strand' *Popular Archaeology* 6.1: 23-27

Biddle, M. and Barclay, K. 1974 'Winchester Ware' in *Medieval pottery from excavations; studies presented to Gerald Clough Dunning* (ed. V.I. Evison *et al.*) London: 137-66

Biddle, M. and Hill, D. 1971 'Late Saxon planned towns', *Ant. J.* 51: 70-85

Biddle, M. and Hudson, D.M. 1973 *The future of London's Past*, Worcester

Biddle, M., Lambrick, H.T. and Myers, J.N.L. 1968 'The early history of Abingdon, Berkshire, and its abbey', *Med. Arch.* 12: 26-69

Biddle, M. and Quirk, R.N. 1962 'Excavations near Winchester Cathedral 1961', *Arch. J.* 119: 150-94

Biek, L. 1958 Notes on preservation in 'Excavations at the South Corner Tower of the Roman Fortress at York, 1956' *Yorkshire Archaeological Journal* 39: 515-38 (appndx.)

— 1978 'A note of preservation' in *Excavations at Little Waltham, 1970-71* (P.J. Drury). CBA Res. Rep. 26: 8-10

— 1979 'A note on preservation' in 'Excavations at 1 Westgate St, Gloucester, 1975' (C.M. Heighway, A.P. Garrod and A.G. Vince) *Med. Arch.* 23: 205-10

Blagg, T.F.C. 1983 'The re-use of monumental masonry in late Roman defensive walls' in Maloney and Hobley: 130-35

Bossuet, G. 1980 *La reconnaissance archéologique des milieux urbains par les méthodes de prospection géophysique:*

L'example de la Charité-sur-Loire. (Memoire de Diplôme de'études Supérieures, Université de Paris I)

Brinklow, D.A. 1978 The environment of Anglo-Scandinavian York' in Hall, R.A. (ed.): 58-70

Brooks, N.P. 1965 'Excavations at Wallingford Castle, 1965: an interim report', *Berkshire Archaeological Journal* 62: 17-21

— 1971 'The development of military obligations in eighth and ninth century England', *England before the conquest: Studies in primary sources presented to Dorothy Whitelock* (ed. P. Clemoes and K. Hughes), Cambridge, 69-84

Brothwell, D. 1972 'Palaeodemography and earlier British populations', *World Archaeology* 4: 75-87

— 1982 'Linking urban man with his urban environment' in Hall and Kenward: 126-29

Bruel, C. 1975 *Palatium und Civitas: studien zur profantopographie spätantiker civitates vom 3 bis zum 13 Jahrhundert Band I: Gallien*

Bu'lock, J.D. 1974 'The problem of post-Roman Manchester' in Jones G.D.B.: 165-71

Buckland, P.C. 1976 'The Environmental Evidence from the Church Street Roman Sewer System', *AY 14/1*

Burnham, B.C. and Kingsbury, J. (eds) 1979 *Space, Hierarchy and Society*, BAR Int. 59 (Oxford)

Cam, H.M. 1963 'The origin of the borough of Cambridge: a consideration of Professor Carl Stephenson's theories', *Liberties and communities in medieval England*, 1-18 (London)

Canterbury Archaeological Trust 1982 *Topographical Maps of Canterbury AD 400, 1050, 1200, 1500 and 1700* (Canterbury)

Carter, A. 1978 'Sampling in a medieval town: the study of Norwich' in Cherry *et al.*: 263-77

— 1983 'The Anglo-Saxon origins of Norwich: the problems and approaches; *Anglo-Saxon England* 7: 175-204

Carter, H. 1976 'The Town in its setting: the geographical approach' in Barley: 7-18

Carver, M.O.H. 1974 'Excavations in New Elvet, Durham City 1961-1973', *Archaeologia Aeliana* 5S 2: 91-148

— 1978 'Early Shrewsbury: an archaeological definition in 1975' *Trans. Shrops. Arch. Soc.* 59: 225-263

— 1979a 'Notes on some general principles for the analysis of excavated data', *Science and Archaeology* 21: 3-14

— 1979b 'Three Saxo-Norman tenements in Durham City', *Med. Arch.* 23: 3-14

— (ed.) 1980 *Medieval Worcester: an archaeological framework*, TWAS 7

— 1981a *Underneath Stafford Town* (Stafford)

— 1981b 'Sampling Towns: an optimistic strategy' in P. Clack and S. Haselgrove (eds.) *Approaches to the Urban Past* (Durham University) 69-92

— 1981c 'Early Medieval Durham: the archaeological evidence' in *Art and Architecture at Durham Cathedral* (BAA)

— 1982a 'The Archaeology of Early Lichfield: an inventory and some recent results', *Trans. S. Staffs. Arch and Hist. Soc.* 22: 1-12

— 1982b 'Excavations South of Lichfield Cathedral, 1976-77', *Trans. S. Staffs. Arch. and Hist. Soc.* 22: 35-69

— 1983a *Two Town Houses in Medieval Shrewsbury*, (*Trans. Shropshire Arch. Soc.* 61)

— 1983b 'Forty French Towns: an essay on archaeological site evaluation and historical aims' *Oxford Journal of Archaeology* 2.3: 339-78

— 1983c 'Theory and Practice in Urban Pottery Seriation', *J. Arch. Sci.* 12: 353-66

— 1986 'Contemporary artefacts illustrated in late Saxon manuscripts', *Archaeologia* 108: 117-45

— (ed.) forthcoming *Early Medieval Stafford*

Carver, M.O.H., Donoghay, S. and Sumpter, A.B. 'Riverside structures and a well in Skeldergate and Buildings in Bishophill', *The Archaeology of York* 4/1

Carver, M.O.H. and Wills, J. 1974 *Shrewsbury; the buried past* (Shrewsbury)

Chadwick, H.M. 1905 *Studies on Anglo-Saxon Institutions* (Cambridge)

Champion, S. 1973 *Andover: the archaeological implications of development*

Cherry, J.F., Gamble, C. and Shennan, S. 1978 *Sampling in Contemporary British Archaeology* (BAR Brit. 50, Oxford)

Clack, P. and Gosling, P.F. (eds.) 1976 *Archaeology in the North* (Durham)

Clark, G. 1979 *Pre-Roman and Roman Winchester Part 2: The Roman Cemetery at Lankhills* (Winchester Studies 3, Oxford)

Clarke, H. and Carter, A. 1977 *Excavations in King's Lynn 1963-1970* (London)

Clifton-Taylor, A. 1972 *The Pattern of English Building* (London)

Collingwood, R.G. and Richmond, I. 1969 *The Archaeology of Roman Britain* (London)

Colvin, H.M. 1958 'Domestic architecture and town-planning', *Medieval England* (ed. A.L. Poole) 3/-97 (Oxford)

Conzen, M.R.G. 1960 *Alnwick, Northumberland: a study in town plan analysis* (Institute of British Geographers)

— 1968 'The use of town plans' in Dyos: 113-30

Corder, P. 1955 'The reorganization of the defences of Romano-British towns in the fourth century', *Arch. J.* 112: 20-43

Coy, J. 1982 'The role of wild vertebrate fauna in urban economies in Wessex' in Hall and Kenward: 107-16

Crossley, D.W. (ed.) 1981 *Medieval Industry* (CBA Research Report 40)

Crummy, P. 1971 'Excavations in Colchester 1964-8', *Trans. Essex Arch. Soc.* 3: 1-130

— 1977 'Colchester, the Roman fortress and the development of the Colonia', *Brit.* 8: 65-105

— 1979 'The system of measurement used in town planning, from the ninth to the thirteenth century', *Anglo-Saxon Studies in Archaeology and History 1* (BAR): 243-83

— 1981 'Aspects of Anglo-Saxon and Norman Colchester', *Archaeology of Colchester* (CBA Res. Rep. 39)

Crummy, P. 1982 'The origins of some major Romano-British towns'; *Brit.* 13: 125-34

Crummy, P. and Terry, R. 1979 'Seriation problems in urban archaeology' in Miller, M. (ed.) *Pottery and the Archaeologist* (London)

Cunliffe, B. 1964 *Winchester excavations, 1960-1963*, I (Winchester)

— 1966 'Excavations at Porchester castle, 1963-5', *Ant. J* 46: 39-49

— 1967 'Excavations at Porchester castle, 1963-5', *Ant. J.* 46: 39-49

— 1969 *Roman Bath*

— 1970 'The Saxon Culture sequence at Porchester castle', *Ant. J.* 50: 67-85

— 1971 *Fishbourne: A Roman Palace and its Garden* (London)

— 1972 'Excavations at Porchester castle, Hants., 1969-1971', *Ant. J.* 52: 70-83

— 1980 'The excavation of the Roman Spring at Bath, 1979', *Ant. J.* 60: 187-206

— 1975-7 *Excavations at Portchester Castle I-II* (Society of Antiquaries Res. Reps. 32-34)

Davison, B.K. 1967 'The late Saxon town of Thetford: and interim report on the 1964-1966 excavations', *Med. Arch.* 13: 189-208

— 1968 'Excavations at Sulgrave, Northamptonshire, 1968', *Arch. J.* 125: 305-7

— 1972 'The Burghal Hidage fort of Eorpeburnam: a suggested identification', *Med. Arch.* 16: 123-27

Dawes, J.D. and Magilton, J.R. 1980 'The cemetery of St Helen-on-the-Walls, Aldwark', AY 12/1

Department of Urban Archaeology 1975 *Archaeological Programme 1974-5* (Annual Report No. 1)

Dixon, P. 1971 'Greenwich Palace Excavations 1970' LA 1.10: 219

Doe, V. 1974 'Late urban landscapes' in Rogers and Rowley: 63-74

Dolley, M. 1978 'The Anglo-Danish and Anglo-Norse coinages of York' in Hall, R.A.: 26-31

Dornier, A. (ed.) 1977 *Mercian Studies* (Leicester)

Down, A. and Rule, M. 1971 *Chichester Excavations Vol. 1*

— 1974 *Chichester Excavations Vol. 2*

Drury, P.J. and Wickenden N.P. 'An early Saxon settlement within the Romano-British small town at Heybridge, Essex', *Med. Arch* 26: 1-40

Drury, P.J. (ed.) 1982 *Structural Reconstruction: Approaches to the Interpretation of the excavated remains of buildings* (BAR 110)

Duby, G. (ed.) 1980 *L'histoire de la France Urbaine* I, II (Paris)

Dunmore, S. and Carr, R. 1976 'The Late Saxon town of Thetford; and archaeological and historical survey' *E. Anglian Archaeology* 4

Durham, B. 1977 'Archaeological investigations in St Aldates, Oxford', *Oxoniensia* 42: 82-203

Durham, B. *et al.* 1973 'A cutting across the Saxon defences at Wallinford, Berkshire 1971', *Oxoniensia* 37: 82-85

Dyos, H.J. (ed.) 1968 *The Study of Urban History*

Esmonde Cleary, A.S. 1979 *Towns and Urbanisation in Roman Britain: the evidence from outside the defences* (unpub. D. Phil. Oxford)

Everitt, A. 1973 *Perspectives in English Urban History*

Farley, M.E. 1974 'Saxon and medieval Walton, Aylesbury, Buckinghamshire' *Records of Bucks.* 20.2: 1-292

Sources

Fasham P.J. 1984 'Groundwater Pumping Techniques for Excavation', *IFA Technical Paper no. 1*

Faull, M.L. (ed.) 1984 *Studies in late Saxon settlement* (Oxford)

Fox, A. 1968 'Excavations at the South Gate, Exeter 1964–5', *Proceedings of the Devon Archaeological Society* 26: 1–20

Freezer, D.F. ND *From Saltings to Spa Town* (Droitwich)

Freke, D.J. 1977 'The origins of Sussex Towns', *Bulletin of the Institute of Archaeology of London* 14: 23–25

Freke, D.J., Martin, D. and Rudling, D. 1977 'Excavations in Winchelsea 1976' *ibid.*: 34–38

Frere, S.S. 1960 'Excavations at Verulamium, 1959. Fifth interim report', *Ant. J.* 40: 1–24

— 1962a 'Excavations at Dorchester on Thames, 1962', *Arch J.* 119: 114–49

— 1962b *Roman Canterbury, the city of Durovernum*, 3rd edn. Canterbury

— 1964a 'Verulamium – then and now', *Bulletin of the Institute of Archaeology*, 4: 61–82

— 1964b 'Verulamium, three Roman cities', *Antiquity*, 38: 103–12

— 1966 'The end of towns in Roman Britain', *The civitas capitals of Roman Britain* (ed. J.S. Wacher) 87–100 (Leicester)

— 1967 Britannia (London)

— 1970 'The Roman theatre at Canterbury', *Brit.* I: 83–113

— 1975 'The Cities of Roman Britain 1960–1974' *Comité International pour L'étude des cités antiques: Lettre d'information III* (Strasbourg) 7–34

— 1983 Verulamium Excavations II (Soc. of Ant. Res. Rep. 41)

Fulford, M. 1985 'Excavations on the sites of the amphitheatre and forum-basilica at Silchester, Hampshire: an interim report' *Ant. J.* 65: 39–81

Gilmour, B. 1979 'The Anglo-Saxon church at St Paul-in-the-Bail, Lincoln', *Med. Arch.* 23: 214–18

Gould, J. 1967 'First report on excavations at Tamworth, Staffs., 1968: The Saxon defences', *Transactions of the Lichfield and South Staffordshire Archaeological and Historical Society* 9: 17–29

— 1968 'Third report on excavations at Tamworth, Staffs., 1968: The western entrance to the Saxon borough', *Transactions of the Lichfield and South Staffordshire Archaeological and Historical Society* 10: 32–43

— 1972 'Letocetum, Christianity and Lichfield (Staffs.)', *Transactions of the South Staffordshire Archaeological and Historical Society* 14: 30–1

— 1976 'The 12th C. Water Supply to Lichfield Close' *Ant. J.* 56: 73–79

Green, F.J. 1982 'Problems of interpreting differentially preserved plant remains from excavations of medieval urban sites' in Hall and Kenward: 40–46

Greig, J.R.A. 1981 'The investigation of a medieval barrel-latrine from Worcester' *J. Arch. Sci.* 8: 265–82)

— 1982 'The interpretation of pollen spectra from urban archaeological deposits' in Hall and Kenward 47–65

Grew, F. and Hobley, B. 1985 *Roman urban topography in Britain and the Western Empire* (CBA Res. Rep. 59)

Grimes, W.F. 1968 *The Excavation of Roman and Medieval London* (London)

Hall, R.A. 1978 'Topography of Anglo-Scandinavian York' in Hall, R.A. (ed.): 31–36

— (ed.) 1978 *Viking Age York and the North* (CBA Res. Rep. 27)

Hall, R.A. and Kenward, H.K. (eds.) 1982 *Environmental Archaeology in the Urban Context* (CBA Res. Rep. No. 43)

Harbottle, B. and Ellison, M. 1981 'An excavation in the Castle Ditch, Newcastle-on-Tyne 1974–6' *Arch. Aeliana* 5s 9: 75–250

Harris, E.C. 1979 *Principles of Archaeological Stratigraphy* (London)

Haslam, J. 1980 'A middle-saxon iron-smelting site at Ramsbury, Wiltshire' 24: 1–68

— (ed.) 1984 *Anglo-Saxon Towns in Southern England* (Chichester)

Hassal, J.M. and Hill, D. 1970 'Pont L'arche: Frankish influence on the west Saxon burh?' *Arch. J.* 127: 188–95

Hassall, T.G. 1970 'Excavations at Oxford, 1969', *Oxoniensia* 35: 5–18

— 1971a *Oxford Castle* (guide)

— 1971b 'Excavations at Oxford 1970. Third interim report', *Oxoniensia* 36: 1–14

— 1972 *Oxford: the city beneath your feet* (Oxford)

— 1973 'Excavations in Oxford 1972. Fifth interim report' *Oxoniensia* 38: 268–98

— 1974 'Urban surveys: Medieval Oxford' in Rogers and Rowley: 49–62

— 1975 'Excavations at Oxford 1973–74. Sixth and final interim report', *Oxoniensia* 39: 53–61

— 1976 'Excavations at Oxford Castle 1965–73', *Oxoniensia* 41: 232–308

— 1977 'Urban archaeology in England, 1975' in Barley: 3–18

Hawkes, S.C. 1982 'Anglo-Saxon Kent c.425–725' in P.E. Leach (ed.) *Archaeology in Kent to AD 1500* (CBA Res. Rep No. 48): 64–78

Heighway, C.M. (ed.) 1972 *The Erosion of History* (CBA)

— 1980 'Excavations at Gloucester: fifth interim report, St Oswald's Priory'

— 1984 'Anglo-Saxon Gloucester to AD 1000' in Faull: 35–54

Heighway, C.M., Garrod, P. and Vince, A.G. 1979 'Excavations at 1 Westgate St Gloucester, 1975' *Med. Arch.* 23: 159–213

Heighway, C.M. and Garrod, A.G. 1981 'Gloucester' in Milne and Hobley

Heighway, C.M. and Parker, A.J. 1982: 'The Roman tilery at St Oswald's Priory, Gloucester' *Brit.* 13: 25–77

Hill, D.H. 1969 'The burghal hidage: the establishment of a text', *Med. Arch.* 13: 84–92

— 1981 *An Atlas of Anglo-Saxon England* (Oxford)

Hilton, R. (ed.) 1978 *The Transition from Feudalism to Capitalism* (London)

Hinton, D.A. and Hodges, R. 1977 'Excavations in Wareham 1974–5', *Proc. Dorset NHAS* 99: 42–83

Hobley, B. 1983 'Roman urban defences: a review of research in Britain' in Maloney and Hobley: 78–84

Hodder, I.R. 1972 'Locational models and the study of Romano-British settlement', *Models in Archaeology* (ed. D.L. Clarke) 887–909 (London)

Hodder, I.R. and Hassall, M.W.C. 1971 'The nonrandom spacing of Romano-British walled towns, *Man* 6: 391-407

Hodder, I.R. and Millett, M. 1980 'Romano-British villas and Towns: a systematic analysis' *World Archaeology* 12: 69-76

Hodges, R. 1981 *The Hamwih pottery: the local and imported wares from 30 years excavations at Middle Saxon Southampton and their European context* (CBA Res. Rep 37)

— 1982 *Dark Age Economics* (London)

Holdsworth P. 1976 'Saxon Southampton: a new review' *Med. Arch.* 20: 26-61

Hope-Taylor, B. 1962 'The "Boat-shaped" house in Northern Europe', *Proceedings of the Cambridge Antiquarian Society* 55: 16-22

— 1971 *Under York Minster. Archaeological discoveries 1966-1971* (York)

— 1977 *Yeavering: an Anglo-British Centre of Early Northumbria* (London)

Hughes, M. 1976 *The Small Towns of Hampshire: the archaeological and historical implications of development* (Hampshire Archaeological Committee)

Hunter, J. 1847 'Hints on the nature, purpose, and resources of Topography', *Proc. Arch. Inst.* : 69-98

Imber, D. 1979 *Lambeth lost and found* (Southwark)

Innocent, D.F. 1906 *The development of English building construction* (Cambridge)

Jarvis, K. 1981 'Excavations in Christchurch 1969-77', *Dorset Nat. Hist. and Arch. Soc.*

Jones, A.H.M. 1966 *The Decline of the Ancient World* (London)

Jones, A.K.G. 1982a 'Human parasite remains: prospects for a quantitative approach' in Hall and Kenward: 66-70

— 1982b 'Bulk-sieving and the recovery of fish remains from urban archaeological sites' in Hall and Kenward: 79-85

Jones, D.M. 1980 *Excavations at Billingsgate buildings Triangle Lower Thames Street 1974* (TLMAS Special Paper No. 4)

Jones, G.D.B. 1974 *Roman Manchester* (Manchester)

Jones, G.D.B. and Webster, P.V. 1968 'Mediolanum: Excavations at Whitchurch 1965-6', *Arch. J.*: 193-252

Jones, W.T. 1923 'The Walls and Towers of Durham', *Durham University Journal* 23: 527

Jope, E.M. 1952a 'Excavations in the City of Norwich, 1948', *Norfolk Archaeology* 30: 287-323

— 1952b 'Late Saxon pits under Oxford castle mound: excavations in 1952', *Oxoniensia*, 22: 77-111

— 1956 'Saxon Oxford and its region', Dark-Age Britain, *Studies Presented to E.T. Leeds* (ed. D.B. Harden), London, 234-58

— 1964 'The Saxon building stone industry in southern and midland England', *Med. Arch.* 8: 91-118

Keene, D.J. 1975 'Suburban growth', *The evolution of towns* (ed. M.W. Barley) (CBA)

— 1979 'Medieval Winchester: its spatial organisation' in Burnham and Kingsbury: 149-59

— 1982 'Rubbish in medieval towns' in Hall and Kenward: 26-30

Keepax, C. 1977 'Contamination of archaeological deposits by seeds of modern origins, with particular

reference to the use of flotation' *J. Arch. Sci* 4: 221-29

— 1978a 'The analysis of archaeological insect assemblages: a new approach', *AY 19/1*

— 1982 'Insect communities and death assemblages, past and present' in Hall and Kenward: 71-78

Kenward, H.K. and Williams, D. 1979 Biological evidence from the Roman wharehouse in Coney Street, *AY*: 14/2

Kenward, H.K., Williams, D., Spencer, P.J., Greig, J.R.A., Rackham, D.J. and Brinklow, D.A. 1978 The environment of Anglo-Scandinavian York' in Hall, R.A. (ed.): 58-70

Lawson, P.J. and Smith, J.T. 1958 'The rows of Chester: two interpretations' *J. Chester North Wales Arch. Soc.* 45: 1-42

Leach, P.J. 1982 *Ilchester I: Excavations 1974-75* (Western Archaeological Trust)

— 1984 *The Archaeology of Taunton* (Western Archaeological Trust)

Leech, R. 1981 'Medieval urban archaeology in the North West, problems and response' in P. Clack and S. Haselgrove *Approaches to the Urban Past:* 55-64

Lobel, M.D. (ed.) 1969 *Historic Towns: maps and plans of towns and cities in the British Isles I*

Loyn, H.R. 1961 'Boroughs and mints AD 900-1066', *Anglo-Saxon Coins* (ed. R.H.M. Dolley), 122-35 (London)

— 1962 *Anglo-Saxon England and the Norman Conquest* (London)

— 1971 'Towns in late Anglo-Saxon England: the evidence and some possible lines of enquiry', *England before the conquest: Studies in primary sources presented to Dorothy Whitelock* (ed. P. Clemoes and K. Hughes), 115-28 (Cambridge)

MacGregor, A. 1978 'Industry and Commerce in Anglo-Scandinavian York' in Hall, R.A.: 37-57

— 1984 *Bone, ivory, antler, horn* (Oxford)

Magilton, J.R. 1980 'The Church of St Helen-on-the-Walls, Aldwark', *AY 10/1*

Mahany, C.M. 1969 *The Archaeology of Stamford*

Mahany, C. et al. 1982 *Excavations in Stamford, Lincolnshire 1963-69* (Society for Medieval Archaeology Monograph 9)

Maloney, J. and Hobley, B. (eds.) 1983 *Roman urban defences in the West* (CBA Res. Rep. 51)

Maltby, M. 1979 *Faunal studies on urban sites: the animal bones from Exeter 1971-75* (University of Sheffield)

Mann, J.E. 'Early Medieval Finds from Flaxengate', *The Archaeology of Lincoln XIV-I* (CBA)

Marsden, P. 1975 'The excavations of a Roman palace site in London 1961-72', *TLMAS* 26: 1-102

— 1976 'Two Roman public baths in London', *TLMAS* 28: 1-70

— 1981 'Early shipping and the waterfront of London' in Milne and Hobley: 10-16

Marsh, G. and Tyers, P. 1976 'Roman pottery from the City of London' *TLMAS* 27: 228-44

Martin, G.H. and McIntyre, S. 1972 *A Bibliography of Britain and Irish Municipal History* Vol. I

Mason, D. 1976 'Chester – the evolution and adaptation of its landscape', *Chester Archaeological Journal* 59: 14-23

McCarthy, M.R. 1980 *Carlisle: a frontier city* (Carlisle)

McGrail, S. 1981 'Medieval boats, ships and landing places' in Milne and Hobley: 17-23

McWhirr, A.D. 1976 *Archaeology and History of Cirencester* (BAR 30)

McWhirr, A. *et al.* 1982 *Romano-British Cemeteries at Cirencester* (Cirencester Excavations II, Cirencester)

Meeson, R.A. 1979 *The Formation of Tamworth* (MA Thesis, University of Birmingham)

Mellor, J.E. and Pearce, T. 1981 *The Austin Friary, Leicester* (CBA Res. Rep 35)

Miles, D.M. and Fowler, P.J. 1972 *Tewkesbury: the archaeological implications of development*

Millett, M. 1975 'The native towns of Roman Britain' CA 52: 134-38

Milne, G. 1981 'Medieval riverfront reclamation in London' in Milne & Hobley: 32-36

— 1982 'Further evidence for London Bridge?' *Brit.* 13: 271-76

Milne, G. and Hobley, B. (ed.) 1981 *Waterfront Archaeology in Britain and Northern Europe* (CBA Res. Rep. No. 41)

Milne, G. and Milne C. 1982 *Medieval Waterfront Development at Trig Lane, London* (TLMAS Special Paper No. 5)

Morgan, R. 1982 'Tree-ring studies on urban waterlogged wood: problems and possibilities' in Hall and Kenward: 31-39

Morris, A.E.J. 1979 *A History of Urban Form* (London)

Mynard, O.C. 1984 *A guide to the Medieval Landscape of Milton Keynes* (Milton Keynes)

Norwich Survey 1980 *The Norwich Survey 1971-1980*

O'Connell, M.G. 1977 'Historic Towns in Surrey', *Surrey Arch. Col.* 5

O'Leary, T.J. 1981 'Excavations at Upper Borough Walls, Bath, 1980', *Med. Arch.* 25: 1-30

Olsen, O. 1982 'The quantitative approach in Urban archaeology' in Hall and Kenward: 6-9

Pantin, W.A. 1963 'Medieval English Town House plans', *Med. Arch.* 6/7: 202-39

Perring, D. 1981 *Early Medieval Occupation at Flaxengate, Lincoln The Archaeology of Lincoln* 9/1

Platt, C. 1976 *The English Medieval Town* (London)

— 1978 *Medieval England* (London)

Platt, C. and Coleman-Smith, R. 1975 *Excavations in Medieval Southampton* (Leicester)

Ponsford, M. 1981 'Bristol' in Milne and Hobley: 103-4

Quirk, R.N. 1957 'Winchester Cathedral in the Tenth Century', *Arch. J.* 114: 28

— 1961 'Winchester New Minster and its Tenth Century tower', *JBAA* 3S 24: 16-54

Rackham, D.J. 1982 'The smaller mammals in the urban environment: their recovery and interpretation from archaeological deposits' in Hall and Kenward: 86-93

Radford, C.A.R. 1955 'Excavations at Glastonbury, 1954', *Antiquity* 29: 33-34

— 1957a 'The Saxon house: a review and some parallels', *Medieval Archaeology* I, 27-38

— 1957b 'Excavations at Glastonbury Abbey 1956', *Antiquity* 31: 171

— 1961 'Excavations at Glastonbury Abbey, 1951-4', *Somerset and Dorset Notes and Queries* 27: 21-24, 68-73, 165-69

— 1968 'Excavations at Glastonbury Abbey 1962', *Somerset and Dorset Notes and Queries* 28: 114-17

— 1970 'The later pre-conquest boroughs and their defences', *Med. Arch.* 14: 83-103

— 1973a 'Excavations at Cricklade: 1948-1963', *Wiltshire Archaeological and Natural History Magazine* 67: 61-111

— 1973b 'Pre-conquest Minster Churches', *Arch. J.* 130: 120-40

— 1978 *The pre-conquest boroughs of England, ninth to eleventh centuries* (Mortimer Wheeler Archaeological Lecture PBA, 44)

Radley, J. 1971 'Economic aspects of Anglo-Danish York', *Med. Arch.* 15: 37-57

Rahtz, P.A. 1968 'Hereford', CA I: 242-46

— 1970 'A possible Saxon palace near Stratford-upon-Avon', *Antiquity* 44: 137-43

— 1977 'The archaeology of West Mercian towns' in Dornier: 107-130

— (ed.) 1974 *Rescue Archaeology* (Harmondsworth)

Rahtz, P. and Fowler, P.J. 1972 'Somerset AD 400-700', *Archaeology and the Landscape* (ed. P.J. Fowler), 167-221 (London)

Rahtz, P. and Sheridan, K. 1971 'Fifth report of excavations at Tamworth, Staffs., 1971 – a Saxon water-mill in Bolebridge Street, An interim note' *Transactions of the South Staffordshire Archaeological and Historical Society* 13: 9-16

Raper, R. 1972 'The analysis of the urban structure of Pompeii: a sociological examination of land-use (semi-micro)' in D.L. Clarke (ed.) *Spatial Archaeology* (London)

Rathje, W.L. 1974 'The garbage project: a new way of looking at the problems of archaeology', *Archeology* 27: 236-41

— 1979 'Modern material culture studies' in Schiffer, M.B. (ed.) *Advances in Archeological Method and Theory* 3: 1-37

R.C.H.M. (England) 1959 'Wareham west walls', *Med. Arch.* 3: 120-38

— 1960 *A matter of time: an archaeological survey* (London)

— 1972 *An inventory of the historical monuments in the city of York, ii. The defences* (London)

Rivet, A.L.F. 1964 *Town and country in Roman Britain*, 2nd edn. (London)

— 1966 'Summing up: some historical aspects of the civitates of Roman Britain', *The Civitates Capitals of Roman Britain* (ed. J.S. Wacher), 101-3 (Leicester)

Roberts, B. 1981 'Of towns and villages' in Clack and Haselgrove: 7-16

Robson, B. 1979 'Towns and typologies: forms and processes' in Burnham and Kinsbury: 187-90

Rodwell, K. (ed.) 1975 *Historic towns in Oxfordshire: a survey of the new county* (Oxford)

Rodwell, W. 1981 *The Archaeology of the English Church* (London)

— 1980 *Wells Cathedral, Excavation and Discoveries* (Wells)

— 1984 'Churches in the landscape: aspects of topography and planning' in Faull: 1-24

Rodwell, W. and Rowley, T. (eds.) 1975 *The Small Towns of Roman Britain* (BAR Brit. 15, Oxford)

Rogers, A. 1970 *The Medieval Buildings of Stamford*
— 1972 'Parish boundaries and urban history: Two case studies', *JBAA* 3S 35: 46-64
Rogers, A. and Rowley, T. (eds.) 1974 *Landscapes and Documents*
Rowley, T. (ed.) 1974 'Early Saxon settlements in Dorchester-on-Thames' in *Anglo-Saxon Settlement and Landscape* (BAR 6) 42-50
Ryder, M.L. 1969 'Changes in the fleece of sheep following domestication (with a note on the coat of cattle)', *The domestication and exploitation of plants and animals* (ed. P.J. Ucko and G.W. Dimbleby), 495-521 (London)
Salusbury-Jones, G. 1975 *Street life in Medieval England*
Salzman, L.F. 1923 *English Industries of the Middle Ages* (Oxford)
— 1967 *Building in England down to 1540* (Oxford)
Saunders, A.D. 1978 'Excavations in the church of St Augustine's Abbey, Canterbury 1955-58', *Med. Arch.* 22: 25-63
Schmid, E. 1972 *Atlas of Animal Bones* (London)
Schofield, J. 1981 'The archive reports of archaeological excavations in the city of London from 1973', *TLMAS* 32: 82-83
Schofield, J. and Dyson, T. (ed.) 1980 *The Archaeology of the City of London*
Sheppard, P. 1980 *The Historic towns of Cornwall: an archaeological survey (Cornwall Committee for Rescue Archaeology)*
Shoesmith, R. 1980 *Excavations at Castle Green. Hereford City excavations vol. 1* (CBA Res. Rep. 36)
— 1982 *Excavations on and close to the Defences. Hereford City Excavations vol. 2* (CBA Res. Rep. 46)
Simpson, C. 1973 *Wallingford: the archaeological implications of development* (Oxford)
Slater, T. 1981 'The analysis of burgage patterns in medieval towns', *Area* 13: 211-16
Smith, J.T. 1951 'A note on the origin of the town-plan of Bury-St-Edmunds', *Arch. J.* 108: 162-64
Somner, C.S. 1984 *The Military Vicus in Roman Britain* (BAR 129)
Southampton Archaeological Research Committee (SARC) 1975 *Saxon Southampton* (Southampton)
Strong, D. and Brown D. *Roman Crafts* (London)
Sumpter, A.B. and Coll, S. 1977 'Interval tower SW5 and the South West Defences: Excavations 1972-75' (AY 3/2)
Sutcliffe, R. (ed.) 1978 *Chronicle* (BBC Publications)
Tait, J. 1936 *The medieval English borough* (Manchester)
Tatton-Brown, T. 1982 'Canterbury and the early medieval towns of Kent' in P.E. Leach (ed.) *Archaeology in Kent to AD 1500* (CBA Res. Rep. 48): 79-83
Thompson, F.M. 1956 'Roman Lincoln, 1953' *JRS* 46: 22-36
Todd, M. 1970 'The small towns of Roman Britain', *Brit.* 1: 114-30
Turner, H.L. 1970 *Town defences in England and Wales* (London)
Unwin, G. 1904 *Industrial Organisation in the Sixteenth and Seventeenth Centuries* (Oxford)
Vince, A.G. 1984 'The Aldwych: mid Saxon London discovered', *CA* 8.10: 310-12
— 1985 'The Saxon and Medieval pottery of London: A review', *Med. Arch.* 29: 25-93
Wacher, J.S. (ed.) 1966 *The Civitas Capitals of Roman Britain* (Leicester)
— 1975 *The Towns of Roman Britain*
— 1978 'Sampling at Ipswich: the origin and growth of the Anglo-Saxon town' in Cherry et al.: 279-86
Wade, K. 1981 'Ipswich' in Milne and Hobley: 130-31
Wade-Martins, P. 1980 'Norfolk: North Elmham Park' *East Anglian Archaeology* 9
Wainwright, G.J. 1978 'Theory and Practice in Field Archaeology' in Darvill, J.T. (et al. eds) *New Approaches to our Past* (Southampton) 11-27
Walthew, C.V. 1978 'Property boundaries and the size of building plots in Roman Towns', *Brit.* 9: 335-50
Ward, J. 1911 *Romano-British buildings and earthworks* (London)
Ward, P. 1968 *Conservation and Development in Historic Towns and Cities*
Watts, L. 1977 *Birmingham Moat. Its history, topography and destruction* (unpub. MA dissertation, Birmingham University)
Webster, G. 1951 'Chester in the Dark Ages', *Journal of the Chester Archaeological Society* 38: 39-48
Wheeler, R.E.M. 1927 *London and the Vikings*, London (London Museum Catalogues: No. 1)
— 1935 *London and the Saxons*, London (London Museum Catalogues: No. 6)
— 1943 *Maiden Castle, Dorset* (Society of Antiquaries Res. Rep. 12)
Whitwell, J.B. 1976 'The Church Street Sewer and an adjacent building in Church Street' (AY 17/1)
Whitelock, D. 1952 *The beginnings of English Society* (Harmondsworth)
— 1955 *English historical documents, c.500-1042* (London)
Wilcox, G.H. 1977 'Exotic plants from Roman waterlogged sites in London' *J. Arch. Sci.* 4: 269-82
Williams, J.H. 1979 *St Peter's Street, Northampton: excavations 1973-76* (Northampton Development Corporation)
— 1982 *Saxon and medieval Northampton* (Northampton)
— 1984 'A review of some aspects of late Saxon urban origins and development' in Faull: 25-34
Williams, J.H., Shaw, M. and Denham, V. 1985 *Middle-Saxon Palaces at Northampton* (Northampton Development Corporation)
Williams, J.H. and Bamford, H. 1979 *Northampton – the first 6000 years* (Northampton Development corporation)
Wilson, D.M. 1966 *The Anglo-Saxons* (Harmondsworth)
— (ed.) 1976 *The Archaeology of Anglo-Saxon England* (London)
Wymer, N. 1949 *English Town Crafts*

Index